Luftwaffe at WAR

Gathering Storm
1933–1939

Emergence
·
The Spanish Civil War
·
The Luftwaffe Strikes - Poland

VOLUME 1

E. R. HOOTON

The Author

E.R. (Ted) Hooton has been a journalist for 40 years and a defence journalist for about 25 years. He has written numerous articles on military history and two earlier highly regarded books on the history of the Luftwaffe, *'Phoenix Triumphant: The Rise and Rise of the Luftwaffe'* (1992) and *'Eagle in Flames: The Fall of the Luftwaffe'* (1997) as well as contributing to several others. He has recently completed a history of air operations over the Western Front, *'War above the Trenches'*.

Acknowledgements

I would like to thank and to acknowledge the help of the following in producing this book:

Alex Vanags-Baginskis, Hans-Eberhard Krüger, Robert Forsyth, Peter Waller (Publisher, Books, at Ian Allan Publishing).

Wolfgang Frey, William Green, José Ignacio González-Aller Hierro, Jörg Huthmann, Admiral Gert Jeschonnek, Peter Kilduff, Ken Munson, Dr Richard Osborne, the late Herr Steffen Papsdorf, Martin Streetley.

The Bundesarchiv Militärarchiv in Freiburg, Imperial War Museum, UK National Archives, US National Archives, Service Historique de Défence, both the Armée de Terre and especially the Armée de l'Air sections, Ministry of Defence Whitehall Library, Library of the Royal United Services Institute, Cuartel General del Ejercito del Aire, Servicion Historico y Cultural Instituto de Historia y Cultura, Instituto de Historia y Cultura Naval, Heeresgeschichtliches Museum, Vienna, Langley Library, Slough

The team at Chevron Publishing and Ian Allan Publishing.

E.R. Hooton
2007

Chevron Publishing wishes to thank the following for their kind contribution to this series: Eddie Creek, Paul Leaman, Kenneth Merrick, Eric Mombeek, J. Richard Smith, Marton Szigeti via Stephen Ransom, John Vasco.

First published 2007

ISBN (10) 1 903223 71 7

ISBN (13) 978 1 903223 71 0

Project Editor: Robert Forsyth

Production: Chevron Publishing

Cover and book design by Mark Nelson

© Colour artwork by Tom Tullis and Fernando Estanislau 2006. Maps and diagrams by Tim Brown.

An imprint of Ian Allan Publishing Ltd, Hersham, Surrey KT12 4RG.

Printed in England by Ian Allan Printing Ltd, Hersham, Surrey KT12 4RG.

Visit the Ian Allan publishing website at www.ianallanpublishing.com

CLASSIC

An imprint of
Ian Allan Publishing

CONTENTS

CHAPTER ONE

POST-WAR TURBULENCE

1919–1923

German air power faced two paradoxes in the aftermath of the Great War; although 'born in war...' it certainly did not '...die in war', indeed it actually expanded while its former enemies evaporated like early morning dew[1]. The second is that the inter-war period began with German airmen fighting the Poles and ended the same way.

The earthquake of the Great War reduced the mighty, prosperous and orderly German Empire to a ruin shuddering under the after-shocks of social upheaval and harassed by former subjects. The German armed forces had been thoroughly beaten and the price of their journey home was paid by the surrender of vast stocks of equipment allowing the Allies to advance unopposed across the western frontier. Yet the army and navy air services managed to hand over only some 574 aircraft out of nearly 2,400 while another 240 were abandoned in the East[2].

They were easily replaced for an inventory of January 1919 reported 6,000 aircraft within Germany's borders including trainers and reserves and, because many manufacturers were continuing

Photographed at Berlin-Döberitz in 1919 after the Armistice, these Fokker D.VIII monoplane fighters were operated by Germany's last Jagdstaffel before being destroyed in compliance with the Treaty of Versailles.

Scenes found at many airfields across Germany in 1918 and 1919. The price of defeat was the surrender and destruction of vast numbers of military aircraft. In these photographs can be seen (below left) partially assembled and abandoned airframes at the DFW factory at Leipzig-Lindenthal, while (above left) Albatros J.I and J.II armoured close-support aircraft are shown in the process of being scrapped at the Albatros factory at Schneidemühl near Eisenach.

A man and small boy saw and chop away at a dump of fixed-pitch wooden propeller blades.

Oberst Hermann von der Lieth-Thomsen, the former chief-of-staff of the Luftstreitskräfte who was appointed head of Department A7L in the Prussian War Ministry. He would spend much of the first quarter of 1919 organising air support for the Freikorps.

A pre-war infantryman, Major Wilhelm Haehnelt was the Inspekteur der Flieger (Idflieg), and was one of Germany's most experienced air leaders.

to meet their wartime contracts, by 2 March 1919 the German Government based in Weimar was informed that the services had 9,000 aircraft[3]. Although the echoes of the last shots of the war had barely disappeared the Prussian War Ministry (*Kriegsministerium*) in Berlin intended using these resources to replace the *Luftstreitskräfte* and created an air department (A7L) under its former chief-of-staff, *Oberst* Hermann von der Lieth-Thomsen.

Within a month of the Armistice, 43-year-old *Major* Wilhelm Haehnelt one of Germany's most experienced air leaders had become director of air production or *Inspekteur der Flieger* (*Idflieg*) replacing the exhausted *Major* Wilhelm Siegert. Haehnelt was a pre-war infantryman who became first an aeronaut and then an aviator briefly commanding FFA 4 before becoming the 5. *Armee's* Aviation Staff Officer (*Stabsoffizier der Flieger-Stofl 5.Armee*) just as trench warfare began. He remained in this post and directed Germany's first air campaign over Verdun in 1916 then became 2nd Army Air Commander (*Kommandeur der Flieger, 2.Armee-Kofl 2.Armee*) on the British front but was relieved in August 1918 following the catastrophic defeat at Amiens[4].

Airmen were needed to secure the infant Weimar Republic from threats internal and external. The radical Left exploited the collapse of the Empire to create a Bolshevik-style social-economic order as in Russia – initially in the Left strongholds of Berlin, the ports and the industrial Ruhr as well as in Bavaria. The external threat came from the newly-emerged Polish Republic which was seeking not only those parts of the German Empire which were predominantly Polish but also areas where there was a German majority. Meanwhile the Russian Bolsheviks were in the Baltic States posing a potential threat to East Prussia.

While many of the troops returning from the front yearned only for peace there was a substantial number of men made restless by war. They responded to the calls from die-hard officers and were augmented by young men who had just missed the war but yearned to fight those whom they blamed for the defeat. With no reliable troops immediately available the *Kriegsministerium* was willing to use this slender reed known as the Volunteer Corps (*Freikorps*) to restore national authority and to provide them with access to weapons including artillery and tanks[5].

Thomsen would spend much of the first quarter of 1919 organising air support for the *Freikorps* and he had the cream of Germany's aircraft designs for the task including Halberstadt C.V, LVG C.V/C.VI corps (multi-role tactical) aircraft as well as close-air support aircraft such as the Halberstadt CL.II/CL.V, the Hannover CL.V and the all-metal Junkers CL.I. There were plenty of disgruntled aviators to fly them and these included some of the cream of the *Luftstreitskräfte* such as *Oberleutnant* Oskar, *Freiherr* von Boenigk, *Oberleutnant* Otto Dessloch, *Leutnant* Werner Junck and *Hauptmann* Bruno Loerzer while from the Navy came *Kapitänleutnant* Friedrich Christiansen and *Leutnant zur See* Gotthard Sachsenberg. Many would be important when the *Luftwaffe* emerged a decade later including *Hauptmann* Ulrich Grauert but especially *Hauptmann* Erhard Milch.

There was an abundance of men and aircraft but getting them to units and ensuring supplies of the fuel and spares needed to keep them in the air was more difficult. Appropriately the 'Red' workers had a tight grip on the means of production as well as storage facilities and the *Freikorps* had to storm some airfields and depots while augmenting their limited supplies through smuggling between the lines. Yet Thomsen was able to create some 35 squadrons with up to 300 aircraft to support them: *Freiwilligen Fliegerabteilungen* (FFA) to meet the internal threat and *Grenzschutz Fliegerabteilungen* (GFA) to protect the eastern borders, although such distinctions were not rigid[6].

The units facing the Poles appear to have been the first into action. The Poles had seized *Flieger Ersatzabteilung* 4's base in Posen (Poznan) on 5 January 1919 and this included some 300 aircraft,

Equipped with a miscellany of tanks and armoured cars, the Freikorps was equipped with restless and frustrated former servicemen led by die-hard officers keen to restore authority over those whom they blamed for Germany's defeat. They were prepared to take their fight to the streets. Von der Lieth-Thomsen worked to support the Freikorps by providing support from the air.

Three leading aviators from the First World War who – all holders of the Pour le Mérite – made their services available to fly von der Lieth-Thomsen's aircraft in 1919.

Oberleutnant Oskar Freiherr von Boenigk, a Silesian, was wounded in action while serving as an army platoon commander in October 1914. He returned to the front to be wounded again the following year, after which he transferred to the air service and became an observer. He later joined Jasta 4 as a fighter pilot in the summer of 1917. By September 1918 he had 26 air victories and was commander of Jagdgeschwader II.

Leutnant zur See Gotthard Sachsenberg from Dessau was a former sea cadet who commenced flying as an observer before flying as a pilot on Eindeckers. In February 1917 he was appointed to command the Marine Field Jasta I with whom he regularly engaged British RNAS aircraft off the Belgian coast. By 17 June 1918 he had 15 victories. Flying a distinctive black and white chequered Fokker D VII he ended the war with 31 victories and in command of the Marine Jadgeschwader.

Born in 1891, Hauptmann Bruno Loerzer spent his formative flying days alongside the young Hermann Göring with whom he became firm friends. He scored his first victory on 21 March 1916 and joined Jasta 5 in the summer of that year. Following service with Jasta 17 and 26, he took command of Jagdgeschwader III equipped with the Fokker D VII and ended the war with 44 victories.

although only 26 were serviceable (including 10 Rumpler C.I and nine Albatros C.I) while 200 were in crates. They also seized a considerable amount of material including 91 tonnes of bombs[7]. They formed the Aeronautical Forces Headquarters (*Dowodztwo Wojsk Aero-nautycznych*) and in three weeks from mid-February created four squadrons which supported operations in East Prussia and Silesia, although one was soon transferred to the east.

In isolated East Prussia, the Northern Border Patrol (*Grenzschutz Nord*) under *General* Hans von Seeckt would ultimately be supported by GFA 402,

403, 404, 405, 406, 407, 408, 409, 411, 431 and 432 with many squadrons concentrated into the Königsberg-based *Fliegergeschwader von Bredow*[8]. In Silesia the Eastern Border Patrol (*Grenzschutz Ost*) was supported by FFA 400, 412 (under Milch), 418 and *Grosshain* all under *Hauptmann* Hugo Sperrle, who assumed command on 9 January having previously been *Kofl* 7. *Armee*. These units went into action on 7 January attacking the former FEA 4 base but with little effect.

The *Freikorps* squadrons had a maximum of 80 aircraft including fighters such as the Albatros

The Junkers J.I (factory designation J 4) entered service in the Infanterieflieger units in 1917. The air-crews viewed the aircraft with considerable favour, due to it being immensely strong and also for the armour protection it afforded. The machine was used to fly low over the trenches and supply troops with ammunition and rations as well as low-level machine gunning of enemy trenches.

The highly manoeuvrable Fokker D.VIII fighter. Designed by Reinhold Platz, it was quick to build and, powered by a Oberursel UR.II engine, it had an impressive rate of climb. Arriving at the Front in late July 1918, there were problems with the wing construction on early examples which were attributed to poor manufacturing standards and production was halted. Output resumed in October, with 85 machines seeing service with the Jagdstaffeln before the end of the war. Others served on in the post-war era including some with the Freikorps squadrons.

D.Va, the Fokker D.VII, the Fokker D.VIII 'Flying Razor', the all-metal Junkers D.I and the Siemens-Schuckert D.IV. But there was little air combat and most of the 150 sorties were reconnaissance and ground-attack missions although a *Flieger-Jagdstaffel des Armee Oberkommando Süd*, was created and Boenigk claimed a Polish aircraft whose crew were apparently taken prisoner.

One reason there was little air fighting was because most of the Polish forces were facing the Russian Bolsheviks and Ukrainian nationalists in the east. The German-Polish conflict ended in the summer when Germany was forced to relinquish 13 per cent of its pre-war territory, including a corridor through West Prussia around Danzig and parts of Silesia, and 12 per cent of its population to Poland. It was galling for many of the airmen knowing that some of their countrymen were willing to assist the Polish enemy with aircraft 'losing their way' and landing in Polish territory where the pilots were well paid for their 'mistake'. By these means the Poles acquired 129 aircraft including 25 Fokker D.VII, 20 LVG C.V, 28 DFW C.IV and even a Friedrichshafen G.III heavy bomber!

One Fokker fighter was delivered by the Alsace-born ace *Vizefeldwebel* Albert Lux. Rootless

after the war, he was briefed by Haehnelt about the *Freikorps* squadrons and joined one in Breslau. But he quickly became disgruntled with his comrades, whom he regarded as little more than a political talking shop, so he contacted the enemy, dropped leaflets for them and then deserted[9].

Within Germany the first air operations against the 'Reds' were flown in mid-January around Berlin. Some units, such as the *Landschützenkorps*, organised their own air support with a *Jagdstaffel* and a *Fliegerabteilung*, while Thomsen organised others including FFA 420 and FFA *Hautpmann* Krocker (later FFA 423), the former formed on 5 January by *Hautpmann* Ulrich Grauert a future *Luftwaffe* general and including *Leutnant* Otto Hoffmann von Waldau a future *Luftwaffe* Operations Chief. The first *Freikorps* operation was to support a successful assault upon Adlershof-Johannisthal airfield from which 'Red' aircraft were operating[10].

The airfield was later occupied by a *Marine Landfliegerabteilung* which helped suppress a second uprising in the first half of March. FFA 420 and 421 (formerly FFA *Möhn*) supported the *Freikorps* augmented by two 'unsanctioned' squadrons, FFA *Loewe* (later FFA *422*) and an unidentified unit supporting *Freikorps Hülsen*. The Left also had air support operating from Kottbus, but both sides used their aircraft only for reconnaissance and ground-attack missions. One of the prisoners taken during this period was the Russian Karl Radek, a member of the Russian Communist Party's Central Committee who was to play a key role in the fortunes of German air power.

From late January the *Freikorps* began to suppress 'Red' risings in other parts of the country of which the most significant were in the northern ports, notably Hamburg, the industrial Ruhr and in Bavaria. One of those involved was the former *Luftstreitkräfte* commander *General* Ernst von Hoeppner, who helped to pacify the area around Baden although without aircraft. The northern assault was led by the hero of East Africa,

Generalmajor Paul von Lettow-Vorbeck, supported by tanks as well as Grauert's FFA 420, Loewe's FFA 422 and FFA *Krocker* with some 30 aircraft which helped him enter the great port in July[11]. The 'Reds' had few aircraft outside Berlin and Bavaria so that most missions continued to be reconnaissance and ground-attack. Ground fire was the greatest peril and the most famous victim was 40-victory-ace *Leutnant* Franz Büchner who fell near Leipzig.

Surprisingly it was Bavaria rather than the Ruhr where most air activity was concentrated[12]. A Socialist Republic of Bavaria proclaimed in Munich had promptly instigated a regime of terror in which hundreds of men, women and children perished. Bavarian *Freikorps* were created and seven squadrons organised to support them including a ground-attack unit *Schlasta Anschütz*. This unit supported the strike force, *Gruppe West* of *Generalleutnant* von Oven's *Korps Oven* together with *Feldabteilung* (FA) *Krausser* (later *Bayerische* FA 1), *Feldabteilung Häfner* (later *Bayerische* FA 2), *Feldabteilung Gersthofen* as well as *Freiwilligen* FA *Dessloch*. Another FA was created in Württemberg while the *Reichswehrministerium* (as the *Kriegsministerium* was named on 6 March) despatched a force which included FFA 409, 421 and 422, all under *Hauptmann* Steffen.

During the late spring the *Freikorps'* noose tightened around the Republic which had a handful of aircraft, mostly trainers from the former *Bayerische Feld-Ersatzabteilung* 1 at Schleissheim. But there were few pilots and the aircraft were mostly used for courier duties although their 'White' opponents sought to engage them wherever possible.

The *Freikorps* air operations, with some 50 aircraft, followed much the same pattern as elsewhere but they are also known to have directed artillery fire by radio. Unusually, their ground-attack missions were urged to direct machine gun fire only on clearly identified military targets, although it is unclear whether these niceties were always observed. There was little air-to-air combat and ground fire brought down a handful of aircraft, the crew of one being rescued from a vengeful 'Red' firing squad only by the prompt and heroic action of staff from a nearby hospital.

In late April the *Freikorps* closed on Munich and their squadrons were ordered to begin an aerial blockade and to fly leaflet missions urging the civilian population to remain indoors. The city was assaulted on May Day and secured after a couple of days. Notably absent from the civil fray were four of the *Luftwaffe's* key figures: *Hauptleute* Hermann Göring and Robert *Ritter* von Greim together with *Oberleutnant* Ernst Udet and *Oberleutnant* Wolfram von Richthofen, although the two former were living in Munich as students.

From the post-war chaos Berlin began to reform a new army, the *Reichsheer*, partly from trusted leaders and carefully selected men and partly from the better disciplined and led elements of the *Freikorps*. The *Reichswehrministerium* (RWM)

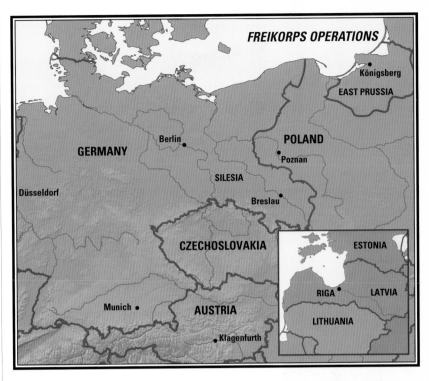

followed the same policy with the nascent air force and many of the *Freikorpsfliegerverbände* were simply renamed *Fliegerstaffeln* in the *Reichsheer*. Planning for the future air force was assigned by Thomsen to *Hauptmann* Helmuth Wilberg, the 38-year-old son of the Württemberg court's Jewish painter[13].

Wilberg was an infantryman who became a staff officer and transferred to the *Fliegertruppe* before the war. He quickly became a *Stofl/Kofl* and especially distinguished himself on the Ypres front as *Kofl 4.Armee* from August 1917, refining close air support operations until they began to unsettle even the phlegmatic British and establishing ground-controlled interception techniques based upon comint similar to the British Compass Stations[14]. After months of work he produced in May 1919 a plan for a force of 1,800 aircraft and 8,000 men but he knew that the plan would never be executed. However, during the early summer, work did begin on converting a number of *Freikorps* squadrons into *Fliegerstaffeln*, usually designated *Truppen-Fliegerstaffel*[15].

As an adviser with Thomsen to the peace conference at Versailles Wilberg had gauged the depth of international bitterness towards Germany. Berlin had anticipated losing territory and paying an indemnity but the Allies, and especially the French who had suffered terribly during the war, were determined no further threats to the Continent's security would emerge from its heart.

The draft peace treaty published on 25 April 1919 shocked all Germany, which was to be emasculated, its armed forces becoming little more than a *gendarmarie* deprived of military aircraft (Article 198). The aircraft industry was to be reduced (Article 201) and all aviation material surrendered (Article 202) with an Inter-Allied Aeronautical Control Commission (IAACC) ensuring that

Freikorps operations occurred not only in Germany but spread as far north as Riga in Latvia and as far south as Klagenfurth in Austria.

Von der Lieth-Thomsen assigned Hauptmann Helmuth Wilberg to lay the foundations of Germany's immediate post-war air arm. During the First World War he gained recognition for the accomplished way in which he developed close-support operations during the Passchendaele campaign on the Western Front. He later became Air Defence Advisor to the Truppenamt.

General Gustav-Adolph Rüdiger Graf von der Goltz who led the German expeditionary force which helped to create an independent Finland in 1918. He subsequently led another force into Latvia which was given air support from some 130 aircraft organised by Haehnelt and Sachsenberg. The mission was successful.

Oberleutnant zur See Theodor Osterkamp was born in Aschersleben in 1892. He served as an observer with a Marine-Feldflieger Abteilung and shot down his first enemy aircraft in September 1916. He subsequently took on pilot training in March 1917 and by September of that year had been credited with six victories. By March 1918 he was in command of Marine Field Jasta II and had a tally of 28 confirmed victories. During the Second World War he served as both commander of a Luftwaffe fighter Geschwader and as a Jagdfliegerführer (area fighter leader) during the Battle of Britain.

June 1919: the Hall of Mirrors at Versailles. It was here that the Allies sought to suppress the threat of German rearmament following the First World War. However, the Reichswehrministerium tried to adjust to what it called the Versailles Imposition or 'Diktat' and sought every avenue to evade its demands.

Germany did not evade these restrictions. The terms were not negotiable and as bad as the ones Berlin had imposed upon Bolshevik Russia at Brest Litovsk a year earlier but, if they were rejected, the Allies threatened to invade Germany and impose the terms at bayonet point. Opposition to the Versailles *Diktat* within Germany was such that Weimar signed the treaty on 28 June only two hours before the French were to begin their invasion. It came into effect on 10 July, although there remained problems.

One was along the Baltic coast north of Germany, whose Empire had helped the non-Serb elements of the Russian Empire to establish new states which the Bolsheviks were determined to liberate from bourgeois independence. Immediately after the Armistice, the Allies insisted that German troops remain in the Baltic States of Latvia, Lithuania and Estonia to secure their independence and Seeckt's *Grenzschutz Nord*, which was responsible for evacuating German troops from occupied Russia, was given responsibility for this task. The new states pressed many German aircraft into service and, to shield themselves from the Bolshevik hordes, the Latvian Government sought German mercenaries, who were offered land in return for help[16].

Their leader was former Guardsman *General* Gustav-Adolph Rüdiger *Graf* von der Goltz, who had led the German expeditionary force which helped to create an independent Finland in 1918. He assumed command as the 'White' forces were being pushed into a coastal bridgehead and assembled 50,000 men (including future *Panzer* leader *Leutnant* Heinz Guderian) with artillery and tanks for a counter-offensive.

With Thomsen's help two squadrons were also organised around the core of Goltz' force, the *Eiserne Division*, under *Hauptleute* Gröckel and Ait as FFA 425 and 433 and later joined by Loerzer's FFA 427 and FFA 424. Another two units were organised as FFA 421 and 426 and together they had some 50 DFW C.V, Fokker D.VII, Halberstadt CL.II/IV and LVG C.Vs. With Seeckt's assistance two squadrons, GFA 408 and 409 would later arrive from East Prussia but the most substantial reinforcement, in February, was *Fliegergeschwader Sachsenberg*[17].

Sachsenberg and his *Marine Jagdgeschwader 4* had returned to Germany for demobilisation and, by happy coincidence, this took place at his home town of Dessau which was also the home of the Junkers aircraft factory. When Sachsenberg was asked, presumably by Haehnelt, to organise a Latvian air expeditionary force he had a ready-made source of supply. Many of his men elected to stay with him, including 32-victory-ace *Oberleutnant zur See* Theodor Osterkamp, and they were augmented by rootless Army aircrew. Sachsenberg created a squadron of Junkers CL I ground-attack aircraft (FFA 417 later *Freiwilligen Schlasta* 417), one of Junkers D.I (FFA 416 later *Freiwilligen Jasta* 416) and a corps squadron with Rumpler C.IV (FFA 413) which sailed to Latvia with 80 aircraft and 700 men.

The reinforced Goltz now struck eastwards towards Riga supported by some 120 single-engined aircraft together with two heavy bombers and six seaplanes, Sachsenberg usually supporting 1. *Garde Reserve Division*. German troops now prepared to storm Riga for the second time in 18 months; the previous occasion had seen the German Army smash the last vestige of Imperial Russian resistance on the Eastern Front aided by an *ad hoc* force of aircraft which exploited their success by bombing and strafing the retreating troops. On 22 May the *Freikorps* repeated this success against Bolshevik forces with Sachsenberg in the vanguard, later dropping supplies to spearhead forces pursuing the enemy.

With few Bolshevik aircraft in Latvia the airmen, as in Germany, discovered ground fire was the major combat hazard but the Junkers, with their steel tube structures covered by sheets of corrugated duralumin, proved robust as the Russians themselves discovered. Another problem for the airmen was the low quality of petrol and oil whose frequent impurities led to clogged fuel lines or seized engines and numerous emergency landings.

After Goltz secured Latvia the Allies demanded his withdrawal but Berlin successfully argued that this would create a power vacuum. Unfortunately Goltz then decided to create a private kingdom and launched a *coup* against the Latvian Government. Then, in June 1919, he attacked neighbouring Estonia but was defeated and saved by a ceasefire imposed by the Allies, who demanded his recall.

They established a blockade which eroded Goltz' strength, notably his air force, but some of his squadrons were withdrawn to Germany to form the new air force with FFA 413 becoming *Truppen-Fliegerstaffel* 34 although it may have been replaced by FFA 429. Goltz was eventually forced to resign (he died in Germany in 1946) and was succeeded on 12 October by *Generalleutnant* Walter von Eberhardt, the *Fliegertruppe* commander at the beginning of the Great War. He now led the *Freikorps* troops on an epic march back to the Fatherland, covered by FFA 424, 425 and 426, with 25 aircraft, some later cannibalised, to provide air cover, until East Prussia was reached in December 1919.

Meanwhile, the RWM tried to adjust to what the Germans called the Versailles Imposition (*Diktat*) and sought every avenue to evade its military excesses. Thomsen's department was disbanded on 11 August 1919 but *Idflieg* remained until the end of the year and Haehnelt loitered around the *Reichsheer* for another year as an officer with special duties. He was demobilised at the end of 1920 but remained prominent in civil aviation, being associated with air sport until 1933 and becoming Vice President of the German Aero-club until 1935. He then became Germany's official air war historian but did not formally rejoin the *Luftwaffe* until July 1938, retiring in March 1942 as a *General der Flieger*. After the war he was taken prisoner by the Russians and died in the former Sachsenhausen concentration camp in March 1946.

Wilberg remained and when the banned General Staff was resurrected as the Troop Department (*Truppenamt*) under *Generalleutnant* Wilhelm Heye, he became its Air Defence Advisor (*Luftschutzreferat*) on 1 March 1920. He continued to plan for a post-war air force to meet internal threats and a potential conflict with Poland, proposing in January 1920 seven air bases and three independent squadrons, but the Allies rejected even this and the Germans had to bend with the wind. As their forces were to be a *gendarmerie* from September 1919, their air squadrons were renamed *Polizei-Fliegerstaffeln* with a total of 10 created in Bavaria (which had two, later reduced to one), Brandenburg, East Prussia (two), Hamburg, Saxony, Silesia, and Westphalia, augmented by a maritime squadron at Kiel[18].

Most *Polizei-Fliegerstaffeln* had single-engined aircraft, although *Polizei-Fliegerstaffel Karlshorst* had Friedrichshafen G.IIIa and *Polizei-Fliegerstaffel Hamburg* had AEG G.V heavy bombers '…to transport a larger number of detectives!'[19] It is probable that these bombers were genuine transports as aerial swords were turned into ploughshares immediately after the Armistice, yet their presence in whatever guise was hardly likely to reassure the Allies.

The new squadrons were given genuine policing roles, no doubt to the irritation of their personnel. These were turbulent times and in March 1920 the *Polizei-Fliegerstaffeln* helped the Government crush a Right-Wing rebellion led by *Doktor* Wolfgang Kapp with reconnaissance, ground-attacks and leaflet drops. The Kapp revolt sparked a Left-Wing insurrection in the Ruhr, which proved the swan-song of the police squadrons with *Polizei-Fliegerstaffeln Böblingen* and *Schleissheim* providing the main air support, the latter coming north from Bavaria. *Gruppe Generalmajor* Haas appears to have had two *ad hoc Fliegerstaffeln. Leutnant* Harding (supporting 3. *Kavallerie-Division*) and *Häfner*. In addition to the 30 or so aircraft, the police air base at Paderborn created another *ad hoc* squadron, *Gefechtsstaffel Münster* under *Major* Wüst, which was expanded to 11 aircraft and flew 129 sorties from 13 March to 4 April 1920. Four aircraft were lost, two in a collision over Merklingsen on 3 April, one to mechanical failure and the last to ground fire, but the only fatal casualties were the three men killed in the collision[20].

However, the police squadron collars were felt by the IAACC, which had begun work in February 1920, under Air Commodore Edward Masterman. To pre-empt intervention the Germans prevaricated, renaming the squadrons *Luftpolizei-abteilungen* on 7 May, but Allied ambassadors demanded their disbandment during the summer of 1920. Berlin continued to prevaricate and on 5 May 1921 the Allies issued the London Ultimatum, demanding disbandment of the *Luftpolizei* and confiscating all 140 of Germany's civil aircraft as security. On 30 June Germany grasped the nettle and created a flightless air traffic control and airport police force as the *Luftüberwachungsabteilungen* from whose ranks several *Luftwaffe* generals would emerge, including Karl Koller who would become the Luftwaffe's Director of Operations in 1943.

Simultaneously, the Germans and IAACC played cat-and-mouse with concealed aviation war material. But aircraft and engines were too difficult to hide and by the end of 1921 Masterman reported that his commission had seized more than 15,700 aircraft and 27,700 engines. On 20 November he reported: "The aerial disarmament of Germany may be regarded as virtually accomplished[21]."

The former Austro-Hungarian Empire, which had dominated central Europe and begun the Great War, also suffered as it fractured along ethnic fault lines leaving Vienna controlling only Austria. Here, too, a Slavic threat emerged in 1919 as Yugoslavia, formerly Serbia, sought the southern province of Carinthia, taking the provincial capital Klagenfurt (Celovec) in December 1918. The *Deutschösterreichische Fliegertruppe*, established on 6 December 1918 under *Hauptmann* Anton Siebert, supported the Nationalist militias (*Volkswehr*) trying to regain the city.

Siebert nominally controlled 1,000 aircraft, the majority trainers, from his headquarters in the Wiener Neustadt *Fliegerarsenal* and most combat aircraft were in storage depots. He salvaged 100 to create six squadron-sized airbases (*Fliegerhorste*), mostly around Vienna but with two (*Fliegerhorste* 3 and 4) at Graz-Thalerdorf[22].

Generalleutnant Wilhelm Heye, head of the Truppenamt.

The head of the post-war Reichsheer, Generaloberst (Hans) von Seeckt who, after his appointment in 1920, immediately collected together a small group of former pilots from the Great War to form the nucleus of a new air force which would lay the foundations for the Luftwaffe.

Hauptmann Julius Yllam's ad hoc *Fliegerhorst* 2a, with 47 men, had 14 aircraft, provided air support for the *Volkswehr* from 20 December and helped it to retake Klagenfurt. It moved into the town's Annabichl airfield and during the uneasy winter lull expanded to 22 aircraft, including some fighters, which opposed a renewed Yugoslav offensive supported by 50 aircraft in April but was unable to prevent Klagenfurt falling again after six weeks. The aircraft were mostly used for reconnaissance and ground-attack but there appears to have been some air fighting, although the Austrians had flown only 96 sorties by the time a ceasefire was organised on 18 June. Yllam lost three men but their sacrifice helped to secure a plebiscite in which the province opted to remain with Austria.

Under the Treaty of St Germaine-en-Laye, signed on 10 September 1919, Austria was also denied an air force although Vienna followed a similar path to Germany in seeking to retain some air power. Most of Siebert's *Fliegerhorste* had been dispersed before the treaty was signed and the remaining aircraft organised into three *Polizei-Flugstaffeln*. But Allied diplomatic pressure was applied and, with Austria dependent upon foreign aid to survive, Vienna was forced to comply in December 1920.

There was one last attempt to retain a post-war air force when the Vienna Security Guard (*Wiener Sicherheitswache*) created a two-squadron (20 aircraft) air unit as *Sicherheitsabteilung 27*[23]. But with Allied eyes everywhere discovery was swift and more pressure was applied until even these units were disbanded in March 1921. Here too an IAACC was established and at one time it was led by Colonel Édouard Barès, who had been Haehnelt's opponent at Verdun and who would later help to create the *Armée de l'Air.*

The IAACC destroyed some 1,200 aircraft and 3,400 engines but sold 71 aircraft to Belgium and Japan. Manufacturers eager to salvage something from the wreckage illegally sold 164 aircraft to customers in Eastern Europe although some would sport the triple-crown insignia of Sweden. By 1922 the IAACC accepted that there was no more contraband and Austria regained control of civil aviation. The St Germaine treaty permitted twelve officers to receive flying training but Vienna's parlous economic state prevented any exploitation of even this loophole for most of the post-war decade.

Faced with similar problems, the Germans took active but covert steps to lay the foundations of future air power. In the meantime, the German Army was reformed by the enigmatic *Generaloberst* Johannes (Hans) von Seeckt, who became Army Commander (*Chef der Heeresleitung*) in the spring of 1920.

Seeckt was a taciturn character who had benefited from a humanist education which broadened his intellectual horizons far beyond those of the average Prussian officer[24]. Most of his wartime experience had been on the more fluid Eastern Front (where he established contact with the Bolsheviks which led to the Treaty of Brest-Litovsk) and in Palestine, which meant his soul was not corroded by Western Front experience which gave him a greater belief in mobile warfare than most of his contemporaries. Yet he remained a curious mixture of the military radical and the reactionary.

His views on air power were fairly conservative and he was content, at the appropriate moment, to resurrect the *Luftstreitkräfte* to support army operations, although he would later recognise that its operations would begin with an air assault upon enemy air power. To lay the foundations he insisted that 180 (5.5 per cent) of the 3,800 front line officers allowed to the *Reichsheer* would be airmen and 10 per cent of the officers responsible for developing military equipment in the Army Ordnance Board (*Heereswaffenamt*) would also be airmen. Among the latter were former air ace *Hauptmann* Kurt Student, who evaluated foreign equipment, while *Hauptmann* Wilhelm Vogt was responsible for procurement and acted as liaison with the industrial rump.

Seeckt also insisted that the *Reichsheer* be 'air minded' with a cadre of air staff officers created in each Military District (*Wehrkreis*) as Experts for Special Employment (*Referenten zbV*) and, like a mother hen, he shielded his airmen from external interference[25]. Yet these officers also had to serve in front line units on traditional duties; Wilberg was transferred to an infantry regiment in 1928 and renewed his air force activities only when the Nazis took power.

One of Wilberg's earliest tasks was to analyse wartime experience to lay the intellectual foundation for the future air force. On 13 November 1919 he drafted a plan, anticipating by a fortnight Seeckt's demand for committees to study the Great War. The first air committee met on 4 December and by the end of the month, 31 specialised groups with some 120 officers were organised to examine specific matters with 27 studying tactical air support but bombing studies focused exclusively on army support[26].

Seeckt was determined to exploit civil aviation[27]. The *Reichsheer's* candidate, retired *Hauptmann* Ernst Brandenburg, wartime leader of the *Englandgeschwader* strategic bombing unit and still on crutches from wartime injuries, was given a key role in the development of civil aviation and ultimately became Ministerial Director for the Transport Ministry's National Air Travel Department (*Ministerialdirigent der Reichsamt für Luftfahrt*) until 1933. This allowed him to supervise the German Aviation Organisation (*Deutschen Luftfahrt-Verband eV* – DLV) established in 1920 to foster young peoples' interest in aviation. It focused upon gliding and encouraging embryo flying training as well as the study of aerodynamics and airframe construction and gliding events were often visited by army officers. An annual glider meeting was organised in the Rhön Mountains east of Fulda with Student and his wife being enthusiastic supporters, along with

The Zögling glider was a familiar sight at the Wasserkuppe. Initial training flights were often less than a minute and sometimes only a few seconds during the late 1920s/1930s.

Von Seeckt gave a key role in the development of civil aviation to Hauptmann Ernst Brandenburg, the one-legged former commander of Bombengeschwader 3 who had pioneered bombing attacks on targets in the south of England. Brandenburg would eventually supervise the Deutschen Luftfahrt-Verband eV (DLV), the organisation responsible for the promotion and development of aviation in Germany throughout the 1920s and 1930s.

Hitler Youth assist one of their fellow trainee pilots from his Zögling glider in the Rhön Valley, as the ground handlers manoeuvre the glider into position for its next flight .

Even rocket-powered tailless aircraft models were tried out on the Wasserkuppe. Seen here in 1928, Professor Wilhelm Schlink, a member of the academic staff of the Technische Hochschule Darmstadt, helps to align a launching ramp while a young Alexander Lippisch, the future designer of the Luftwaffe's Me 163 rocket interceptor, crouches behind a 4.05 m span model to make necessary adjustments.

Wilberg. The experience helped the eccentric Günter brothers, Siegfried and Walter, to design their elegant He 70 and He 111.

Surprisingly, some German manufacturers continued to produce military aircraft openly and with Allied support. Ernst Heinkel sold his submarine-borne floatplanes to both Japan and the United States, which also acquired Dornier flying boats and fighters. The Japanese market would prove a valuable legitimate outlet for Heinkel's military designs in the coming decade[28].

German manufacturers also illegally exported some 1,500 military aircraft leading to Allied hands gripping their throats for many years. They disrupted German aircraft production until May 1922 and then restricted the performance of new aircraft, making grudging minor changes in June 1925. These were enforced by IAACC which was renamed

A glider named 'Moritz' piloted by Arthur Martens takes off at Wasserkuppe in the Rhön Valley in Germany. This was the favoured place for trainee glider pilots due to the ideal conditions encountered there.

The Heinkel He 1 seaplane. Built under licence in Sweden for Ernst Heinkel, it first flew in May 1923. Its role was not intended as combat, though ten such machines were acquired by the German Navy in the mid-1920s.

the Aeronautical Guarantee Committee on 5 May 1922 and acted as a dead hand upon German aircraft development; indeed by the end of 1921 all the great wartime aircraft manufacturers had vanished.

The new Navy (*Reichsmarine*) was dominated by conservatives and only 20 of its 1,500 front line officers (1.5 per cent) had aviation experience, of whom a third were from the *Marine Luftschifferabteilung*. *Kapitänleutnant* Walther Faber, a 31-year-old former training advisor to the Naval Aviation Chief (*Marineflugchef*) was responsible for naval aviation, heading a department in the Admiralty (*Reichsmarineamt*) from March 1919 until September 1920 before becoming *Flottenabteilung Referent für Seeflugwesen* with a tiny staff. He had entered the Navy in 1906 before learning to fly in 1913 and saw front line service at List and Zeebrugge in 1916 before joining the *Marineflugchef*. He would remain *Referent* until 31 March 1923 and

then pursued a non-aviation career in the Navy specialising in torpedoes and mines, heading the Naval High Command's (*Oberkommando des Marines*) science department throughout the war. He retired a month before the war's end and died in December 1945[29].

Yet he managed, by some sleight of hand, to retain six Friedrichshafen FF.49 floatplanes at Norderney and Holtenau and used them for second-line duties; indeed they were still in service in 1934! As the Navy was also permitted to retain a few anti-aircraft guns at Königsberg he played an important part in the clandestine development of these weapons. He also created a minute air staff through offices in the two naval commands[30].

Germany's covert attempts to acquire air power were almost forced into the open. Europe's leading pre-war economy was now in ruins and unable to pay the reparations demanded by Versailles. However, neither Paris nor Brussels wished to recognise the truth and in January 1923 their troops marched into Germany's industrial heartland, the Ruhr, while Berlin's Slavic neighbours in Poland and Czechoslovakia made threatening noises. The Government responded with a policy of non-cooperation while the more adventurous conducted a campaign of sabotage bringing the prospect of full-scale invasion.

In response the *Reichsheer* secretly mobilised and swelled its ranks with former *Freikorps* militias. As a shield against French bombers, President Friedrich Ebert authorised the covert acquisition of aircraft and with money from Ruhr industrialist Hugo Stinnes an order was placed (ostensibly by Argentina) with Fokker for 100 fighters, half D.XI and half D.XIII. Some military aircraft had been ordered already, including 53 Dietrich DP IIa (a development of the Fokker D.VII) for fighter training while Student ordered reconnaissance aircraft from Heinkel, although the first did not appear until 1924 after the crisis had passed[31].

The veteran airmens' organisation, *Ring Deutscher Flieger*, under Siegert with 2,500 men, provided a ready-made pool of manpower. Siegert selected some 100 former fighter pilots and the *Wehrkreise Referent zbV's* organised refresher training for them at private air schools but also for reconnaissance crews on Albatros B.II trainers. The Navy acquired ten Heinkel He 1 seaplanes, although their 'Brazilian' owners assembled and based them across the Baltic in Stockholm.

The situation was diffused by the conciliatory approach of the new German Chancellor, Gustav Stresemann, who was appointed in August 1923 as the German economy went into meltdown with hyper-inflation. Stresemann lasted only four months but was then appointed Foreign Minister and in 1924 negotiated the Dawes Plan which matched reparations with Germany's ability to pay them, while opening the country to substantial American investment.

He was always a nationalist but convinced the Allies that Germany had not only disarmed but also was no longer a threat to European peace, leading to the dismantling of the Allied monitoring organisation. His final triumph was the Treaty of Locarno signed on 1 December 1925 which guaranteed Germany's western borders and ended any further threat of French military action while guaranteeing that the Rhineland would remain demilitarised when France withdrew in 1930. This would be underlined when he accepted the Young Plan in 1929 which not only reduced reparation payments but set a deadline of 30 June 1930 for the evacuation of the Ruhr.

Yet the eastern borders remained menaced by Poland and Czechoslovakia for most of the decade and the *Reichsheer* regarded them, as well as France and Belgium, as the prime threats to German security[32]. Poland was like the bullying child of over-indulgent parents, its position guaranteed by France, and Seeckt observed in 1922: "Poland's existence is intolerable, incompatible with the survival of Germany. It must disappear…" When he made this observation he was already taking steps both to neutralise the threat and to develop forbidden technology, including aircraft, his hand strengthened by Locarno.

NOTES FOR CHAPTER ONE

[1.] The words were famously scrawled on the status board of *Jagdgeschwader 1* late on 11 November. Bodenschatz, *Jagd in Flanders Himmel*, p.141ff. For post-war chaos see Hooton, *Phoenix Triumphant* pp.17-19.

[2.] Morrow, *German Air Power in World War I* pp.146, 236 f/n 13. UKNA Air 9/24.

[3.] Morrow p.154.

[4.] Morrow pp. 92, 126, 150. See Haehnelt's entry in Collins and Miller *Axis Biographical Research* website *(Luftwaffe)*.

[5.] See Koch and Scott, *The origins of the Freikorps. A re-evaluation*. University of Sussex Journal of Contemporary History. A list of major *Freikorps* units is in Wendel: *Axis History Factbook*. Germany & Austria, Freikorps 1918-1923. Website: www.axishistory.com.

[6.] For the *Freikorps* squadrons see Hooton pp.20-22. Schliephake, pp.11-16. Völker, *Entwicklung* pp.124-125, f/n 2, 4. Much of the information comes from the research of Hans-Eberhard Krüger and I would like to praise his unstinting generosity in supplying information and material. See also his articles in *Jägerblatt*.

[7.] For the Poles see Belcarz and P?czkowski, pp.20, 25-26, 41-42, p.292. Cynk pp.39, 45.

[8.] *FFA 418* included many former members of JG II.

[9.] For Lux see Franks, Bailey & Guest. *Above the Lines* p.160. Hooton pp. 20-21. Lux p.134ff. Visiting Germany in the 1930s he was briefly arrested for espionage but released.

[10.] For air operations see *Darstellungen aus den Nachkriegskämpfen deutscher Truppen und Freikorps. 4. Band.* Hereafter Official History.

[11.] (*op.cit.*)

[12.] For air operations see Official History *Band 4 and 5*. Pletschacher p.152.

[13.] For Wilberg see Collins & Miller *Axis Biographical Research* website. Corum, *The Luftwaffe* pp.21, 30-32, 34, 299 f/n 17.

[14.] *Luftstreitkräfte Nachrichtenblätter 28, 34 & 36/1917.*

[15.] Hooton pp.24.

[16.] Johnson. *The White Falcons* in Worldatwar website.

[17.] For air operations. Official History. *Band 2*. Hooton pp.22-23. Krüger. *Jagdstaffeln über Kurland und Oberschlesien*. Wendel *Axis History Factbook*. Germany & Austria, Freikorps 1918-1923. Kampfgeschwader Sachsenberg. Website: axishistory.com.

[18.] Hooton pp.29-31. Völker, *Dokumente*, pp.51-52, 55-57. Krüger, *Die Reichswehr- und Polizeiflieger-Staffeln*. SHAD 7N2611.

[19.] Krüger *op cit* p.10.

[20.] Official History, *Band 9*.

[21.] SHAD 4N80-I, 4N96-I, 4N96, 7N2611. UKNA Air 9/24, FO 371/4752 C12077, 371/4757 C11056, 371/4872.

[22.] Gabriel pp.220, 229. Hooton pp.25-26. Green, *Alpenstock*, SHAT 4N97, 4N105.

[23.] Hooton pp.40-41.

[24.] For Seeckt see Corum, *Blitzkrieg*, Carsten pp.104-108, 115, 213-214. Seaton, pp.6-10.

[25.] Corum *op cit*. pp.31, 148-149. Hooton pp.27-28.

[26.] Corum, *Blitzkrieg* pp.144-14.

[27.] Homze, pp.10-15. Hooton pp. 31-35. Suchenwirth pp.8-10, 14-16.

[28.] For the German aero-industry Homze is indispensable. For the post-war industry see pp.3-4.

[29.] See his entry in Collins & Miller's website *Axis Biographical Research. Kriegesmarine*.

[30.] Hooton p.29. Völker, pp.135-136.

[31.] For the Ruhr Crisis see Carsten pp.154-155; Völker, pp.133-134, 138, 200. Also Lennart Andersson's article *Secret Luftwaffe*.

[32.] Corum, *Blitzkrieg* p.170.

CHAPTER TWO

DRANG NACH OSTEN

1923-1932

An aerial view of the training centre at Lipetsk. When the centre was first taken over by the Germans, it had one hangar, a workshop, an old factory shed for supplies and an administration building. By the summer of 1925, a second runway, new hangars, repair depots, an engine test-bed, barracks, medical quarters and a rail connection to the nearby station had been completed.

Karl Radek would be the key to Russo-German cooperation, for after his capture in 1919 he turned his Berlin cell into a salon attracting a wide range of visitors including Seeckt's old friend the former Turkish War Minister Enver Pasha.

He was probably acting as Seeckt's proxy and later flew to Moscow where he met Defence Commissar Leon Trotsky and proposed that Soviet Russia help the Weimar Republic develop forbidden military technology. Trotsky agreed in principle but was preoccupied with fighting the Poles, 'Whites' and other threats to the regime. But he did send his friend Victor Kopp to Germany to visit arms manufacturers and aircraft plants and his April 1921 reports had many suggestions including the use of the Albatros factory in Memel, Lithuania, to produce aircraft for the Russians.

The Russians were especially interested in Junkers all-metal aircraft which they had encountered when fighting Goltz. During 1920 they captured an incomplete CL.I and a D.I in Latvia and were eager to exploit the technology. This desire was shared by Dr Hugo Junkers whose business was hovering on the brink of bankruptcy despite every effort at diversification including an airline, *Junkers Luftverkehr*, under Sachsenberg.

In July 1921 he was approached by *Major Dr* Oskar *Ritter* von Niedermeyer, famous for his undercover wartime operations in Afghanistan and Persia, who was leading a delegation to the Soviet Union to examine the Russian armament and aircraft industry with a view to collaboration. Junkers was more than willing to support the RWM's aims as the Russians and Germans began to hammer out details of their military co-operation during the autumn using the Berlin apartment of Kurt von Schleicher, founder of the *Freikorps,* who fought the Bolsheviks' German allies!

The German delegation was led by *Oberst* Otto Haase, who would lead the *Truppenamt* from 1922 to 1926, while Kopp was joint leader of the Russian delegation with Leonid Krassin, Chairman of the Foreign Trade Council. In November the delegations visited Dessau and concluded a verbal agreement by which Junkers would build aircraft and aero-engine factories in Russia in return for government funds and a share of the profits[1].

But without a German government guarantee other manufacturers were unwilling to commit their limited funds into a country which had recently nationalised all foreign enterprises and their caution proved justified. Early in 1922 this problem was resolved when the Chancellor/Foreign Minister (he had previously been Chancellor/Finance Minister) Joseph Wirth allocated the Army RM150 million ($2.8 million) to support collaboration with the Russians. He also opened negotiations with Moscow to formalise diplomatic and commercial relations leading, on 16 April, to the Treaty of Rapallo which renounced war reparations, improved trade relations and provided for what would later be described as technology exchange.

Rapallo removed the last obstacles to military cooperation, the details of which were already being completed. A *Sondergruppe R* was established under Seeckt's former adjutant *Major* (later *Oberst*) Veit Fischer who would later join the *Luftwaffe* and command a *Luftgau*. Fischer had arranged preliminary agreements with both Albatros and Junkers in mid-March 1922 to establish factories in the Soviet Union, the latter in return for a down-payment of RM40 million ($746,000) and RM100 million ($1.86 million) in capital. The Albatros deal collapsed for unknown reasons but other manufacturers were interested in working in Russia and one of them, Friedrich ('Fritz') Siebel, represented the Foreign Ministry in negotiations.

The pace now grew and on 22 November 1922 Junkers signed an agreement with the Russians in which he would establish factories in Russia to build his aircraft and aero-engines in return for Moscow's guarantee of work. Barely a week later, on 4 December, the Russians ordered 100 aircraft, including 50 Junkers J.21 corps aircraft, 30 J.22 fighters and 20 J.20 seaplanes although Moscow did not actually ratify the order until February, by which time the French occupation of the Ruhr was giving new urgency to the Soviet-German talks on collaboration.

The importance of aviation was underlined when Hasse led a delegation, including Student, to Moscow in February 1923 where they met the head of the Workers' and Peasants Red Air Fleet (*Voenno-Voozddushnye Sily Roboche-Krest'yanski Krasnyvozdushny Flot-VVSRKKF*), A.P. Rosengol'ts

A line-up of Fokker D.XIIIs photographed at Lipetsk.

A Fokker D.XIII, coded '6', of the 'Fliegerschule Stahr' in flight over Lipetsk. The school was often known after its first commander, Major Stahr.

Fokker D.XIII, Lipetsk, 1932.

on until August 1942, becoming an honorary *General der Flieger*.

To help staff work, seven officers were assigned as advisors and instructors to the VVSRKKF from the mid-1920s including a *Hauptmann* Martin Fiebig. During the war he had become a bombing expert and by the Armistice was commanding *Bogohl* 9. Between 1925 and 1926 he was air doctrine lecturer at the Soviet Air Commanders' Academy and also advised Soviet air leaders on bombing[2].

Air training and aircraft development were the priority and, after rejecting Odessa, the two sides agreed on 15 April 1925 to establish a base at Lipetsk, some 500 kilometres south-west of Moscow. A disused factory on the outskirts became the heart of the establishment which was gradually expanded to include two runways, hangars, repair sheds, an engine test bed and a hospital – indeed after the Germans departed it remained in Soviet Air Force hands and even at the beginning of the 21st Century is a major base[3].

The Ju 22 was to have been the backbone of Lipetsk activities but it was extremely unstable and prone to spinning. Fortunately the 50 Fokker D.XIIIs acquired during the Ruhr Crisis were still available and they were shipped in crates from Stettin to Leningrad in May then railed to Lipetsk for re-assembly. Only a third were used at any one time, two replacements were received, and extensive rotation meant that when the last Germans departed in September 1933 some 40 aircraft remained airworthy.

The German Army assigned between 60 and 70 staff under *Major* Stahr to the Lipetsk establishment which was designated the *Wissenschaftlichliche Versuchs- und Prüfanstalt für Luftfahrzeuge* (*Wivupal*). It would cost Germany RM 2 million ($478,000) a year but proved a lifeline for German air power, initially providing operational training within a few weeks of its establishment[4]. The instructors were nominally civilians on contract either from civilian flying schools or from an airline and, again for security reasons, were paid in US dollars.

Each summer until 1927 *Wivupal* received 30 veteran ('Old Eagles') fighter pilots for a course lasting up to 22 weeks operating in a fighter squadron (*Jagdstaffel*) and a fighter demonstration squadron (*Jagdlehrstaffel*) with the highlight being a dogfight between two squadrons of nine aircraft equipped with camera guns. By the time Lipetsk closed, some 120 fighter pilots had been either trained or received refresher training at the base and the excellent safety record meant that there were only three fatalities, two in a mid-air collision and the third being 35-victory ace *Leutnant* Emil Thuy killed in the vicious Albatros L.76 on 11 June 1930.

(Trotsky's brother-in-law) and the Red Army Chief-of-Staff, P. P.Lebedev and established a liaison office, *Zentrale Moskau* (ZMo) which was responsible to the *Truppenamt*. Thomsen was selected head of ZMo and arrived in Moscow in November.

ZMo supervised not only the creation of an air-training and aircraft development establishment but also chemical warfare and armoured vehicle establishments. Governmental support remained half-hearted; Stresemann believed it would undermine his attempts to regain Germany's political standing and many begrudged any form of military expenditure, but the position eased following the formal rapprochement with Russia in the Treaty of Berlin in April 1926. ZMo was a demanding position and it undermined Thomsen's health – he may have been suffering from diabetes, and was steadily losing his sight. In 1929 he was forced to hand over to Niedermeyer but lived

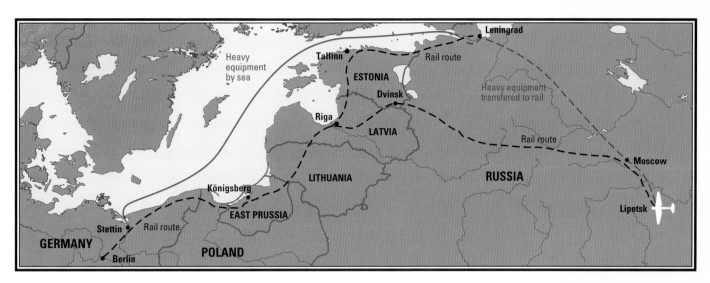

From 1927 the emphasis switched to 'Young Eagles' and Lipetsk attracted not only would-be fighter pilots but also artillery observers for a six-month course in an observer squadron (*Beobachterstaffel*) and observer demonstration squadron (*Beobachterlehrstaffel*), their training culminating from 1928 in live firing training with Russian batteries at Voronezh. The aircraft included six or seven Heinkel HD 17 corps aircraft later augmented by a similar number of Albatros L.76/78 but thanks to Stresemann's diplomatic efforts observer training returned to Germany in 1930.

The inventory was augmented by a variety of trainers and transports including Albatros L.68as, Heinkel HD 21s, Junkers F.13s, Junkers A.20s and even two Fokker D.VIIs transferred from the Soviet Air Force! By 1 October 1929 there were 66 aircraft at Lipetsk. They were needed because the numbers of potential aircrew in Germany were slowly declining; some 'Old Eagles' died or were killed in accidents (notably Lothar von Richthofen, brother of the 'Red Baron'); others had to keep body and soul together. By 1926 only 100 members of the Army were eligible for flying duty and, despite

Lipetsk, by November 1930 the 'flying officers' list had only 168 names against a target of 180, although 77 of these would later become generals in the *Luftwaffe*[5].

Only 6 per cent of the Army officers holding a pilot's licence flew in their spare time while the number of officers actually seeking flying training dropped from six in 1926 to three in 1931. This was a consequence of the *Reichswehr*'s low pay rates, for officers had to pay for most of their training and, without private means, few

Routes to the East: the covert German channels to the Lipetsk training base 1925-1933

The Heinkel HD 17 two-seat reconnaissance aircraft was designed in 1924 by Ernst Heinkel. Powered by a 450 hp Napier Lion engine, the aircraft had a maximum speed of 385 km/h at sea level. A Beobachterstaffel was established at Lipetsk in 1926 and the type became the unit's main equipment.

Camera gun film of Fokker D.XIIIs taken at Lipetsk during gunnery training. Many of the centre's aircraft had different coloured fins and rudders including green and white vertical stripes and red and white horizontal stripes. Fuselages were often marked with white fuselage bands.

Two of the finest aerobatic pilots of their generation, Ernst Udet (left) and Willi Stör pose for photographers at the Deutsche Verkehrsfliegerschule (DVS) or Commercial Pilots School at Schleissheim. Those who saw Udet's flying displays never forgot the skill shown by the First World War fighter ace, whose score of 62 victories was second only to von Richthofen in the German Air Service.

Arranged in two neat rows, these Udet U 12 a Flamingos were operated by the DVS at Schleissheim. From April 1927, the DVS began training new, young pilots or 'Jungmärkern'. After a year's instruction the pilots earned their B-2 certificates having passed the commercial pilot's course.

could afford to fly, a problem exacerbated by the Depression.

Yet the RWM subsidised civilian flying training organisations to help with clandestine military air training. Basic flying training was provided by around six private flying schools, including that of Ernst Udet, and by *Sportflug GmbH*, which was established in 1924 by Siebel. This had seven schools each with approximately six single-engined aircraft such as the Heinkel HD 21, the LVG B.III and Udet U12, while the associate *Aerosport GmbH* at Warnemünde used war-surplus Friedrichshafen FF.49s for naval seaplane training. Each *Sportsflug* school was conveniently close to a *Wehrkreis* (Military District) headquarters which sent officers for initial pilot and observer training, but when the Allies discovered the subsidies they compelled *Sportsflug* to close [6].

Most of its assets were absorbed by the *Deutschen Verkehrsfliegerschule GmbH* (DVS) which

was established at Berlin-Staaken in 1925 as an international centre of excellence for advanced air training, whose comprehensive course included instrument training. It was *Major* Alfred Keller, a famous bomber pilot (whose nickname was Bombshelter or '*Bombenkeller*') and holder of the *Pour le Mérite*, who oversaw a significant expansion during the late 1920s matching that in civil aviation which was boosted in Germany by DVS aircraft orders. Schools were opened at Schleissheim (near Munich) and in Brunswick and the organisation received secret RWM subsidies.

Wilberg arranged with Brandenburg for 40 *Offizieranwärter* students each year to train at DVS Schleissheim while from 1928 DVS Berlin-Staaken and Brunswick were used for clandestine observer training, the latter providing practical training from 1931 and qualifying some 80 officers, including *Major* Student, in the next two years. The best *Offizieranwärter* students at Brunswick were sent for fighter training at Lipetsk and upon joining the army they received refresher training courses at a new training organisation *Luftfahrt* (later *Deutsche Luftfahrt*) *GmbH*.

It was not until 1928 that Berlin began evaluating new combat aircraft at Lipetsk, with technicians and scientists as well as military observers swelling the numbers at Wivupal to an average 200 men, rising to 300 in 1931. Single-engined aircraft were flight-tested in Germany, dismantled, shipped to Leningrad and then railed to Lipetsk for re-assembly and testing with weapons, bomb racks and sights.

Secrecy was paramount, although it was spectacularly breached twice in December 1926; first by an extremely accurate report in the British newspaper the *Manchester Guardian* and then by Social Democrat Deputy, Philipp Scheidemann, in

Parliament. The Government was forced to ban active-list officers from attending but the Army, which conducted a vigorous damage-limitation exercise, circumvented this by having these men temporarily resign their commission which they regained upon their return. Many *Offizieranwärter*, who were not officially in the Army, were selected for Lipetsk and in 1929 there were 10 on a course with 36 other pupils and six instructors.

All travelled under an alias and while a few sailed to Leningrad in a cruise ship or a freighter (disembarking at night to avoid detection), most travelled on the *Nord Express*, the Paris to Riga trans-European rail service. At Riga they would take a train to Russia via Daugavpils (Dvinsk). Unlike most travellers, they were not subject to the paranoiac attentions of the Soviet border guards who treated them with courtesy and once their names were checked off the list they continued to Lipetsk via Moscow.

Lipetsk had few facilities, indeed some newcomers were met by a sign: *'A warm welcome to the world's arse'* (*'Herzlich Willkommen am Arsch der Welt'*). Parties and receptions provided some form of social life and sometimes there were movies. While Moscow might have been enthusiastic about Russo-German fraternal relationships the Germans had little contact with the general population apart from the pretty maids with whom many relationships went beyond the fraternal.

Lipetsk also helped to train a core of ground crews, some 450 by 1933, who gained experience in the very latest all-metal airframe technology. They could also practise on a wide variety of aero-engines

including the Fokker D.XIIIs' and HD 17s' Napier Lions, which were originally returned to England for overhaul until the Germans were sufficiently confident to perform this task themselves at Lipetsk.

Yet despite the most stringent security prec-autions, British and French intelligence built up a comprehensive picture of activities in Lipetsk; the British Secret Intelligence Service produced two reports in November 1929 and August 1932 as did French military intelligence, although mistakenly suggesting Lipetsk was also used as a bomber school[7]. The British noted the disappearance and reappearance of Army officers from the active list and they correctly deduced this was for flying training. The Ambassador, Sir Horace

Newcomers to the Lipetsk site were met by a cheerful sign: 'Herzlich Willkommen am Arsch der Welt' ('A warm welcome to the world's arse').

A group of former Liptesk pilots in DVS uniform are reviewed by Hermann Göring in 1933. From the right of the picture are Wolfgang Falck and Günther Radusch who were to become pioneer night fighter pilots in the Luftwaffe. Sixth from the right is Günther Lützow who later became Kommodore of JG 3 and the second Luftwaffe pilot to score 100 victories. To his right is Hannes Trautloft who was to lead JG 54 and, like the other three, was awarded the Ritterkreuz.

In the background is Ju F 13, D-410, W.Nr. 740/1924, 'Steppenhuhn'. Powered by a BMW IIIa engine, this aircraft started its service life with Südwestdeutsche L.V. AG, Frankfurt/Main in 1925. It then passed to Europa-Union in January 1926 and was retired from service with DLH in November 1932. In the foreground is Dornier Do B Merkur, W.Nr. 128/1929 'Wiessfuchs' ('White Fox'). Powered by a BMW VI engine, the aircraft was registered in April 1929 with Deruluft, Berlin. In August 1928, the aircraft transferred to DLH AG and in April of the following year, returned to Deruluft.

As a way of circumventing the crippling restrictions imposed by the Versailles Treaty, Junkers, amongst other companies, opened subsidiaries in Sweden and Turkey. The Junkers G 24 was a popular design which found markets with several foreign countries, being operated by Swiss, Swedish and Turkish airlines until the lifting of restrictions allowed the type to be registered in Germany. This line-up of S-AAAL, S-AAA?, S-AAAS and S-AAAT shows the standard pale grey finish with black trim that became the hallmark of Deutsche Lufthansa when it formed in 1926.

Erhard Milch, the Commercial Director of Lufthansa at his desk in the late 1920s/early 1930s. Milch was a shrewd administrator with little concern for displaying ruthlessness when required. Later, he would work with Göring as Secretary of State for Aviation.

Erhard Milch (centre) talks with pilots and fellow Lufthansa staff next to a Junkers G 24 three-engined airliner, a development of the F 13. During 1926 Lufthansa used two G 24s, D-901 and D-903, to fly from Berlin to Peking and back to test the possibilities of establishing a regular Far Eastern service.

Rumbold, noted on 29 May 1931 that 66 officers had gone through the process and named seven who had 'returned to the fold'. In fact six were on a secret list drawn up in 1930 of officer airmen and they included *Rittmeister* Pflugbeil and *Oberleutnant* Schulze-Heyn who would become *Kommodore* of KG 51 in August 1940 [8].

The French mistake was understandable for in 1928 and 1929 the Germans evaluated civil airliners including the Dornier Do B *Merkur*, the Rohrbach Ro XII and the Junkers G 24 which might be converted into bombers. They would pose as part of a civil airline, such as the Russo-German *Deruluft*, and fly from Königsberg to Velikye Luki which would be the scene of an epic siege involving *Luftwaffe Transportgruppen* between November 1942 and January 1943 [9].

The auxiliary bomber (*Behelfsbomber*) was a way of circumventing the Versailles Treaty and, while none of the Lipetsk aircraft proved suitable, the concept was validated later with the Junkers Ju 52/3m which would be the backbone of the state airline *Lufthansa*. *Lufthansa* was created in the aftermath of the disappointing Junkers aircraft factory venture established at Fili but lost money because Berlin ordered no aircraft while Russian orders were limited. On 1 March 1927 Fili was taken over by the Russians and placed under Andrei Tupolev whose earliest designs, including the TB-1 long-range bomber, reflected the Junkers influence. Junkers sued both governments but lost both the cases and official German support [10].

Ernst Brandenburg was already seeking to merge his airline, *Junkers Luftverkehr*, with *Deutsche Aero Lloyd* and the court case gave him the lever he needed. Faced with the banks cutting his credit Junkers capitulated and *Deutsches Luft Hansa AG* or

DLH (more commonly *Lufthansa*), was created on 6 January 1926. The new airline had an annual subsidy of RM18 million ($4.3 million) until 1929 and its Operations Director (Commercial Director from 1929) was a former Junkers man and *Polizeiflieger*, 33-year-old Erhard Milch, a friend of Wilberg [11]. The baby-faced Milch, was a shrewd manager who recognised that the way to make the new airline profitable was to keep its aircraft in the air as long as possible

Because of their longer range he expanded the multi-engined aircraft fleet, later including the Ju 52/3m, to lay the foundation for the *Behelfsbomber*. For maximum flying time, even at night and in bad weather, he introduced a system of visual and radio navigation beacons as well as providing landing aids at all his main airports to ensure that by 1929 all *Lufthansa* pilots were instrument rated. This philosophy would have an impact upon *Luftwaffe* bomber development the following decade allowing it to make a quantum leap beyond its rivals. The Commander of the RAF's Air Defence of Great Britain observed in October 1934 that *Lufthansa's* nightly service between Cologne and Croydon had been cancelled on only four occasions in the previous year, a capability which the RAF could not match [12].

While *Lufthansa* embraced technology the Army under Seeckt preferred to keep its distance, reflecting his curious dichotomy. In one breath he embraced mechanised mobile warfare and laid deep foundations but failed to address the General Staff's ignorance of industrial and economic factors. This fundamental ignorance was a major contributor to Germany's second defeat together with his over-selective rebuilding of the General Staff which produced well-trained men, but few of them [13].

By the mid-1920s some of the younger officers were becoming restive and seeking a more modern approach. They created a loose grouping of modernisers who were nicknamed the *Fronde*, after French 17th Century rebels and one of their leaders was the *Truppenamt's* Head of Operations, *Oberst* Werner von Blomberg who would play a key role in *Luftwaffe* development and whose son, Axel, would perish as a *Luftwaffe* officer in 1941 leading a mission to Iraq [14].

The *Fronde* also sought to broaden the officer base in contrast to Seeckt who, while demanding well-educated Army officers, preferred those of an aristocratic background. The aristocracy dominated the Army providing nearly a quarter of the officers and, even in 1932, more than a third of the officer cadets. Fighter ace's Günther '*Franzl*' Lützow's cousin, *Oberstleutnant* Eberhard Kinzel, was the head of Foreign Armies East (*Fremde Heeres Ost*) from November 1938 to May 1942, while Blomberg's nephew would be the future *Generalfeldmarschall* Walter von Reichenau [15].

Air planning reflected the growing divide between the conservatives and the modernisers. During the war the *Luftstreitkräfte* suffered from piecemeal deployment with the largest permanent unit being the *Geschwader* of no more than 50 aircraft. By contrast the Allies, and especially the French, had concentrated most of their air power into formations of 100 to 150 aircraft which were often grouped into larger commands[16]. By 1925 Wilberg was proposing a similar structure for a future air force but Army conservatism was demonstrated in June 1927 only eight months after Seeckt's departure with the publication of the Outline Mobilisation Plan for Wartime Armed Forces (*Aufstellungsplan einer Kriegswehrmacht*) or *A-plan*.

This envisaged a 21-division army with air squadrons in each *Wehrkreis* and some 247 aircraft of which 47 would be fighters (Fokker D.XIII transferred from Lipetsk) and 57 *Behelfsbomber*, the remainder would be corps aircraft. The *A-plan* air scheme was revised in 1929 into a force with 22 *Staffeln*, each of six aircraft, mostly corps squadrons but including six with fighters and three with heavy night bombers. Even the Operations Branch recognised the imbalance of corps aircraft forming 59 per cent of the squadrons and in April 1930 proposed cutting overall strength to 18 *Staffeln* but with only four corps squadrons, a third each being fighters and bombers, the latter reflecting the growing recognition of the bombers' importance[17].

This was the first official move towards an independent air force but even in 1931 the most senior 'air' officer was only an *Oberstleutnant*, whose status remained advisory. But with Blomberg's support in 1924 Wilberg's TA (L) organisation was expanded into a full department with Operations, Personnel, Technical and Administration desks to which an Air Defence desk was added the following year to create an embryo air staff. In 1927 it received an Intelligence desk and was made responsible for operational training and on this high note Wilberg, an *Oberstleutnant* since 1926, departed for an infantry regiment and did not return to aviation until 1933.

He was replaced by 42-year-old Württemberger, *Major* Hugo Sperrle, who had joined the infantry in 1903 but received flying training while with the War Academy (*Kriegesakademie*) on the eve of the Great War. During the war he became first a squadron commander and then in March 1917 one of the new Group Aviation Leaders (*Gruppenführer der Flieger*). In 1918 he became *Kofl 7. Armee* on the French front and afterwards held a similar position supporting the *Freikorps* in Silesia. Subsequently he served as *Wehrkreis V Referent zbV* and in an artillery regiment before replacing Wilberg but his abrasive personality meant he lasted barely a year before also being posted to an infantry regiment[18].

Hauptmann Helmuth Felmy, aged 39, replaced him at T2 III (L), as TA(L) was renamed, in 1925. An infantryman born in Berlin, he was involved in aviation by 1912 as well as qualifying as a staff officer and then commanded air squadrons, notably in Palestine. In the *Reichsheer* he ostensibly joined the Motor-Transport organisation but from 1924 was Wilberg's planning officer. He and Blomberg, who visited Lipetsk in 1928, increasingly favoured the creation of a single air force and as the first step they proposed combining all air activity within an inspectorate, an idea backed by the *RWM*'s efficiency expert *Major* Albert Kesselring[19].

On 30 September 1929 Blomberg was transferred to East Prussia's *Wehrkreis I* but the following day the *Inspekteur der Waffenschule* became the *Inspekteur der Waffenschulen und der Luftwaffe*. Not only did this have equal status with the remaining *Truppenamt* departments but it was under the 50-year-old Bavarian staff officer, *Generalmajor* Hilmar *Ritter* von Mittelberger, who had ended the war, like Haehnelt, in 2. *Armee* and then held a variety of positions[20].

Earlier, the *Heereswaffenamt* split Student's aircraft and equipment development organisation and while he retained responsibility for development/testing *Hauptmann* Helmuth Volkmann took over acquisition/economic planning. Volkmann later assumed control of both and on 1 October 1929 this became an embryo aircraft development and procurement organisation. Its head was to have been Wilberg's former Operations officer, *Hauptmann* Paul Jeschonnek, but he had been killed in a flying accident some four months earlier and replaced by another Bavarian 'Old Eagle' *Major* Wilhelm Wimmer[21]. Although not a staff officer Wimmer proved more than capable of converting staff requirements into aircraft with almost all of the *Luftwaffe*'s wartime combat aircraft being developed under his auspices.

By 1930 the *Reichswehrministerium* was poised to resuscitate German air power barely 11 years after the Versailles *Diktat*. Three 'advertising' squadrons' (*Reklamestaffeln*) were created on 1 October in *Wehrkreise* I (Königsberg), II (Berlin) and III (Nuremberg) each with 11 men (including recalled instructors from Lipetsk) and four Albatros L 75a/L 82 biplane trainers based upon the 1927 *Fliegerkurierstaffeln*. Ostensibly owned by *Luftfahrt GmbH*, they were cadres for corps squadrons with qualified observers but would also tow targets for the anti-aircraft batteries[22].

Seeckt's policies meant the *Reichsheer* recognised the importance of air power and air officers had their own war games early in each year. Most of the *Luftstreitkräfte* officers whom Seeckt had inserted into the *Reichsheer* were still alive by the early 1930s and they had been augmented by some 550 potential aircrew who had been through either Lipetsk or the *Sportsflug/DVS* organisations. Curiously a high proportion of air officers, up to 20 per cent, tended to be attached to the cavalry divisions[23].

On 29 November 1930 a key meeting was held in Berlin with Defence Minister Wilhelm Groener (a former *Generalleutnant* who had succeeded Ludendorff as Army Chief-of-Staff in 1918), the Foreign Minister Julius Curtius and the Transport

Major Hugo Sperrle was a front line veteran having served as an infantry officer, air squadron commander and staff officer as Kofl 7. Armee on the French front. A caustic and bombastic man, he served only briefly as Wilberg's replacement before being moved to the infantry.

Hauptmann Helmuth Felmy, a former infantryman who had worked closely with Wilberg, replaced Sperrle as head of T2 III (L) and, in the late 1920s, pushed for the creation of a stand-alone air force.

In late 1930, the energetic former bomber pilot, Ernst Brandenburg, played an instrumental role in advising the German government on how best to proceed with the production of military aircraft in discreet contravention of the Versailles Treaty.

Minister Theodor von Guerard. Expert advice was provided by Brandenburg and Mittelberger and, while the participants reluctantly agreed with Curtius that there should be no open defiance of the Versailles Treaty, the meeting did agree to begin production of military aircraft and equipment developed at Lipetsk for storing at secure facilities [24].

Less than a month later Mittelberger published and circulated a document 'Training Guidelines for the Luftwaffe's Role within the Armed Forces' (*Richtlinien für die Ausbildung in der Reichswehr auf dem Gebiet der Luftwaffe*). But already questions were being raised about the organisation of air power and while many of Mittelberger's officers were seeking an autonomous air force this idea raised a storm of objection when the *Truppenamt* leader, *Generalleutnant* Kurt *Freiherr* von Hammerstein-Equord canvassed his department heads in mid-May 1930 [25].

Opponents were led by *Oberstleutnant* Wilhelm Keitel, Head of Organisation (and future leader of *Oberkommando des Wehrmacht* - OKW), who feared the airmen would fight a private war and abandon the Army. They sought to copy the wartime organisation but Mittelberger skilfully diverted their wrath by assuring his colleagues that the airmen would never abandon their comrades. Hammerstein-Equord's successor, *Generalleutnant* Wilhelm Adam, was persuaded and his policy published on 21 April 1931 (the 13th anniversary of the Red Baron's death) stated that the airmen and the anti-aircraft forces should be unified. Adam would later face down a rebellion by some departmental heads on this issue.

Mittelberger completed the rout of his opponents on 24 February 1932 when Hammerstein-Equord, now head of the Army, stated that the air arm (still referred to variously as *Fliegertruppe* [the title from 1914-1916], *Flugwaffe* and *Luftstreitkräfte* [the term from 1916 to 1918]) would be a separate service equal in status to the Army and the Navy. Six months later one of Mittelberger's officers, *Hauptmann* Hans Jeschonnek, made the logical proposal that an air ministry based upon Brandenburg's organisation be established for the new service [26].

Interestingly, Keitel's old department endorsed the plan in October and proposed absorbing naval aviation, long a goal of the Army 'Old Eagles', the only significant dissenter within the *Truppenamt* being training chief, *Oberstleutnant* Walther Wever, who described the idea as 'nonsense'. On 28 October the *Truppenamt* decided to sell the idea to the Government but the politicians were more concerned with the deepening political crisis, although the appointment of Blomberg as Defence Minister in December 1932 was a straw in the wind.

Felmy was already demanding implementation of the 22-*Staffeln* plan to begin German aerial re-armament. This became the rallying point for the nascent *Luftwaffe* and Adam formally made the

request when he met new Defence Minister and *Freikorps* father, Kurt von Schleicher on 11 July 1932. Adam wanted to complete the plan by 1936 and also to create a training organisation of seven units with 140 aircraft and 4,600 men. After pondering the programme for three days Schleicher rubber-stamped it on 14 July (Bastille Day) and also authorised the creation of anti-aircraft gun (*Fliegerabwehrkanone-Flak*) batteries from October 1933 [27].

Work was to begin the following financial year and by 1936 there would be 280 aircraft including some 70 reserves. Adam's and Felmy's organisational plans reflected traditional German military thought with the front-line squadrons (150 aircraft) and schools (60 aircraft) under separate commands, the squadrons being assigned to regional commands (*Fliegergruppenkommando*) with headquarters at Königsberg, Berlin and Nuremberg and the bomber squadrons (which would also provide long-range reconnaissance) being augmented by converted *Lufthansa* aircraft. But Felmy was already looking to the future and in February 1932 proposed an 80-*Staffeln* force (720 aircraft) from 1938 of which more than half would be bombers at the disposal of general headquarters and this would form the basis for the next generation military aircraft [28].

While the Army could look forward with confidence to the new decade, the Navy was less sanguine. In June 1925 Faber's organisation was incorporated under the naval administration's (*Allgemeines Marineamt*) sea transportation organisation (*Seetransportabteilung*) and assigned to *Kapitän zur See* Rudolf Lahs, a destroyer commander at the Battle of Jutland, as *Gruppe BSx*. In September 1929 Lahs was promoted to *Konteradmiral* and retired to become head of the National Association of the German Aviation Industry (*Reichsverband der Deutschen Luftfahrtindustrie* - RDLI). The following day, 1 October, his organisation was renamed *Gruppe LS* under *Kapitän zur See* Konrad Zander, previously commander of the Baltic Naval Station (*Marinestation des Ostee*).

All flying training was performed within Germany with *ab initio* work at a yacht club near Lübeck. Most training was performed by *Seeflugzeug-Versuchsabteilung GmbH* (*Severa*) which Osterkamp had established at Kiel-Holtenau in 1924 ostensibly as a civilian air freight organisation with a contract to tow targets for navy gunnery training. *Severa* provided air- and ground-crew training and provided a cover for naval air bases which were established during the next five years at Norderney, Wangerooge and Wilhelmshaven-Rüstringen although it had ceased to exist when the latter base opened [29]. This was because the head of the *Seetransportabteilung Kapitän zur See* Günther Lohmann lost control of covert investment which caused a RM26 million ($6.19 million) loss. When this was revealed the resulting scandal swept away Lohmann, the Navy commander (who was replaced by *Admiral* Erich Raeder) and even the Defence

Minister. Groener had to resolve the crisis by winding up Lohmann's organisations including *Severa*, which ultimately became *Luftdienst GmbH* and continued its overt and covert activities unhindered until absorbed by DVS in 1933.

The Navy exploited the Paris Agreement of 1926 to begin ordering seaplanes and flying boats. Evaluation was performed in Travemünde and in 1928 the first nine Heinkel He 5s were acquired with 10 He 9s the following year, while six Dornier R *Superwals* were also acquired 'for *Severa* and *Lufthansa*.' Because they had to operate in Germany these aircraft were unarmed although from the late 1920s, as the Navy began to evaluate fighter designs, Lipetsk was used in the weapon development process while sea trials were conducted either on Swiss lakes or in Scandanavian fjords. In 1932, for example, a Swedish-registered Ju 52ce was used for torpedo-bomber trials in Oslo Fjord using Norwegian Navy torpedoes.

Work began on developing land-based torpedo-bombers in 1928 but an increasingly cost-conscious government sought rationalisation of the two services' air programmes. Raeder and most of his senior officers were battleship men and to secure funding for the first of the new light battleships (*Panzerschiffe*) they agreed on 1 October 1929 to rationalise aircraft development, with the Army being responsible for landplanes and the Navy for seaplanes. But this innocuous agreement would set the Navy on the slippery slope which would eventually end in it losing all control of air power, as will be discussed in a later volume.

The German Navy's continued indifference to aviation was demonstrated when Zander was

The sleek profile of a Heinkel He 5 floatplane on the water. This is the fourth prototype of 1926, powered by a 450 hp Napier Lion engine. The He 5 became noteworthy for the fact that during a competition at Warnemünde in 1926, one such aircraft rammed a motor cruiser and sank, while another won the competition! This did not prevent the German Navy from subsequently operating nine He 5s two years later.

replaced in October 1932. The new aviation head was a former U-boat ace, *Fregattenkapitän* Ralf Wenninger who had won the *Pour le Mérite* during the Great War, together with his father. He became Zander's Chief-of-Staff a year earlier, selected more for reasons of seniority than experience, of which he was totally lacking.

A Heinkel He 9 speeds across a gentle swell demonstrating the high performance with which it attained six world seaplane records. Fitted with a BMW VIa 660 hp 12-cylinder engine, the He 9 reached speeds in excess of 230 km/h in the summer of 1929. That year the German Navy acquired ten such machines.

Fregattenkapitän Ralf Wenninger, holder of the Pour le Mérite in recognition of his service as a U-boat commander, was appointed to head German naval aviation in October 1932. However, he lacked experience for the post and by 5 May 1933 had been sidelined to head up the Zentralabteilung (Z-Amt) in the Reichsministerium.

He 60 B, W.Nr. 416, was registered D-2325 in December 1932 to the RDL (Reichsverband der Deutschen Luftfahrtindustrie, Berlin) at the Erprobungsstelle Travemünde – the marine testing facility at Travemünde on the Baltic coast. By mid-1936 the BMW VI-powered He 60 began to equip a number of the fledgling Küstenfliegergruppen. By the the end of 1937 four such Staffeln existed equipped with the type as well as two shipboard Bordfliegergruppen. The aircraft behind the He 60 is a He 59 registered in June 1932 as D-2215 W.Nr. 379.

A view of Lipetsk airfield and its hangars taken in mid-1933 shortly before the Germans left the facility.

Land-locked Austria also covertly re-established its air arm during the late 1920s despite severe funding problems. Vienna regained control of national aviation with a separate Paris Agreement signed on 27 October 1927 and this included a provision that a maximum of 12 soldiers might hold civilian pilots' licences over the next seven years. The task of covertly creating an air force was assigned to *Oberst* Alexander Löhr a staff officer and 'Old Eagle' who promptly created an *Abteilung* L and began to create a training organisation. His officially authorised pilots were to be the instructors and were trained in Switzerland as well as by DVS while a school nominally owned by the national airline ÖLAG was established at Graz-Thalerhof[30].

Army cadets could volunteer for the school where instruction with DVS support began in 1930 using war-surplus Brandenburger C.Is augmented by Hopfner HS 8-29 and Phönix L2cs. Despite cash shortages the school was slowly expanded and by 1932, Löhr had 46 airmen. The previous year an operational unit was created under *Major* Yllam with a single Junkers A 35b which was augmented by six Fiat-Ansaldo A120 corps aircraft. From May 1930 police airmen were trained at Graz-Thalerhof and a *Polizei-Fliegerstaffel* was created with 12 war-surplus aircraft.

Vienna's financial resources were stretched to the limit and it proved impossible to expand the miniature air force during 1932; indeed by the end of the year two of the Fiat-Ansaldos had to be grounded to save money. Germany maintained links with the new air force and during 1931 Sachsenberg gave lectures on air warfare while Wimmer visited the country during July.

As the RWM slowly rebuilt German air power, Lipetsk's days were obviously numbered although a new director, 41-year-old *Major* Hellmuth Bieneck, was appointed in May 1929. An airman who had worked alongside Felmy in Palestine, he was the *Wehrkreis VI Referent zbV* and

later played a major role in establishing the *Luftwaffe's* training organisation[31].

The late 1920s saw intense activity as aircraft competed to win contracts for the new air force with the Arado SD IV/V and Heinkel HD 38 (later He 38) being developed into the Arado Ar 64/65 and the Heinkel He 51, while for the reconnaissance contracts Heinkel had two winners with the HD 41 becoming the He 45 long-range reconnaissance (*Fernaufklärung*) and the HD/He 46 becoming the short-range reconnaissance (*Nahaufklärung*) or corps role. The Dornier Do F 'air freighter' would be selected for the bomber role as the Do 11 but the lack of powerful engines, a result of the Versailles Treaty, proved worrying while both the He 46 and Dornier suffered serious shortcomings.

The base was costing the cash-strapped RWM RM3 million ($714,000) a year, 20 per cent of total military aviation expenditure and with the Depression blasting capitalist economies Berlin needed to make better use of the funds. By 1932 German activity at Lipetsk was clearly at an all-time low and in October the Russians demanded that the Germans restore their use of the base and return all their military aircraft which had returned to Germany after testing.

During the year Mittelberger met Yakov I. Alksnis, the visionary head of the Russian air force who was of Latvian extraction and spoke fluent German, while Wimmer met Alksnis' former Chief-of-Staff, Sergei Mezhenikov. As the Russians demanded a German return to Lipetsk, Felmy was proposing its closure and this was implemented the following year. The news was broken to the Russians during the summer of 1933 and the last Germans departed in September leaving their hosts with the facilities and the remaining Fokker D.XIII. The Germans reoccupied Lipetsk in 1941 but lost it permanently in 1943 and the base continues to be operated by the Russian air force to this day.

Their success owed much to the Stalinist Purges which began three years later and lasted until the outbreak of war. Almost all the Russian military leaders, including Alksnis, fell into the bloody maw, Radek suffering a show trial and disappearing in a prison camp either in 1939 or 1940. The important and the insignificant were all carried away and it is very likely the victims included all the young maids whom the Germans had wooed in Lipetsk.

NOTES TO CHAPTER TWO

1. For the negotiations see Carsten pp.67-68, 70-71, 116, 135-138, 142-143, 147, 234, 362. Erickson, *The Soviet High Command*, pp. 92, 109-110, 144-163. Homze pp.7-9, 8-11. Lennart Andersson, *Junkers Two Seaters*.

2. Corum pp.163-164.

3. For Lipetsk see Braatz pp 53ff. Carsten pp.236-237; Homze p.9; Hooton, pp 44-49; Schliephake pp.14, 17-18, 21, Appendix B; Suchenwirth pp. 11-13.Völker pp.134-135, 140-142, 156, 158-159; Lennart Anderson, *The Secret Luftwaffe*; Speidel, *Reichswehr und Rote Armee*. Johnson, *Planting the Dragon's Teeth*. Website: worldatwar.net. Vercamer and Pipes, *German Military in the Soviet Union 1918-1933*. Website: feldgrau.com.

4. No further information on Stahr appears to have been published.

5. Völker, Anlage 15.

6. For *Sportsflug* and its successors see Hooton pp.57-59. Völker pp.137-140, 145-146, 149-151, 154.

7. UKNA Air 2/1353: report 0160/1825 of July 5 1933, Appendices A-F; SHAT 7N2620.

8. Information kindly supplied by Mr Richard Smith.

9. The future *Lufttransportchef* Friedrich 'Fritz' Morzik flew for the rival Russian airline Dobrolet during the 1920s- Alexandrov, *Junkers Planes in Russia*.

10. Hooton p.48.

11. For Milch and *Lufthansa* see Irving's biography. See also Corum pp.150-151, 153.Völker pp.152-153.

12. UKNA Air 2/13889.

13. Corum pp.94-95.

14. For the *Fronde* see Carsten pp.245-248, 253, 261; Seaton pp. 15-16, Deist pp.5-6.

15. Kinzel became Chief-of-Staff of *Heeresgruppe Nord* then *Heeresgruppe Weichsel* and finally *OKW-Führungsstab Nord*. He and his mistress committed suicide on June 24 1945.

16. Corum, pp.153-154.

17. Carsten p.27, Homze pp.30-31, 43;Völker, pp.159-160, 166-169.

18. Mitchell p.35.Völkers p.136, 143-144, 161.See Sperrle's entry in Collins & Miller's website *Axis Biographical Research*.

19. Völker p163.

20. Hooton pp.51-52. Suchenwirth pp. 16-21. I am indebted to Mr Wolfgang Frey of the *Bundesarchiv* for providing a resumé of Mittleberger's career.

21. Suchenwirth pp.34-37.Völker pp144, 155-156, 164. Jeschonnek's younger brother *Hauptmann* Hans Jeschonnek would join Mittelberger's organisation in charge of tactics and training in 1931.

22. Völker p.171. Useful information on clandestine German air activity may also be found in Nowarra, *Verbotenen Flugzeuge* and Ries, *Maulwürfe*.

23. Corum p.149, 162-163.

24. Völker pp.159-160.

25. For this debate see Corum, *Luftwaffe* pp.86-88;Völker pp.173-180. Hooton pp.71-74.

26. Hooton p.75;Völker p.195.

27. Hooton pp.73-74. Völker pp.188-189.

28. Völker pp171-172.

29. For naval aviation see Corum, *Luftwaffe* pp.78-81; Hooton pp.59-61, 65-66 Suchenwirth pp.41-45.Völker pp.135-136, 139, 145, 151, 156-158, 164-165.

30. Gabriel pp.230-232; Hooton pp 79-80; Mitcham p.133; Green, *Aerial Alpenstock*.

31. See his entry in Collins & Miller's *Axis Biographical Research* website.

CHAPTER THREE

THE WEVER
YEARS

1933–1936

General der Flieger Walther Wever

Three days before Adolf Hitler became Chancellor, Hammerstein-Equord informed the *Reichswehr* leadership on 27 January that the training of air- and ground-crews would have absolute priority.

While the aristocratic officers regarded the Nazis with contempt, the party's egalitarian policies attracted many middle-class officers who also responded to the siren song of defiance to the Versailles *Diktat*. None more so than Defence Minister Blomberg who had become a Nazi sympathiser while commander of *Wehrkreise* I in East Prussia.

Europe was in the throes of the Depression and the Nazis offered a dynamic solution to the nation's social and economic problems. This was underlined by Hitler's use of aircraft provided by Milch to make whistle-stop tours around the country during the 1932 election. Many 'Old Eagles' were either Party members or sympathisers including the Deputy *Führer*, Rudolf Hess (who had been a *Freikorps* pilot), Greim (who had taken Hitler on his first flight), Heinrich Müller (who would later run the *Gestapo*) and former air ace Bruno Loerzer (who commanded the Party's aviation organisation the *SA Fliegersturm*), while future *Luftwaffe* general Günther Korten had been linked with the Party since the early 1920s. The aviation spokesman was Hermann Göring.

By the Armistice Göring held the *Pour le Mérite* and was the Red Baron's heir commanding JG I although scoring no victories in the last four months of the war[1]. While studying in Munich after the war he came into contact with the Nazis and headed their *Sturm Abteilung* (SA) 'bully-boys' but was seriously injured in the Munich coup farce of 1923 in which Korten was also involved.

His injuries left him a lifelong drug addict on 'hard' and then 'soft' drugs which further warped his personality and caused his weight to balloon until by 1933 he weighed some 125 kilos. Göring regarded himself as 'The Iron Man' (*Der Eiserne*) but his weight led to the less flattering nickname of 'The Fat Man' or 'Fatty' (*Der Dicke*)[2]. Yet this gave him the *persona* of the bluff, good-humoured aristocrat who was more acceptable to the Great and the Good. In reality he remained a thug and blustering bully; he was the first head of the Prussian *Gestapo* and would control the national telephone interception service whose headquarters would be installed in the basement of

the Air Ministry (*Reichsluftministerium* - RLM). In the 1920s he became a Parliamentary deputy while supplementing his income by acting as part-time agent for both Heinkel (although he was uneasy at the designer's semitic appearance) and BMW while Milch, in his hunt for *Lufthansa* subsidies, also provided bribes. Göring was eventually receiving RM50,000 ($11,900) a year at a time when a night out with a meal, beer and a visit to the cinema cost only RM5.00 ($1.19).

Göring's megalomania made him determined to benefit from the Party's pledge to create an air ministry controlling all aspects of aviation, although he never gave any thought to air power applications. When Hitler came to power Göring became National Commissar for Aviation (*Reichskommisar für die Luftfahrt*) within Brandenburg's organisation but with Milch as his deputy, and in March the *Reichsluftfahrtkommissariat* was established in Behrenstrasse. That month Göring visited the German

Ltn dR Rudolf Hess of Jasta 35b, seen here with an unarmed triplane of Jastaschule II. Hess saw active service with Jasta 35b, flying Fokker D.VIIs. He survived the war and became Hitler's deputy in the Nazi Party. He became a POW in Britain in 1941 and died in Spandau Prison on 17 August 1987.

When he became deputy leader of the NSDAP, Rudolf Hess was a very keen aviator and in February 1935 won the Zugspitzflug flying the Messerschmitt-built M 35.

Hermann Göring (right) returns from a ride in the country with the ageing President Paul von Hindenburg. On 31 August 1933, von Hindenburg promoted Göring from his wartime rank of Hauptmann to no less than a General der Infanterie. But just under a year later on 1 August 1934, Hindenburg died and Adolf Hitler assumed the title of Reich President as well as Chancellor. Göring's path to power was assured.

Relaxing in deckchairs in front of Hermann Göring's triplane 206/17 with its white cowling are, on the left, Hptm Bruno Loerzer (44 victories), Staffelführer of Jasta 26, and Obltn Göring (22 victories), Staffelführer of Jasta 27. Loerzer would survive the war and remain a firm friend of Göring.

Robert Ritter von Greim was born in 1892, joining the Bavarian Army in 1911. In 1916 he transferred to the Flying Service, rising to command first Jasta 34 and then Jagdgruppe 10. By the end of the war he had 26 victories and had been awarded the Pour le Mérite on 10 October 1918. After helping Chiang Kai-shek to organise an air force in China, he returned to Germany and formed the DVS at Berlin-Staaken. While serving there he established Reklamestaffel Mitteldeutschland which became the Luftwaffe's first fighter Gruppe. He led this unit until he became Inspector of Fighters and Dive Bombers in April 1935. In 1936 he was made Inspector of Equipment and Flight Safety and next year became Luftwaffe Head of Personnel.

A stern-faced Hermann Göring walks with his new Führer, Adolf Hitler, on an 'Erinnerungsmarsch', a march to commemorate the Beer Hall Putsch, with other Alte Kämpfer – 'old fighters' – from the Nazi Party in Munich on 9 November 1934.

Göring would be rewarded for his loyalty: here Adolf Hitler shakes hands with the newly promoted Commander-in-Chief of the Luftwaffe in 1938, Generalfeldmarschall Hermann Göring.

flight test centre at Rechlin to demand greater progress on military aviation.

Meanwhile, his control over aviation became absolute. On 25 March 1933 the DLV absorbed all private aviation organisations and was retained as the German Air Sport Association (*Deutschen Luftsportverband e.V*). Its 12 (later 16) *Luftsportlandesgruppen* retained the ethos of the original DLV but added paramilitary training together with subtle political indoctrination for boys as young as ten. The president was Göring's pre-war friend, Bruno Loerzer, with whom he had joined the *Fliegertruppen* and who was once his pilot. The 44-victory 'ace' commanded JG III during the war but had difficulty

settling down afterwards and became a heavy drinker. After serving in Goltz' *Freikorps* he became a cigar salesman before throwing in his lot with the Nazis. Despite his doubtful competence he now controlled the framework of an *ab initio* flying training organisation.

The RWM welcomed the idea of an air ministry but it did not wish for a civilian overlord, even one with so distinguished a war record. Mittelberger now made his last contribution to German air power and at his suggestion all military and naval aviation, as well as *Flak*, were to be merged into the Air Defence Department (*Luftschutz Amt*) on 1 April while the *Heereswaffenamt* remained responsible for development and production. Mittelberger retired and spent the next ten years advising the Turkish Government and instructing at its War Academy. His contacts were exploited in 1939 when he became Head of the Liaison Staff in Ankara until he returned to Germany in February 1943 and died there ten years later.

But Blomberg, Göring and Milch were already outflanking the services with Blomberg, who had been 7. *Armee* head of operations when Sperrle was *Kofl*, sabotaging the new organisation. Instead of assigning it to Milch's old friend Felmy, as the Army intended, it went to *Oberst* Eberhardt Bohnstedt, a wartime *Flak* officer due to retire in September and described, probably unfairly, by Reichenau as a 'stupid clot'. Felmy was transferred to an infantry regiment and while Milch hypocritically expressed surprise, he wrote in his diary following a meeting with Blomberg on April 25: "*We get the lot!*[3]" Two days later Göring became *Reichsminister für die Luftfahrt*, nominally under Blomberg who curtly informed Bohnstedt a fortnight later that the *Luftschutz Amt* would be transferred to the RLM on 15 May, which became the *Luftwaffe*'s official birthday[4].

Despite the setbacks, the RWM's plan continued to take shape. One of the few Nazi cabinet meetings approved the expenditure of RM40 million ($9.52 million) on the rapid expansion of the Air Force and Göring would ensure the *Luftwaffe*'s share of the defence budget would rise from 10 per cent (RM 76 million or $18.1 million) in 1933 to 38 per cent (RM2.23 billion or $897 million) in 1936. In Dollar terms this compares with British expenditure of $66.5 million (15.6 per cent of the defence budget) to $247.2 million (26 per cent) in the same period and French expenditure of $5.8 million (12.7 per cent) and $17.4 million (18.5 per cent).

To supervise the reformation of the German Air Force, Göring wanted to use the most senior representative of the aircraft industry, *Konteradmiral* Lahs. But Lahs recognised that the RLM would be a poisoned chalice and politely declined. Brandenburg was too conservative and too stubborn, so Göring proposed Milch as State Secretary for Aviation (*Staatssekretär der Luftfahrt*) and Blomberg sanctioned this on 19 October 1933 by promoting him to *Oberst*, with Göring having been promoted to *General der Infanterie* on 31 August.

Milch's cherubic features concealed a heart of stone wrapped in a huge ego based upon a justified belief in his own dynamism and organisational skills. He was abrasive with equals, overbearing with subordinates and oversensitive to sleights real or imagined. This meant he collected enemies like others collected stamps until the irresistible force of his ego would run into the immovable object of the *Führer*'s will over the issue of Me 262 jet bombers in 1944 and, as a delighted observer commented, he was 'shot down in flames'.

Milch's father (like Wilberg's) was Jewish, a significant hurdle in the anti-semitic regime but both officers became *kosher* Ayrans by decree, although they were not strictly Jews and their exemplary war records should have shielded them from the stream of Nazi race regulations. Göring himself once stated he would decide who was, or was not, Jewish and he shielded many people, partly influenced by his second wife Emmy. By contrast Milch made little effort to protect those tarnished with racial impurity and in 1935 purged even the air defence warning organisation. It should be remembered that the *Luftwaffe* used the Nazi Party salute until it was unveiled on 1 March 1935 and both Hitler and Göring had wanted this adopted by the other services[5].

Göring played little further part in the development of the *Luftwaffe* until 1936 and Milch was *de facto* air minister until the autumn of 1937. Initially he directly controlled Bohnstedt's and Brandenburg's departments which became separate directorates responsible for military and civil aviation and were joined on 1 October by Wimmer's organisation from the *Heereswaffenamt*.

Bohnstedt and Brandenburg quickly faded from the picture and with Wimmer's arrival and the former's old organisation was renamed the Air Command Directorate (*Luftkommandoamt*) under 47-year-old *Oberstleutnant* (*Oberst* from April 1934) Bernhard Kühl who joined the *Luftwaffe* in September 1933. Kühl, whose round cheeks and large spectacles gave him a curiously amiable appearance similar to Dickens' Mr Pickwick, was born in Memel and after

The heavy-drinking, former cigar salesman, Bruno Loerzer, seen here as head of the DLV (Deutsche Luftsportverband), at the left of this photograph. He is talking to Wolfgang Späte (right) at the 1935 Rhön trials on the Wasserkuppe. Späte, who was at this time one of Germany's best known glider pilots, eventually joined 5./JG 54 on the Eastern Front, becoming its Staffelkapitän in the autumn of 1941. In July 1942 he was transferred to the Rechlin Experimental Station where he formed Erprobungskommando 16 responsible for developing the Me 163 rocket fighter.

With the rank of Oberst (Colonel), Erhard Milch was propelled to the position of Secretary of State for Aviation by Göring on 19 October 1933. The fact that Milch's father was Jewish did not stop his meteoric rise to the very pinnacle of the Nazi system, and ultimately, along with Albert Speer, he was in control of transportation throughout the Third Reich.

As Reichskommisar für die Luftfahrt, Göring, seen here, far right, visiting a factory with Nazi officials in 1936, made sure that the German economy increased its spending on aviation dramatically in the mid-1930s. By 1936 expenditure on the Luftwaffe had reached RM2.23 billion, just under forty per cent of the national defence budget.

Oberst Bernhard Kühl, a First World War squadron commander and former infantry officer, joined the Luftwaffe in September 1933 to head the fledgling Luftkommandoamt. Kühl saw his department expand to become the Luftwaffeführungsstab in June 1935. By April 1936 he was serving as the Höherer Fliegerkommandeure II as part of General der Flieger Leonhard Kaupisch's Luftkreis II based in Berlin.

Hans Jürgen Stumpff, who eventually reached the rank of Generaloberst, was born in 1890, serving with the German Army and appointed to the General Staff in 1916. In 1933 he transferred to the Luftwaffe, becoming head of the Personnel Office. From June 1937 to January 1939 he was Chief of the General Staff and then took over Luftflotte 1 early in 1940.

infantry service he became a staff officer and then an air observer. He became a squadron commander in 1916 and ended the war as a *Grufl* (*Gruppenführer der Flieger* or 'Group Aviation Leader') responsible for co-ordinating air operations at army corps level. After *Freikorps* service in Silesia he rejoined the infantry and then became *Referent zbV Wehrkreis II* before returning to the infantry[6].

The naval air organisation was absorbed, with Wenninger and his deputy, *Korvettenkapitän* Ulrich Kessler, sidelined as air attachés covering London, Brussels and the Hague. The organisation remained unchanged for a year when in June 1935 the expanded *Luftkommandoamt* created a Command Staff (*Luftwaffenführungsstab*), with intelligence and administrative elements, as an operational headquarters under Kühl who handed over to *Oberst* Wilhelm Mayer in October 1935.

More important than the Air Force organisation were the men who ran it. Blomberg had available some 550 officers with flying experience but between 1933 and 1934 transferred only 182 soldiers and 42 sailors, the majority (175 or 78 per cent) being reserve officers. The Defence Minister clearly, and understandably, had no intention of undermining the expansion of the traditional services but what they lacked in quantity was compensated by the quality and they helped to lay a firm foundation for the new service[7].

The congenial, yet self-effacing Pomeranian head of the *Personnelamt* (Personnel Department) was *Oberstleutnant* Hans-Jürgen Stumpff who arrived on 1 July and celebrated his 42nd birthday a fortnight later. Stumpff was the second son of an infantry officer in whose footsteps both he and his brother, Horst, naturally followed. He fought the British at Mons in 1914 and in August 1916 began staff officer training, ending the war with OHL. He then served in the *Reichsheer* and joined the Army Personnel Department (*Personalamt*) in 1929 and so he easily transferred to the *Luftwaffepersonalamtes*. In September 1941 he and Horst, commander of 20. *Panzer Division*, were awarded the *Ritterkreuz* before the latter became *General der Panzertruppe* in the *Ersatzheer*[8].

The younger Stumpff possessed considerable vision and ability while also having the confidence of both Blomberg and Göring. Although very capable, Stumpff aptly looked like a senior bureaucrat and appears to have preferred administrative to operational work, while proving a capable if not charismatic front line leader[9]. He appointed *Oberst* Albert Kesselring head of administration in October, a month before his 48th birthday but his most surprising selection was that of Bohnstedt's successor in the person of *Oberst* Walther Wever who, only a year earlier, had opposed the concept of an independent air force.

Wever's appointment on 1 September 1933 marked the peak of a career which seemed devoid of promise before the war. The West Prussian infantryman of middle class background blossomed in war by displaying clarity of thought and organisational talent. He worked in OHL becoming Ludendorff's

adjutant then became almost a one-man fire brigade during the defensive battles of 1917. He had risen steadily in the *Reichsheer* to become Head of Training, his nationalism fuelled by the loss of his birthplace of Posen (Poznan) to newly-emerged Poland and like Blomberg he became sympathetic to the Nazis without being their puppet[10].

To gain operational freedom the stocky, open-faced officer, who held the persona of a managing director, was happy to become the *éminence grise* and he deftly avoided confrontation with his masters who gave him *carte blanche*. He was blessed with intellectual curiosity and, unlike many modern managers, he was willing to listen to his subordinates, testing their arguments by playing Devil's Advocate and accepting a well-reasoned argument even when not fully convinced.

Working in harness with Milch he remorselessly drove the *Luftwaffe*'s expansion and when subordinates complained that there were only 24 hours in the day, he would curtly advise them: "*Work at night!*" Wever was willing to work behind a desk but, following the Prussian tradition of setting an example, he learned to fly although in three years he had only 200 hours, less than many new *Luftwaffe* pilots. Yet he would often fly out to his growing empire to discuss matters informally in the German tradition of coffee and cake, usually providing the cake himself[11].

Wever's greatest contribution was to combine wartime experience with imagination to develop a unique air doctrine. During the war, the key factor was defensive power based upon artillery which became Queen of the Battlefield by delivering accurate fire at long ranges and at high volumes to create barriers of fire and steel[12].

At what the German Army described as Tactical Level – ie. at divisional and army corps operations – the defence proved a huge hurdle until late 1917 when overcome through covert concentrations of overwhelming force combined with sophisticated artillery techniques, which destroyed command and control. During 1918 Tactical Level breakthroughs became routine but exploitation at what the Germans termed the Operational (*Operativ*) Level (army and army group operations) proved fleeting as the defenders could easily re-weave their webs by exploiting rail systems augmented by automotive power over undamaged roads.

Automotive power promised faster exploitation of tactical breakthroughs at the Operational Level. Indeed, writing of the first German breakthrough in March 1918, the British Official Historian, General Sir James Edmonds, prophetically wrote in 1937: "*In future, it would seem that improvised Armies will have little chance, even if there is time to create them, against an enemy who is in possession of aeroplanes, tanks, armoured cars and mechanised troops to exploit a gap...*[13]". The proviso about 'improvised Armies' reflected the post-war belief that the reformed defensive crust would remain impenetrable to exhausted attackers, a view shared even by Germany's senior military leaders in 1940. *See page 41.*

Many generals, including *Generalleutnant* Ludwig Beck who was chief of the *Truppenamt*/General Staff until 1938, believed that air power should largely support Tactical Level operations. Reconnaissance and close air support were the prime roles, executed mostly by the corps aircraft shielded by fighter screens, a view underlined by the earliest post-war doctrinal documents published in September 1921 and June 1923. The emphasis upon Tactical air power was also repeated about 1925 in an air operations manual published by Wilberg's department. Bombers were long-range guns engaging targets 'beyond artillery range' such as supply dumps and railway marshalling yards, although a counter-air element was included with attacks on airfields and army headquarters[14].

But the bomber was at the heart of the doctrine at the other end of the air power spectrum with the traditional services reduced to little more than spear carriers. The disciples of the Italian Giulio Douhet believed wars would be decided by striking the enemy's industrial heartland to deprive their forces of the sinews of war. Wartime experience appeared to show that exposure to air attack demoralised civilians and Douhet believed that future attacks upon cities would be heavier and force the terrified populace to sue for peace.

The siren song of air power supremacy provided the rationale for autonomous air forces, notably the Royal Air Force (RAF), which followed it unquestioningly. The image of bomber fleets razing cities to the ground, most strikingly shown in the British 1936 film 'Things to Come', loomed large in the public mind fed by ever-more apocalyptic visions in fiction, much as the horrors of nuclear war were highlighted after the Second World War. In February 1932 the World Disarmament Conference, attended by Blomberg and Brandenburg, vainly proposed a total ban on bombers.

The German Army was aware of Douhet's ideas; indeed *Hauptmann* Wolfram von Richthofen, who would soon head technical development, was attached to the Embassy in Rome between April 1929 and September 1932 partly to discover as much as possible about them and their importance to the Italian Air Force. His future boss Wimmer had long advocated a strategic bombing force and on 18 February 1932 argued that the future belonged to those nations which could strike fear in the civilian population.

Within a month Felmy wrote on 12 March that bombers were the only means of neutralising the air threat to Germany; indeed Mittelberger had sought a heavy bomber based upon the Dornier *Superval* (Super Whale) flying boat[15]. The day Hitler came to power the *Heereswaffenamt* issued a directive for a long-range heavy bomber (*Langstrecken-Grossbomber*) capable of reaching targets in northern Scotland or the Urals, the latter earning the requirement the nickname of '*Ural Bomber*.'

Another bomber advocate was *Dr* Robert Knauss, *Lufthansa*'s Traffic Manager and a part-time writer on aeronautics. In May 1933 he proposed an

Dr Robert Knauss (left) was a friend of Milch's and was employed as Lufthansa's Traffic Manager. He was to write a major study analysing the strategic concept of Germany's air power, proposing the creation of an air force, whose decisive element would be a fleet of 400 long-range four-engined 'strategic' bombers. He is seen here in 1926 as the leader of a team which made a 10,000 km aeronautical expedition from Berlin to Peking.

autonomous air force based upon heavy bombers which, like *Grossadmiral* Alfred von Tirpitz' Grand Fleet, would hold the balance of power and prevent Germany succumbing to a two-front threat. Knauss joined the *Luftwaffe* late in 1933 and commanded *Behelfskampfgeschwader* KG 172, the headquarters staff who would form a bomber unit from requisitioned *Lufthansa* Ju 52s upon mobilisation, before becoming *Kommodore* of the *Lehr Geschwader Greifswald* in October 1937. In 1940 he became head of the *Luftkriegsakademie* and died in 1955.

Milch was closely in tune with the wishes of his political masters and knew that they desired an air force which could cow its neighbours. But he also recognised that German industry at that time could not produce a fleet of heavy bombers and so his industrial plans focused upon medium bombers which could strike targets within 500 kilometres of the border and which could be produced quickly[16].

With air power debates polarised between the conservatives and the radicals it was Wilberg who had suggested a middle way in May 1926[17]. This envisaged opening attack upon the enemy heartland to hinder mobilisation and strategic movement, then striking enemy air forces and rear areas to impede their Operational Level movement and finally an all-out assault upon logistics, units and reserves throughout their Tactical and Operational depth in support of friendly operations.

Following his appointment Wever read voraciously about air power in order to meet the demands of his office. He probably became aware of Wilberg's directive but as former Head of Training he was also aware of moves to create mechanised mobile

The Italian air power theorist, Marshal Guilio Douhet, established an air doctrine which supposed the invincibility of mass formations of heavily-armed heavy bombers deployed against centres of civilian population and industry.

During WW1, Walther Wever, although only a Hauptmann, had been appointed as Ludendorff's Adjutant. In 1935 this able and far-sighted officer was appointed as the Luftwaffe's first Chief of Air Staff.

A group of personalities from Deutsche Lufthansa pose with a Turkish flight engineer during the 1920s. From left to right are: Bredow, Krüger, Direktor Milch, Flugkapitän Klaus, Dr. Robert Knauss, the Turkish flight engineer Fehmi Mehhed, Walter Angermund and future Luftwaffe Generalmajor, Carl-August Freiherr von Gablenz. Like Milch, von Gablenz had flown as a combat pilot during the First World War. An extremely accomplished aviator, he was also no stranger to the challenge of long-distance flight, having flown in a Ju 52 from Berlin-Tempelhof, via Belgrade, Athens, Cairo, Baghdad, Calcutta, Bangkok and Canton to Shanghai – a distance of 14,000 km – in August 1934. In 1936 he had made the 3,850 km flight from the Azores to New York. He had worked for Junkers as a technical assistant before joining Deutsche Lufthansa in 1924, rising to its Executive Board in 1933, a position he maintained until his death in an air crash in August 1942.

formations to exploit Tactical Level breakthroughs at Operational Level. Air operations at this level offered him a means of squaring the circle.

He tested the concept in a war game on 27 September 1934 based upon a French offensive and 'hit' first their air force infrastructure and then the army throughout its Tactical-Operational depth to help drive them across the Rhine[18]. He then repeated this success before Beck in a tour de force at the *Reichswehr's* Winter War Games held in Berlin between 6 November and 11 December 1934. For the first two days he played the conservatives' game by focusing upon tactical air support, with an occasional attack upon the enemy bridges across the Rhine.

On the third day he again unleashed a storm of attacks throughout the French Tactical-Operational depth and also struck Paris and industrial centres, the latter mostly to ensure temporary disruption in the supply chains. This brought the enemy to their knees and they sued for peace and while the referees concluded that the *Luftwaffe* had suffered 80 per cent losses Wever brow-beat them into reversing their views[19].

The experience was rapidly incorporated into a new doctrine, drawn up by a committee headed by Wilberg, and published within months of the exercise as *Luftwaffe* Regulation 16: 'The Conduct of the Air War' (*Luftwaffedienstvorschrift 16: Luftkriegführung*)[20]. This accepted the general doctrine that the destruction of the enemy armed forces was the primary goal while Paragraph 10 stated: "*The mission of the* Luftwaffe *is to serve these goals by combining the war in the air within the framework of combined operations*[21]." This would be achieved by securing air superiority then hamstringing enemy mobile forces. This meant attacking road and rail communications between the supply dumps and the front line, especially 'choke points', communications centres and any troop concentrations encountered. At sea it would strike the enemy fleet and its bases, or at ports if the navy was attacking enemy maritime commerce[22].

This doctrine was accepted by all but the most reactionary staff officers, although they included Beck who once sought control of all the fighter squadrons. But as a 'concession' Wever gave them operational control of corps squadrons (*Nahaufklärungsstaffeln*) and some long-range reconnaissance squadrons (*Fernaufklärungsstaffeln*) which actually removed any excuse for interfering in the *Luftwaffe's* operations.

Wever also used his war games success to play for higher stakes. He recognised the strategic potential of air power but, unlike many air leaders, he believed this should be harnessed to an integrated war strategy. Operational Level support could be used as an interim step towards developing a long-range strategic bombing force and *Luftwaffedienstvorschrift 16* anticipated the existence of such a force; indeed as early as May 1934 Wever confirmed a seven-year development programme for the '*Ural Bomber*'.

The strategic element in Operational Level support was clearly described in Paragraph 21 which noted: "*It is more effective to set the air force against a distant target if, by its destruction or closure, it can decisively influence the fighting power of the enemy army or navy*". It added: "*Even during combined operations with the army and navy, the air force should not give up the campaign against the sources of enemy power. One stipulation should be to select targets so that the air force's battle will have a rapid effect upon the ground and sea battle*". The document frequently used Operational terms which had Strategic interpretations[23].

But without infrastructure and aircraft these were mere words. When the Nazis came to power the Army was just beginning to implement Felmy's 22-*Staffeln* plan but a *Truppenamt* meeting on 9 March 1933 amended this to 32 *Staffeln* within two years. Hitler, Göring and Milch had no time for Army caution and within two months Milch revamped the plan to a 51-*Staffeln* force by August 1936 with a strong bomber element[24].

In a 72-hour brainstorming session Milch drafted a production plan costing RM170 million ($40.5 million) to support this programme, which began on 29 June and focused on off-the-shelf designs, some from Lipetsk and others already being marketed. He organised funding for the expansion of existing production facilities and for expansion through the acquisition of related facilities to create production complexes with cost-plus contracts, with industrial manpower rising from some 17,000 at the end of 1933 to nearly 125,000 by mid 1936.

The Lipetsk-developed Arado Ar 64/65 and Heinkel He 51 fighters, together with the Heinkel

The Do 11 C continued the German trend towards development of aircraft with para-military capacity. It had entered service with the Deutsche Reichsbahn (German State Railway), which had commenced an air freight service in November 1933 and also provided covert training for bomber crews.

He 45/46 reconnaissance aircraft, would equip many of the squadrons but the Arado proved delicate, and the He 51 would prove inferior to its contemporaries, while the He 46 vibrated badly. The Dornier Do 11C 'freighter' was selected as the foundation of the bomber force but proved structurally weak and was dubbed the 'Flying Coffin' by its luckless crews. Strengthened versions, the Do 11D and Do 13 (Do 23 from 1935), proved little better. Fortunately the robust and reliable Junkers Ju 52/3m airliner and *Behelfsbomber*, universally dubbed 'Aunty Yu (*Tante Ju*)' by the *Luftwaffe*, proved an adequate substitute.

From 1934 the Technical Office (*Technisches Amt*) under Wimmer was responsible for aircraft development. Wimmer was a 44-year-old Bavarian who learned to fly just before the war and held a variety of front line and staff positions during the war. He had been an air staff officer during the *Freikorps* era and then served in various positions within the Bavarian *Wehrkreis VII*, formally joining the *Luftwaffe* in September 1933 and he was regarded as having the best technical mind in the service [25].

New aircraft development was under 39-year-old *Major* Wolfram von Richthofen, a cousin of the Red Baron, whom he had accompanied on his last flight. He had been a cavalryman until 1917 and after the war gained an engineering degree before returning to the Army, although between 1929 and 1932 he was *de facto* air attaché in Rome [26]. Despite his experience in motorised infantry in 1933 he transferred to the *Luftwaffe* where his ability both to make decisions and to ingratiate himself with his superiors helped his rise up the ladder although he could be extremely impatient and even rude. His voluminous diaries acted as a lightning rod for his professional frustrations and while, like many officers, he played cards off duty, he also played the flute.

He was well aware that the infant *Luftwaffe* was poorly equipped but argued: "Better to have second-rate equipment than none at all." He was at a turning point in aviation technology for in the late 1920s the US aircraft industry revolutionised aircraft design. The traditional airframe was made of alloy tubes and spars strengthened internally and externally with steel rigging wires and covered in fabric, light wood or alloys. It was usually a biplane design to provide greater aerodynamic lift, although the early 1930s saw the appearance of more monoplanes with wings braced by fuselage struts. Both biplanes and monoplanes usually had open cockpits and fixed undercarriages.

But the Americans developed semi-monocoque or stressed skin construction which reversed the traditional concept and was usually incorporated into a monoplane design. The airframe was now based upon the metal skin with some internal stiffening, while the wing was formed around a steel spar which ran through the fuselage. The lightweight structure increased the power-weight ratio to make these aircraft faster than traditional machines and speed was further increased through the introduction of enclosed crew compartments and retractable undercarriages. The increased internal volume could be used for greater fuel and payload capacity but the technical sophistication of the new aircraft was reflected in its increased price.

The Martin 139 bomber was the first combat aircraft to use the semi-monocoque construction technique and to enter volume production. It was capable of outrunning even the fastest fighter and underlined the message of British Premier Ramsay MacDonald that "The bomber will always get through".

In July 1932 the *Heereswaffenamt* issued a specification for a high-speed twin-engined medium

Mechanics at work on the starboard 750 hp BMW VI engine of a Dornier Do 23 bomber. The somewhat clumsy fixed, spatted undercarriage is notable as is the four-bladed wooden propeller and generator mounted under the wing centre section near the fuselage.

Wilhelm Wimmer, head of the Technisches Amt from 1934 was regarded as as having the best technical mind in the Luftwaffe.

bomb load, the '*Ural Bomber*' programme being downgraded to one of evaluation [27].

For Tactical air support a requirement was issued in May 1934 for a multi-role twin-engined aircraft, but within a month this was revised with the reconnaissance role assigned to the Do 17 and close air support assigned to both light and heavy dive-bombers. The former was renamed *Schlachtflugzeug*, while the latter became the *Stürzkampflugzeug* or '*Stuka*'. The former was a single-seat aircraft carrying light bombs and the He 50 was augmented by fighters until the Henschel Hs 123 arrived. The latter led to a slightly revised requirement in January 1935 for a two-man aircraft with longer range and capable of carrying a heavier bomb load, although Richthofen remained dubious about the whole concept.

The Inspector of Fighters and Dive-Bombers (*Inspekteur der Jagd- und Sturzkampfflieger*) *Oberst* Ernst Udet made his most significant contribution to the *Luftwaffe* through the development of the Messerschmitt Bf 109 fighter. The first generation of German fighters reflected a traditional fighter design philosophy emphasising manoeuvrability for dogfights and an open cockpit for all-round vision. But the second generation had to intercept the new bombers, and this required designs that emphasised both speed and firepower, and semi-monocoque construction was employed. A fighter requirement specifying only an all-metal monoplane with retractable undercarriage was issued in December 1933 and led to the Heinkel He 112 and the Messerschmitt Bf 109.

Although no intellectual, Udet made a significant mental leap to appreciate the advantages of the Bf 109 which was designed by his friend Willi Messerschmitt. He 'sold' the Bf 109 at a demonstration before Göring and Blomberg on 3 July 1936 when he combined his own flying skills and the aircraft's superb performance to 'shoot down' not only a bomber formation but also its He 51 fighter escort. However, it is worth noting that the Bf 109 B-1 was a matron with a facelift for, like most biplane fighters it featured only two rifle-calibre machine guns which had to be

Generaloberst Göring's Ju 52/3m, W.Nr. 4022 takes off. This aircraft was allocated exclusively for Göring's use and was named 'Manfred von Richthofen'. His other two machines, W.Nr. 4066 registered D-ABAQ, and W.Nr. 4069 registered D-ABIK, were named 'Manfred von Richthofen II' and 'Manfred von Richthofen III' and were used by senior staff of the RLM as well as by Göring.

bomber, leading to the development of the Dornier Do 17, the Heinkel He 111 and the Junkers Ju 86. However, development was plagued by the difficulty of developing high-power engines, a legacy of the Versailles Treaty, and the Junkers Jumo 205 diesels would prove unreliable. Yet Wimmer and Richthofen recognised the need for a complementary heavy bomber and accelerated the '*Ural Bomber*' programme during 1935, leading to the Do 19 and Ju 89 prototypes appearing in 1936, although both proved under-powered. Consequently, Wever issued a new heavy bomber requirement in April 1936 for 'Bomber A' with a range of 6,700 kilometres with a 900 kilo

"Better to have second-rate equipment than none at all…": Wolfram Freiherr von Richthofen seen here with the rank of General der Flieger and 'wearing' a Ritterkreuz which has been applied after the photograph was taken, although he was awarded that decoration on 17 May 1940 as commander of the VIII Fliegerkorps. A distant cousin to Manfred von Richthofen whom he had accompanied on his last flight, he had been a cavalryman until 1917 and after the war gained an engineering degree before returning to the Army. Known for his temperamental moods, he would rise to become a Generalfeldmarschall in the Luftwaffe.

Heinkel He 111 C-04, D-ABYE 'Königsberg', which was delivered to Lufthansa in the summer of 1936. The aircraft could carry ten passengers at a maximum speed of 315 km/h but was considered by the airline to be too expensive for commercial operation. Nevertheless by the summer of 1937 the type was operating on no fewer than 16 routes.

The Heinkel He 50 biplane was used in small numbers to experiment with dive-bombing. Originating from a Japanese specification for a two-seat dive-bomber, it was a particularly strong aircraft able to withstand high diving speeds. It played a key role in Germany's pre-role dive-bombing development. Trials were conducted using cement 'bombs' at Rechlin and Warnemünde. This example, LP+GY, was attached to a training unit based in Czechoslovakia in 1939-40.

A busy scene at the Junkers airfield at Dessau as the Ju 89 V1 is prepared for a test. These tests were to show that the aircraft had a maximum speed of 390 km/h, but installation of armament would have reduced this performance considerably. It was similar to the Do 19 with a 7.9 mm machine-gun in the nose and tail and a 20 mm cannon in a dorsal and ventral turret. The aircraft in the background of this photograph is the Ju 88 V1 which was also undergoing tests at this time. The Ju 89 was designed to the same 'Ural Bomber' specification as the Do 19 but proved to have a much better performance than its rival. Basically an enlarged Ju 86, the prototype Ju 89 V1 was powered by four 1,075 hp Jumo 211 engines driving three-bladed Hamilton propellers. It made its first flight in December 1936.

Ernst Udet (right) was one of Germany's leading First World War fighter aces, whose score of 62 victories was second only to von Richthofen in the German Air Service. In the post-war years he was an aerobatic pilot and a playboy. A charming and extrovert 'pilot's pilot' and holder of the Pour le Mérite, he captivated and enthralled those who saw his flying displays. One of his most spectacular stunts was to pick up a piece of cloth from the ground with the wingtip of his aircraft. Göring gave him the rank of Oberst and he was appointed Chief of the Technisches Amt of the RLM on 9 June 1936. He was an advocate of of small, fast aircraft and had little understanding of Wever's earlier plans for a long-range, heavy bomber.

During 1934 the Luftwaffe Chief-of-Staff, General Walter Wever, proposed the construction of a long-range strategic bomber able to attack targets in the north of Scotland or in the Urals from German bases. The specification for such an aircraft was placed with the Dornier and Junkers companies, both of whom had experience with long-range multi-engined aircraft. The Dornier project, the Do 19, was a somewhat ugly mid-wing monoplane with slab-sided fuselage and twin fins and rudders. It was powered by four 715 hp Bramo 322 H-2 radials and had a retractable undercarriage. A crew of nine was to be carried, comprising pilot, co-pilot/navigator, bomb-aimer, radio operator and five gunners. Armament was to comprise a nose turret housing a 7.9 mm MG 15 machine gun, a similar gun in the tail and two large two-man turrets in both the dorsal and ventral positions each housing a single 20 mm cannon. It was quickly realised that the heavy and cumbersome two-man turrets would further reduce the aircraft's effectiveness and these were removed from the design. Wever's death in an air crash in June 1936 forced a rethink of the original 'Ural Bomber' proposal and the type was abandoned and all existing prototypes were scrapped.

The Heinkel He 112 V4, D-IZMY, was the fourth prototype of the type which competed with the Bf 109. This aircraft was intended to serve as forerunner of the A-series and was later fitted with an experimental rocket engine.

Championed by Udet, the Messerschmitt Bf 109 V1 – the first prototype – was powered by an imported 695 hp Rolls Royce Kestrel engine and made its first flight in September 1935. It was this aircraft type that more than any other was to make the name of Messerschmitt a household name, and not only in Germany.

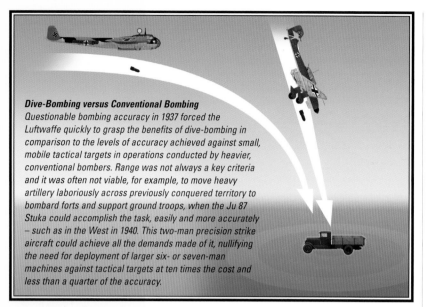

Dive-Bombing versus Conventional Bombing
Questionable bombing accuracy in 1937 forced the
Luftwaffe quickly to grasp the benefits of dive-bombing in
comparison to the levels of accuracy achieved against small,
mobile tactical targets in operations conducted by heavier,
conventional bombers. Range was not always a key criteria
and it was often not viable, for example, to move heavy
artillery laboriously across previously conquered territory to
bombard forts and support ground troops, when the Ju 87
Stuka could accomplish the task, easily and more accurately
– such as in the West in 1940. This two-man precision strike
aircraft could achieve all the demands made of it, nullifying
the need for deployment of larger six- or seven-man
machines against tactical targets at ten times the cost and
less than a quarter of the accuracy.

*An early production Do 17 E-1, D-A+OTM, which had probably
been delivered to KG 255. Although painted in the three-colour
camouflage scheme introduced in 1936, many such aircraft were
delivered with civil registrations combined with Balkenkreuz
national insignia.*

*During 1931 Ernst Udet
had visited the USA and
had become very
impressed with the diving
characteristics of the
Curtiss FIIC Hawk biplane.
At his instigation two
aircraft – one of which is
seen in the photograph –
were bought by Germany
and used by Udet in his
aerobatic shows. The
success of these
machines was eventually
to lead the RLM to put
forward the idea of a dive-
bomber, which resulted in
the Ju 87. Even before this
however, the Heinkel
company had built the
He 50 dive bomber for a
Japanese contract, that
nation also having been
impressed by American
work in the field.*

cocked manually as well as a wooden propeller;
however, variable pitch propellers and 20 mm cannon
were soon introduced.

Messerschmitt also met another requirement,
issued in March 1934, for a 'heavy' fighter. The
Germans had wanted two-seat long-range fighters
since the mid 1920s and a requirement was issued in
August 1932 for a 'heavy' fighter which was quickly
renamed Combat Destroyer (*Kampfzerstörer*). The idea
fascinated Göring and, in a rare moment of
exuberance, Wimmer let his imagination run free and
the roles were expanded from long-range escort and
interception to reconnaissance, ground-attack and

high-speed bombing. Wever came to oppose what he
called 'a forlorn hope' but could not dissuade Göring
and the outline requirement was redrafted in May
1934 to seek a twin-engined, multi-role aircraft armed
with cannon[28].

Richthofen managed to head off the stampede
to mediocrity in January 1935 by splitting the
requirements into a heavy fighter, a high-speed
reconnaissance bomber and a Fast Bomber
(*Schnellbomber*). Although Udet was still a civilian at
the time he is reported to have influenced selection of
the Bf 110 for the heavy fighter requirement with the
prototype flying in May 1936, while the *Schnellbomber*
shortlist, including the Junkers Ju 88, appeared at the
end of 1936.

Yet there was deep concern about bombing
accuracy – indeed even in 1937 an elite unit with the
most modern aircraft could put barely 2 per cent of
their bombs within a 200 metre diameter target from
4,000 metres. Greater accuracy could be achieved by
diving on the target and Heinkel had been developing
dive-bombers for the Japanese Navy. Their accuracy
impressed the RLM which ordered 111 He 50s and
the popularity of the concept led to two Curtiss
Hawks being bought by dive-bomber enthusiast Ernst
Udet with RLM funds and they were demonstrated at
Rechlin in October 1933[29].

Surprisingly, Fascist Italy provided little support
for Nazi Germany despite their joint ideology and
Göring's close links with the Fascists since 1923. In
mid April 1933 Göring returned to Rome to seek
Mussolini's help with aircraft and training. Despite
promises, no aircraft were provided but in July
Pflugbeil led some German pilots, including a future
Inspekteur der Jagdflieger, Adolf Galland, for fighter
training. They qualified in the autumn but no
more followed because DVS Schleissheim proved
more suitable.

Italy preferred to provide military aid to its
northern neighbour, and former sworn enemy,
Austria. The Austrian Air Force slowly expanded and
in 1933 added two squadrons of fighters (*Gruppe C*)
and corps aircraft (*Gruppe A*) which were placed
under *Lehrabteilung II* (LA II) at Graz in March 1934
together with a primary training squadron.
Administration was under *Lehrabteilung* III at Vienna
which also controlled an advance training squadron,
and by March 1934 the Austrian air service had 30

*A Ju 52/3m, W.Nr. 4019, D-2468, of Luft Hansa sits on watery
concrete at an airfield in Germany while undergoing checks
some time during the mid-1930s.*

aircraft and 440 men. In May 1934 the Air Defence Command (*Luftschutzkommando*) was created and between July and December flew its first operational missions; the first against Austrian Nazis who had murdered Chancellor Engelbert Dollfus, and the second against Socialists who had rebelled against his Right-wing successor Kurt von Schuschnigg[30].

Hitler's public revelation of the *Luftwaffe* on 1 March 1935 encouraged Vienna to follow suit on 19 June as the *Österreichische Luftstreitkräfte* under *Generalleutnant* Löhr and by the end of the year it had 78 aircraft and 686 men. Expansion was slow because of the country's financial situation and by the summer of 1936 it had 1,000 men and in addition to ordering Fiat CR. 32bis fighters it had also ordered Caproni Ca. 133 bombers.

By contrast the *Luftwaffe*'s expansion was dramatic but, until conscription was introduced in March 1935, it relied largely upon volunteers although the *Wehrkreise* were assigned quotas for transfer. Some 2,000 soldiers and sailors, including some 300-400 aircrew, were transferred in 1933. The Police, *Lufthansa* and *DVS* provided more, including some 100-200 aircrew, while an increasing number of 'Old Eagles' were persuaded to join the fold, most notably Udet[31].

Loerzer's DLV provided a growing stream of young men and also began training reservists and by October 1935 it had some 28 training centres. Regular training was centralised from November 1933 when the naval air ace, *Oberst* (*Generalmajor* by 1937) Friedrich Christiansen, was appointed *Inspekteur der Schulen der Luftwaffe* with six DVS schools. However, from October 1935 a process of decentralisation began when each Air Region (*Luftkreis*) created an Air Replacement Battalion (*Flieger Ersatz Abteilung* - FEA later *Flieger Ausbildungs Regiment* - FAR) to provide basic training. *Fliegerschulen* were attached to each unit to provide basic and advanced flying training and they were augmented by specialist schools[32].

At the same time, Milch exploited his *Lufthansa* experience to create a network of well-equipped bases and by 1936 he had 36, each costing the same as an infantry division. Each had accommodation for man and machine, workshops, storage facilities, an extensive communications system with radios, telephones and teletypes, and radio and visual navigation aids. Seeckt had encouraged the development of modern communications; Guderian's rise within the armoured forces began because he was a signaller, and the importance of communications led to the creation in December 1933 of the Air Signal Service (*Luftnachrichtenwesen*) under one of the original qualified aviators, *Oberstleutnant* Wolfgang Martini, who had celebrated his 42nd birthday two months earlier.

Born in what later became Poland, Martini joined the army in 1910. He served in signal units during the Great War and later with *Freikorps* units fighting the Poles before joining the *Reichsheer*. He learned to fly in the 1920s and transferred to the *RLM*

Luftwaffe expansion in Staffeln 1934-1936

Type	1934	1935	1936
Fighter	3	8	22
Bomber	8	20	48
Stuka/Schlacht	-	-	9
Reconnaissance	2	5	10
Corps	2	6	11
Transport	-	-	6
Naval	1	5	5
Total	**16**	**44**	**111**

All strengths on April 1 of each year. It should be noted that these figures include *Staffeln* raised on that date.
Bombers in 1934-1935 include equivalent of two *Behelfskampfstaffeln*.

Table 3-2: Flak expansion in batteries 1934-1936

Type	1934	1935	1936
Gun Batteries	9	32	72
S/L Batteries	7	11	20
Total	**16**	**43**	**92**

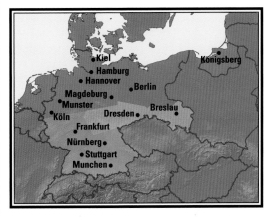

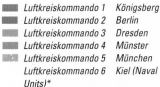

Luftkreiskommando areas 1 April 1934

- Luftkreiskommando 1   Königsberg
- Luftkreiskommando 2   Berlin
- Luftkreiskommando 3   Dresden
- Luftkreiskommando 4   Münster
- Luftkreiskommando 5   München
- Luftkreiskommando 6   Kiel (Naval Units)*

* Naval units had no designated area

Luftkreiskommando areas 1 November 1937

- Luftkreiskommando 1   Königsberg
- Luftkreiskommando 2   Berlin
- Luftkreiskommando 3   Dresden
- Luftkreiskommando 4   Münster
- Luftkreiskommando 5   München
- Luftkreiskommando 6   Kiel (Naval Units)*
- Luftkreiskommando 7   Hamburg

* Naval units had no designated area

in 1933, remaining its unchallenged signals specialist until the end of the Second World War. He was promoted steadily and on 20 September 1941 his 50th birthday present from Göring was a promotion to *General der Luftwaffennachrichtentruppen*[33].

Martini and Milch together exploited the navigation aids to improve bomber performance. Unlike most of their European contemporaries each German bomber had a direction-finding (DF) antenna and was supposed to have a fully-qualified navigator to ensure it could operate both in cloudy

In 1933 the naval air ace, Friedrich Christiansen, was appointed Inspekteur der Schulen der Luftwaffe and later,Korpsführer of the National Socialist Fliegerkorps. Christiansen is seen here shaking hands with a passenger following a flight in a Do X flying boat.

Oberstleutnant Wolfgang Martini, commander of the Luftnachrichtenwesen. A former member of the Freikorps, he worked to improve aircraft performance through new navigation technology and developments in the field of communications. He would end the Second World War having been responsible for devising measures to counter or exploit Allied electronics systems.

weather and at night[34]. From November 1933 *Lufthansa* organised blind-flying training under the guise of State Railway Extensions (*Reichsbahnstrecken*) and this continued until the outbreak of war. The navigation system technology would be further exploited later in the decade to create electronic bombing aids allowing specialised aircraft to strike targets even on the darkest nights or in the thickest cloud.

As men and machines arrived, the *Luftwaffe* began to expand. On 1 March 1934 it had only 77 aircraft, rising to 800 within a year and by April 1936 the figure was nearly 2,700 including 1,000 bombers. The *Flak* arm, which was an Army organisation, initially came under the *Luftwaffe*'s operational control but in February 1935, Göring assumed absolute control of the arm, although the Army would later re-create its *Flak* batteries. Initially the handful of squadrons were concentrated from 1 April under Sperrle's 1. *Fliegerdivision* because Sperrle was one of the most experienced air commanders in the *Reichsheer* and, therefore, the *Luftwaffe*.

At the same time the *Luftwaffe* created its equivalent of the *Wehrkreise* as *Luftkreise*, with the Kiel-based *Luftkreis* VI being a purely naval organisation. Initially these were largely administrative, logistics and training organisations but as the squadrons and *Flak*

batteries expanded from October 1935 they were given an operational role with a Senior Air and Flak Commander (*Höhere Fliegerkommandeur*, *Höhere Kommandeur der Flakartillerie*) and for greater efficiency the administrative and routine work was devolved into sub-districts (*Luftgaue*) from April 1936; organisation would remain substantially unchanged for the next two years. There was no air commander in either the East Prussian or Naval regions, the latter (now under *Konteradmiral* Zander) having instead a *Führer der Seeluftstreitkräfte* (Naval Air Corps Leader) who was former *Fregattenkapitän* Hermann Bruch. All units were given cover-names, most purporting to be part of DVS, DVL or *Lufthansa*[35]. This did not deceive either the French or the British, both of whom received what the British called 'secret information' which included details of the 51-*Staffeln* plan. The British air attaché, Group Captain J.H.Herring, was actually told by Milch's assistant, Carl Bolle in June 1933, that Germany had begun air re-armament. It was an open secret even within Germany and a week after Bolle's admission Herring observed two unknown 'express postal aircraft' (one a He 51 fighter) at an air display at Tempelhof. He asked the senior air official sitting beside him about the aircraft but before he could answer his bored wife responded: "Oh, those will be two of the new single-seat fighters I suppose[36]."

The Allied response when Hitler revealed the *Luftwaffe* was therefore muted, encouraging Berlin to

ORDER OF BATTLE
April 1 1934

Luftkreis I (Konigsberg): Generalleutnant Edmund Wachenfeld
No squadrons
Flakabt (Heer) 1

Luftkreis II (Berlin): Generalleutnant Leonhard Kaupisch
Berlin-Döberitz: I/JG 132 (Fliegergruppe Döberitz)
Tutow: I/KG 152 (Fliegergruppe Tutow)
Berlin-Tempelhof: BKG 1
Prenzlau: 1(F)/AufklGr 222
Flakabt (Heer) 2, 3, 6

Luftkreis III (Dresden): Oberst Karl-Friedrich Schweickhard
Grossenhain: 1(F)/AufklGr 324
Kottbus: 1. (H)/AufklGr 114 (Fliegergruppe Kottbus)
Gotha: 2. (H)/AufklGr 114
Flakabt (Heer) 4

Luftkreis IV (Münster): Generalleutnant Hans Halm
Fassberg: I//KG 154 (Fliegergruppe Fassberg)
Flakabt (Heer) 5

Luftkreis V (Munich): Generalleutnant Karl Eberth
No squadrons
Flakabt (Heer) 7

Luftkreis VI (Kiel): Konteradmiral Konrad Zander
Warnemunde: Seefliegerübungsstaffel

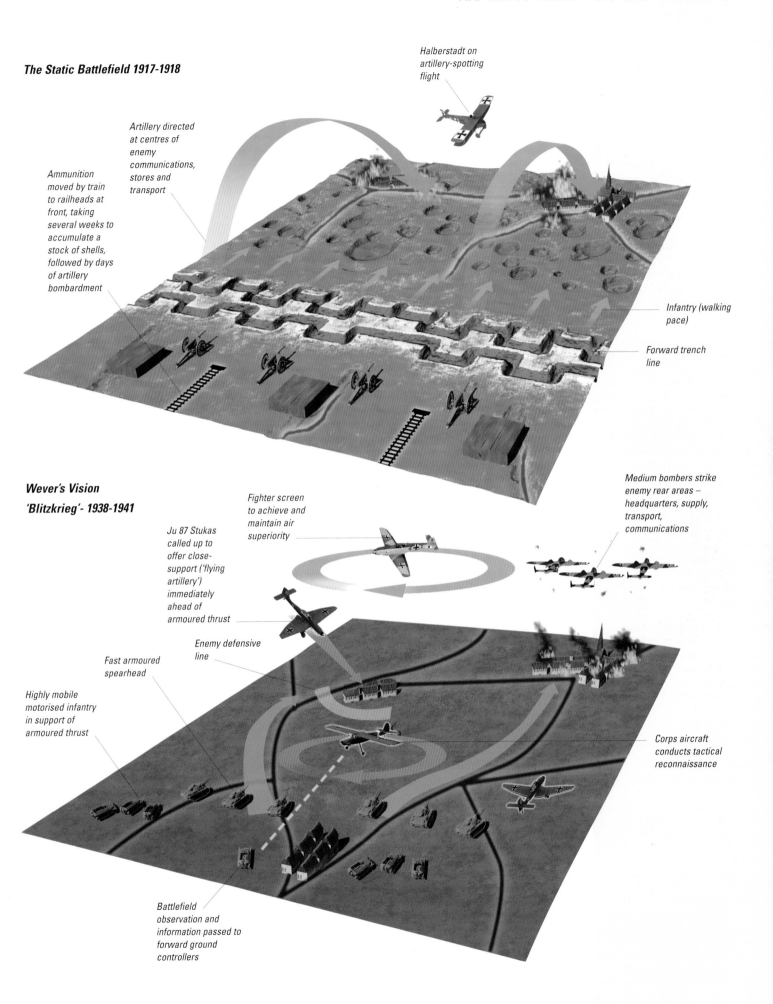

The Static Battlefield 1917-1918

Halberstadt on artillery-spotting flight

Artillery directed at centres of enemy communications, stores and transport

Ammunition moved by train to railheads at front, taking several weeks to accumulate a stock of shells, followed by days of artillery bombardment

Infantry (walking pace)

Forward trench line

**Wever's Vision
'Blitzkrieg'- 1938-1941**

Medium bombers strike enemy rear areas – headquarters, supply, transport, communications

Fighter screen to achieve and maintain air superiority

Ju 87 Stukas called up to offer close-support ('flying artillery') immediately ahead of armoured thrust

Enemy defensive line

Fast armoured spearhead

Highly mobile motorised infantry in support of armoured thrust

Corps aircraft conducts tactical reconnaissance

Battlefield observation and information passed to forward ground controllers

41

By the autumn of 1933 three Reklamestaffeln - literally 'Advertising Squadrons' had been established in Germany as clandestine fighter units. The three squadrons were: 'Reklamestaffel Ostdeutschland' at Neuhausen near Königsburg, 'Reklamestaffel Mitteldeutschland' at Berlin-Staaken and 'Reklamestaffel Süddeutschland' at Fürth near Nuremberg. On 1 April 1934, the second two Reklamestaffeln were transferred to Döberitz near Berlin where they were eventually to form the nucleus of the Luftwaffe's first fighter Gruppe, I./JG 132. This photograph, which was taken during this period, shows the unit's He 51s.

In formation, Ju 52/3m bombers of the fledgling Luftwaffe make a demonstration flight over the heads of the crowd in the stadium at one of the Nürnberg Nazi Party rallies during the latter half of the 1930s.

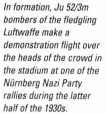

Three pre-production He 51s roar into the air, all wearing a standard silver-coloured aluminium dope finish, with the nearest machine, D-IQEE, carrrying standard port side tail markings.

These two pictures below taken at Döberitz near Berlin show He 51s of Reklamestaffel Mitteldeutschland being readied for operations. Note that the aircraft carry German civil registrations and black, white and red bands on the starboard side of their vertical tail surfaces.

accelerate the expansion programme. A decree establishing the new service was signed by Hitler on 26 February (he preferred the title *ReichsLuftwaffe* but this was soon formally reduced to *Luftwaffe*), its uniform based upon that of DLV, as the third element of the *Reichswehr* which would be renamed the *Wehrmacht* on 1 June 1935. To facilitate expansion the ever-helpful Blomberg provided 6,000 technically-trained men, including 4,300 aircrew volunteers, between May and September, but with the German Army itself expanding this was 'Fatty's' last favour.

The need for strategic reconnaissance led to the creation in January 1935 of a covert reconnaissance unit under *Oberstleutnant* Theodor Rowehl with a

ORDER OF BATTLE
April 1 1935

Luftkreis I (Konigsberg): Generalmajor Karl-Friedrich Schweickhard
    Neuhausen: 1.(F)/AufklGr 121 (Fliegerstaffel Neuhausen)
Höherer Kommandeur der Flakartillerie im Luftkreis I
    I./ FlakRegt 1; I./ FlakRegt 11

Luftkreis II (Berlin): Generalleutnant Leonhard Kaupisch
Höhere Fliegerkommandeure II: Oberst Hugo Sperrle
    Döberitz: I./JG 132 (Fliegergruppe Döberitz)
    Jüterborg-Damm: II./JG 132 (Fliegergruppe Damm)
    Tutow: I./KG 152 (Fliegergruppe Tutow)
    Finsterwalde: I./KG 652
    Berlin-Tempelhof: BKG 274
    Prenzlau: 1.(F)/AufklGr 122
Höherer Kommandeur der Flakartillerie im Luftkreis II
    I./FlakRegt 2; I./FlakRegt 12; I., II./FlakRegt 22

Luftkreis III (Dresden): Generalleutnant Edmund Wachenfeld
Höhere Fliegerkommandeure III: Oberst Hellmuth Volkmann
    Merseburg: I/KG 553
    Gotha: 2 (H)/ AufklGr 114
    Kottbus: 1. (H)/AufklGr 114 (Fliegergruppe Kottbus)
    Grossenhain: 1. (F)/AufklGr 323
Höherer Kommandeur der Flakartillerie im Luftkreis III
    I./FlakRegt 10; I./FlakRegt 13

Luftkreis IV (Münster): Generalleutnant Hans Halm
Höhere Fliegerkommandeure IV: Oberst Alfred Keller
    Fassberg: I/KG 154 (Fliegergruppe Fassberg)
    Kassel: 1. (F)/AufklGr 124 (ex 424)
    Münster: 1., 2. (H)/AufklGr 214 (Fliegergruppe Münster)
Höherer Kommandeur der Flakartillerie im Luftkreis IV
    I./FlakRegt 7

Luftkreis V (Munich): Generalleutnant Karl Eberth
Höhere Fliegerkommandeure V: Oberst Hellmuth Felmy
    Giebelstadt: I./KG 155
    Landsberg: Stab, I/KG 255
    Wurzburg: 1. (F)/AufklGr 525
    Göppingen: 1., 2. (H)/AufklGr 315
Höherer Kommandeur der Flakartillerie im Luftkreis V
    I./FlakRegt 8; I./FlakRegt 25

Luftkreis VI (Kiel): Generalleutnant Konrad Zander
Führer der Marineluftstreitkräfte (FdL)
    Kiel-Holtenau: KüJGr 136 (1., 2.)
    Holtenau: 2./ KüFlGr 106
    Norderney: 2. (M) / FlGr (*See*) 116
    List/Sylt: *Stab*, 1./ FlGr (*See*) 106
    KüAufklStaffel 126
    Seefliegerstaffel 186

One of several He 51 B-2 floatplanes which were delivered to 1./Küstenjagdgruppe 136 at Keil-Holtenau for coastal defence is rolled toward the waterline on its ground-handling dolly. The unit was later redesignated I./JG 136 and, although the home base was Jever on the North Sea coast, the aircraft operated from Holtenau which had the necessary harbour facilities. The addition of floats reduced the maximum speed of the He 51 from 330 km/h to 318 km/h.

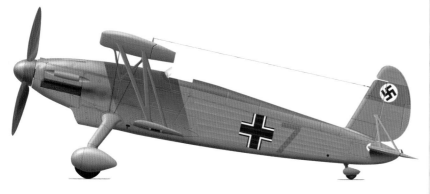

A line-up of Ar 68 Es of Jagdgeschwader 134 'Horst Wessel.' On 7 March 1936 Germany re-occupied the Rhineland which had been declared a demilitarised zone by the Versailles Treaty. The occupying troops were supported by the He 51s of II./JG 132, the Ar 68s of III./JG 134 and the He 51s from I./St.G 162 'Immelmann.' After circling Cologne cathedral at midday, several Ar 68s and He 51s landed at the city's Butzweilerhof airfield. Hannes Trautloft, who was serving with III./JG 134 at the time, described the operation as "…a great moment". Following its arrival at Cologne the unit was to fly several exercises and manoeuvres. The aircraft shown here are carrying the markings adopted for one of these exercises.

Four Do 23 G bombers of II./KG 153 in flight over the Finsterwalde area some time in 1936. The aircraft are painted pale grey overall with the black and white Swastika emblazoned across a bright red band across the fin and rudder.

The death of Walther Wever in June 1936 in a flying accident was a shock to the Luftwaffe which lost one of its most intelligent and reasoned senior officers. When he heard the news Göring reportedly burst into floods of tears.

variety of aircraft. Ostensibly part of Lufthansa, *Kommando Rowehl* or *Fliegerstaffel zbV* would roam the skies of Europe on 'route-proving' trials and supply the *Luftwaffe* with the foundation of its target folders. Its growing importance was underlined when the *Luftwaffe* was committed for the first time a year after its existence was revealed.

On 2 May 1935 France had signed a mutual assistance pact with the Soviet Union which had a first-line strength of 6,672 aircraft. Right-wing opposition delayed French parliamentary ratification of the agreement until 11 February 1936 which was completed 16 days later. Hitler ordered the re-occupation of the Rhineland on 11 February and Blomberg drafted the directives on 28 February for what was officially called the 'Winter Exercise (*Winterübung*).

On 7 March German troops marched into the Rhineland shielded by the Ar 65s of III./JG 134 and He 51s of I./St.G 165 and some *Flak* batteries, the aircraft initially lacking ammunition and operating with neither guns nor sights harmonised. To give the illusion of strength the aircraft switched airfields frequently and were hastily painted with new markings. Although France partially mobilised there was no political will to fight the re-occupation, although fear of potential French bomber attacks reportedly led to KG 253 being alerted to attack Paris [37].

ORDER OF BATTLE
April 1 1936

Luftkreis I (Konigsberg): Generalleutnant Karl-Friedrich Schweickhard
    Neuhausen: Stab, 1. (F)/AufklGr 121
Höherer Kommandeur der Flakartillerie im Luftkreis I:
    Generalmajor Friedrich Hirschauer
    I./FlakRegt 1; I., II./FlakRegt 11

Luftkreis II (Berlin): General der Flieger Leonhard Kaupisch
Höherer Fliegerkommandeure II: Generalmajor Bernhard Kühl
    Berlin-Döberitz: Stab, I./JG 132
    Jüterbog-Damm: II./JG 132
    Bernburg: I./JG 232
    Greifswald: Stab, II., III./KG 152
    Neubrandenburg: I./KG 152
    Tutow: III./KG 152
    Schwerin: Stab, I./St.G 162
    Lübeck-Blankensee: II./St.G 162
    Prenzlau: 1., 2., 3. (F)/AufklGr 122
    Stargard: Stab, 1., 2. (H)/AufklGr 112
    Kottbus: 1., 2. (H)/AufklGr 212
    Berlin-Tempelhof: Stab KG zbV 172
    Tutow:I./KG zbV 172
    Fassberg: II./KG zbV 172
Höherer Kommandeur der Flakartillerie im Luftkreis II : Generalmajor Hubert Weise
    I./FlakRegt 2; I./FlakRegt 12 ; I., II./FlakRegt 22;
    I., II./Regt General Göring
    Luftgau Kommando 4 (Berlin)

Luftkreis III (Dresden): General der Flieger Edmund Wachenfeld
Höherer Fliegerkommandeure III: Oberst Hellmuth Volkmann
    Merseburg: Stab, I./KG 153
    Finsterwalde: II./KG 153
    Altenburg: III./KG 153
    Liegnitz: IV./KG 153
    Gotha: Stab, I./KG 253
    Erfurt: II./KG 253
    Nordhausen: III./KG 253
    Grossenhain: Stab, 1., 2. (F)/AufklGr 123
Höherer Kommandeur der Flakartillerie im Luftkreis III: Oberst Rudolf Bogatsch
    I./FlakRegt 3; I./FlakRegt 10; I./FlakRegt 13; II./FlakRegt 23
    Luftgaukommando 6 (Breslau)
    Luftgaukommando 7 (Dresden)
    Luftgaukommando 8 (Weimar)

Luftkreis IV (Münster): Generalmajor Hubert Weise
Höherer Fliegerkommandeure IV: Generalmajor Alfred Keller
    Dortmund: Stab, I./JG 134
    Werl: II./JG 134
    Köln-Burzweilerhof: III./JG 134 (- 7.)
    Dusseldorf: 7./JG 134
    Hannover-Langenhagen: Stab, I./KG 154
    Wunstorf: II./KG 154
    Kassel: Stab, 1., 2. (F)/AufklGr 124
    Munster: Stab, 1., 2., 3. (H)/AufklGr 114
    1., 2. (H)/AufklGr 214
Höherer Kommandeur der Flakartillerie im Luftkreis IV:
Generalleutnant Johannes Lentzsch
    I./FlakRegt *4*; I./FlakRegt *5*; I./FlakRegt *6*; I./FlakRegt *7*;I./FlakRegt *9*
    Luftgaukommando *9* (Hannover/Brunswick)
    Luftgaukommando *10* (Münster)
    Luftgaukommando *11* (Giessen)

Luftkreis V (Munich): Generalmajor Hugo Sperrle
Höherer Fliegerkommandeure V: Oberst Hellmuth Felmy
    Ansbach-Neukirchen: Stab, II./KG 155
    Giebelstadt: I./KG 155
    Schwäbisch-Hall: III./KG 155
    Kitzingen: I./StG 165
    Wurzburg: Stab 2., 3. (F)/AufklGr 125
    Göppingen: Stab, 1., 2.(H)/AufklGr 115
Höherer Kommandeur der Flakartillerie im Luftkreis V:
Oberst Friedrich Heilingbrunner
    I./FlakRegt 8; I./FlakRegt 25
    Luftgaukommando 13 (Nuremberg)
    Luftgaukommando 14 (Munich)
    Luftgaukommando 15 (Stuttgart)

Luftkreis VI (Kiel): Generalleutnant Konrad Zander
Führer der Marineluftstreitkräfte: Oberst Hans Geisler
    Jever: KüJGr 136 (1-4.)
    Nordenay: Stab, 2.(M)/FlGr (See) 116
    List/Sylt: 1.(M), 2.(F), 3.(Mz) / FlGr (See)106
    Wilhelmshaven: 1./BordFlGr 196

The occupation of the Rhineland led the *Luftwaffe* to expand the *Luftkreis* IV and V infrastructure across the Rhine. From April 1936 there was a further expansion frenzy with an 18 per cent increase in aircraft strength with 54 'daughter' *Staffeln* being created from 'mother' *Geschwader* and *Gruppen*. But within three months of the Rhineland success the *Luftwaffe* suffered its greatest tragedy.

Wever had learned to fly when he became Chief-of-Staff but had little experience. On 3 June he flew his He 70 to Dresden to lecture officer cadets at the local *Luftkriegschule* but he was anxious to return to Berlin for a state funeral. In his hurry he neglected pre-flight checks, forgot to release the aileron lock and the 3 tonne Heinkel failed to take off and crashed at the end of the runway killing him and his flight engineer. When he heard the news Göring reportedly burst into floods of tears for Wever had been unique, a fact which was to become only too apparent in the following years.

NOTES FOR CHAPTER THREE

1. Franks, Bailey & Guest. p.117.
2. For Göring see the biographies by Irving, Manvell & Fraenkel.
3. Irving, *Milch* p.32, 357 n.16 and *Göring* p.113. UKNA Air 118/33.
4. For the *Luftwaffe* 1933-1936 see Corum, *Luftwaffe*, pp.124-181; Homze pp.46-138 (the definitive work on the aero-industry and production); Hooton pp.94-119; Schliephacke pp.31-40, 44-47, Appendix G; Suchenwirth pp.57-60, 74-80, 84-90;Völker, *Entwicklung* pp.201-230, while the definitive work on *Luftwaffe* pre-war organisation isVölker, *Luftwaffe* pp.11-158. For aircraft see Green's *Warplanes of the Third Reich* and for units see both Rosch and Holm's website. See also Nowarra, *Verbotenen Flugzeuge* and Ries, *Die Maulwürfe* and *Luftwaffen-Story*.
5. O.Niell Appendix A.
6. For Kühl see Collins' & Miller's website.
7. Corum p.157.Völker, *Luftwaffe*, p.52.
Corum 157, 331 f/n 6. Faber pp. 25-26. Mitcham p.27, Hooton p.118 f/n 9. Collins & Miller's website. Also web site: ritterkreuztraeger 1939-45.de.

One of the most beautiful aircraft of the inter-war period, the Heinkel He 70 was designed by the Günter brothers as a fast transport. The first passenger-carrying He 70s were used by Deutsche Lufthansa on its Berlin-Hamburg-Cologne-Frankfurt-am-Main service, and later other routes inside Germany. With the birth of the Luftwaffe, two military versions were produced, the He 70 E and F, these being tested as fighter, reconnaissance and bombing aircraft. The machine seen here is W.Nr. 403, the third aircraft to wear the civil registration 'D-3'. It was operated by DLH and re-registered as D-2537 and then as D-UHUX. The aircraft wears the characteristic DLH pale grey and black finish and lightning-bolt design with 'Blitz' and 'Luft Hansa' applied to the engine cowling.

9. Irving, *Milch* p.359/n.46.

10. Corum p.315 f/n 47. Mitcham p.15.
    For Wever see Deichmann p.69. Faber pp.23-24. Homze pp.60, 99-100, 133/n.4. Mason pp.183-184. Völker, *Luftwaffe* pp.31-32.

12. For doctrine the definitive work is Corum's *The Luftwaffe*, especially pp.124-154.

13. Edmonds. P.481.

14. The texts are in Corum and Muller, pp72-76, 86-90.

15. Homze pp.33-34.

16. Homze p.56. Völker, *Luftwaffe* pp.28-31.

17. Corum & Muller. pp.91-115.

18. Corum pp.152-153.

19. Deichmann p.53, Mason p.212, Völker, *Luftwaffe* pp.32-33.

20. For the text see Corum pp.140-144. Corum & Muller pp118-157.

21. Corum & Muller p120.
    Op cit pp.130-133.

23. *Op cit* pp.123, 133-143.

24. Hooton pp. 101-106.

25. For Wimmer see Corum, pp.165, 174. Collins & Miller's website.

26. Corum p.307 f/n 75. I am deeply indebted to Robert Forsyth's researches into Richthofen. See also Collins & Miller's website.

27. Faber pp.160-162. Green, *Warplanes* pp127-129, 483-484. Homze pp.121-123. Mason pp.191-192.

28. The French issued a similar requirement in October 1934 for what became the Potez 63.

29. For dive-bombing see Faber pp.149-155. Homze p.127. Ishoven pp. 289-290, 295-298, 306. Smith pp.8-10.

30. For the Austrian air force see Gabriel and Green, *Alpenstock.*

31. Corum pp.157-161. O'Niell p.126.

32. For *Luftwaffe* training see Faber pp. 141-148. Hooton pp.110-111. Ketley & Rolfe, Rosch pp.384-413.

33. Mitcham, p.325 f/n 21. Collins & Miller's website.

34. Hooton p.106.

35. See Schliephake Appendix C.

36. UKNA Air 2/1353.

37. For *Winterübung* see Hooton p.115. Schliephake p. 41. Völker p.148.

CHAPTER FOUR

BAPTISM OF FIRE: SPAIN

1936–1939

*Members of the Republican semi-Trotskyist POUM Militia display
a show of force at the Karl Marx barracks in Barcelona.*

Six weeks after Wever's death the *Luftwaffe* entered its baptism of fire, not against the French or the new Eastern European states, but in Spain where a failed military *coup* had set the scene by 19 July for a full-scale civil war.

The rebels, under General Emilio Mola, controlled a large slice of northern Spain; there was a bridgehead around Seville in southern Andalucia while General Francisco Franco held the Canary Islands and the colony of Morocco with the Army of Africa, Spain's only professional troops. The remainder of the country was under nominal government hands although real power was held by Left Wing militias. Both sides sought foreign military aid: Madrid looked north to socialist France and to Germany (it sought He 51 fighters), Mola sought help from Italy, while the Moroccan rebels, or rather local Nazis, turned towards Berlin and here serendipity would play a part.

A passing *Lufthansa* Ju 52 piloted by *Flugkapitän* Alfred Henke had been commandeered to transport a rebel general to Morocco. Two German Nazi businessmen then used the aircraft to fly to Berlin to persuade Hitler to aid the rebels. Yet diplomatic protocol meant Berlin continued to recognise the Madrid Government and *Lufthansa* would operate commercial flights through Barcelona until 8 August.

Hitler met the delegation on 25 July at Bayreuth, where he had been mainlining on Wagner, but he was cautious. Arguing, correctly, that Communist power was growing in the government (later Republican) area but unwilling to intervene directly for fear of forcing France into premature intervention, he authorised covert military support for the rebels (who would soon be called Nationalists), although only to Franco.

The priority was to tip the balance of power by getting the Army of Africa across the Straits of Gibraltar over the Republican Fleet. Blomberg and Göring thrashed out the details in a meeting which continued into the early hours of Sunday 26 July, to provide air transport facilities with a self-defence capability. Blomberg was enthusiastic while Göring's initial reluctance (he had wanted to use *Lufthansa* aircraft rather than erode *Luftwaffe* strength) was rapidly overcome upon hearing of Hitler's support for the project which the RLM would control.

Ostensibly the operation would be run by a Spanish organisation, the *Hispano-Marroqui de*

General Francisco Franco (left) and General Emilio Mola emerge from a conference at Burgos on 1 October 1936. Franco had just been elected Commander-in-Chief and Head of Government by the Spanish rightist generals, giving him complete control of Nationalist Spain.

Göring, who was initially reluctant to send Luftwaffe aircraft to Spain in July 1936, was overruled by Hitler who was in favour of lending air support to the Spanish rebels in an operation which would be placed under RLM control. Göring pushed for aircraft to be diverted from Lufthansa, but the Führer disagreed.

Transportes SL (HISMA) and all German personnel would wear its white uniform. Milch was summoned to Bayreuth, briefed and, as church bells summoned the faithful to prayer, he tackled the project with the verve of a hell-fire preacher. The programme was dubbed Operation 'Magic Fire' (*Unternehmen 'Feuerzauber'*) and operational control was assigned to

Generalleutnant Helmuth Wilberg, a First World War pilot who was appointed head of the Special Staff W for German-Spanish Military Aid. Prior to his appointment, Wilberg had been commander of a Luftkreisschule.

Wilberg and his newly created Special Staff W (*Sonderstab W*) as RLM ignored the day of rest[1].

To even the burden three *Kampfgruppen* (I./KG 153, II./KG/155 and I./KG 253) each supplied three Ju 52/3mg3e, the last having received the honorary title '*General Wever*' only days before, while I./JG 132 and I./JG 134 supplied He 51B-1 fighters and 20 *Flak* 30 2 cm light anti-aircraft guns were added to defend their bases. HISMA chartered a ship in Hamburg for them and 91 men, including the future 'aces' *Leutnant*s Hannes Trautloft and Hans-Joachim 'Hajo' Herrmann. Many of the men were 'volunteered' by their commanding officers who made some sign declarations of secrecy before giving them the good news[2]. They changed into civilian clothes and travelled as a 'Strength Through Joy' (*Kraft durch Freude*) tourist group to embark, where they met their commanding officer, *Major* Alexander von Scheele.

Scheele was a *Schlasta* veteran who had emigrated to Latin America after the war. As the Nazis regained German pride, Scheele returned to offer his services and now he briefed the '*Feuerzauber*' team. They were to be purely a transport and training mission, he said, and they were forbidden to participate in combat missions although the fighters could escort the transports until Spanish pilots could master the Heinkels.

After an inspection by Milch and Wilberg the 'tourists' sailed out of the Elbe on 1 August. Meanwhile another 11 demilitarised Ju 52 bombers painted in *Lufthansa* colours flew to the Nationalist enclaves via San Remo in Italy, which was also aiding the rebels. One aircraft accidentally landed at a Republican airfield and the crew were arrested, then taken to Madrid only to be released under German diplomatic pressure. The Junkers itself remained at the airfield and was destroyed in an air attack.

By the time the '*Feuerzauber*' team reached Seville on 6 August the airlift was actually under way. Franco had six aircraft but it was the reluctant Henke who flew the first German mission on 28 July with some 35 men sitting on the floor with their knees drawn to their chins. He flew several flights a day, joined by a second *Lufthansa* '*Tante Ju*' and over a fortnight they transported 2,489 men[3].

When the '*Feuerzauber*' team arrived Henke was drafted to train the Spanish how to use half the Junkers as bombers. *Hauptmann* Rudolf 'Bubb' *Freiherr* von Moreau commanded the remaining Junkers which assembled in Morocco at Tetuan, while *Oberleutnant* Kraft Eberhardt began fighter training at Tablada airfield outside Seville as well as being responsible for communications and supplies through a depot at Salamanca. Luckily there was already a

Lufthansa maintenance depot at Seville and this supported the expeditionary force until HISMA could establish dedicated facilities.

The transports flew the hour-long 180 kilometre route from Tetuan to Seville for the first five days, then used a temporary airstrip at Jerez de la Frontera which cut the journey by 50 kilometres and 20 minutes. As it was the height of summer, flights had to be made in the mornings and evenings when the maximum number of sorties were flown. Maintenance facilities were crude, work being carried out at night under vehicle headlights or even lanterns, but acquiring aviation fuel and then filling the aircraft proved the most serious problems.

The airlift concluded on 11 October with the delivery of 13,900 men and 270 tonnes of equipment including 36 guns. The peak in personnel transport was reached in the week of 10-16 August when 2,853 men were flown in and from September the emphasis was on bringing in material with a peak in deliveries during the week 14-20 September when 69.5 tonnes were carried across the Straits. The effort involved 868 sorties and only one aircraft was lost, at Jerez on 15 August with the deaths of two men. As Hitler rightly said: "Franco ought to erect a monument to the glory of the Junkers 52. It is this aircraft which the Spanish Revolution has to thank for its victory[4]."

Although Scheele said that combat operations were '*verboten*' he interpreted his orders to authorise bombing. The anti-aircraft guns of Republican warships forced Moreau's transports to fly at 2,500-3,500 metres and the battleship *Jaime I* based at Malaga posed an especially serious threat. To neutralise her, two Junkers were fitted with crude racks and loaded with 250 kg bombs. On 13 August Moreau and Henke set off to attack the battleship, but only the *Lufthansa* pilot found her and struck her with two bombs which severely damaged her upper deck and killed 47 of her crew. The battleship promptly withdrew to Cartagena[5].

Scheele's fighters were also sucked into the conflict. The Heinkels proved too demanding for the Spanish and rather than leave them grounded Eberhardt created an operational flight with himself, Trautloft and *Leutnant* Herwig Knüppel. On 24 August they escorted Ju 52s of the new Nationalist air force in a raid on the Getafe airbase outside Madrid while the next day both Eberhardt and Trautloft claimed their first victories, with the German tally extended to six within three days. Moreau flew a night attack which hit the War Ministry in Madrid on 27/28 August, but it was not until the following day that Hitler formally sanctioned the use of Germans in combat missions.

In the following month the Luftwaffe drip-fed material into Spain including another 44 aircraft, mostly He 51s and He 46s, the latter for the Spanish. In addition *Hauptmann* Aldinger brought a battery of 8.8 cm *Flak 36* anti-aircraft guns and some searchlights and the reinforcements helped Franco's forces to secure much of Andalucia and then drive northwards to take Toledo on 27 September.

Hauptmann Rudolf 'Bubb' Freiherr von Moreau, (second from left) of the Luftwaffe Technisches Amt and Flugkapitän Alfred Henke of Lufthansa (far right), seen here waiting to receive a celebratory drink on 11 August 1938 shortly after landing at Floyd Bennett Field in New York having flown non-stop for 24 hours, 56 minutes from Berlin in a Focke-Wulf Fw 200 – a record-breaking non-stop flight of 6,370 km. It was a propaganda coup for the Nazis and the resurgent German aviation industry. Exactly two years earlier von Moreau and Henke had flown some of the first semi-clandestine flights of German air involvement in the Spanish Civil War from Morocco and southern Spain using Ju 52s as both bombers and transports.

In July 1936, Oberst Alexander von Scheele established the Reisegesellschaft which co-ordinated the transport of German volunteers to Spain.

"Franco ought to erect a monument to the glory of the Junkers 52...": so said Adolf Hitler of the twenty aircraft which carried Moorish Spanish Nationalist troops of the Army of Africa from Morocco to Spain.

During September Moreau created a bomber *Kette* nicknamed Pauls (*Pablos*) which flew its first mission on 15 September, while a *Versuchskommando* or '*Mechelis Kette*' was created with three dive-bombers, a He 50Gs and a pair of Hs 123As, but saw little service possibly due to a lack of spares. The arrival of He 59B and He 60E floatplanes saw the creation of a maritime patrol unit whose strength doubled the following month.

With the capture of Toledo the Germans were rested for almost a month while Wilberg despatched reinforcements, allowing Scheele to reorganise his force. Additionally, two squadron-sized units; *Gruppe Eberhardt* with 14 fighters, and *Gruppe Moreau* with 20 bombers and a pair of He 70F reconnaissance aircraft were formed, the second bomber squadron being dubbed the Peters

Just after this photograph was taken at Ávila on 13 November 1936, Oblt. Kraft Eberhardt (centre), one of the first German fighter pilots to arrive in Spain, was killed when his He 51 collided with a Republican fighter. His place as Kapitän of 4.J/88 was taken by Herwig Knüppel. To the left of this picture is Lt. Dietrich von Bothmer with Lt. Hennig Strümpell to the right.

A Heinkel He 70 reconnaissance aircraft of A/88 being escorted by two Italian Fiat CR. 32 fighters. The Fiat could hold its own with the early Russian aircraft that were sent to Spain and was far superior to the He 51.

The first six German fighter pilots were sent to Spain in their civilian clothes. From left are: Lt. Gerhard Klein (shot down and killed by flak on 18 January 1938 on the Teruel front), Lt. Ekkehard Hefter (killed in an accident on 28 September 1936 due to engine failure at Vitoria, the first fighter pilot to be killed in Spain), Oblt. Hannes Trautloft, Oblt. Herwig Knüppel, Oblt. Kraft Eberhardt (killed in combat on 13 November 1936 at Casa de Campo) and Lt. Wolf-Heinrich von Houwald.

One of the first batch of six He 51s which arrived in Spain in August 1936, this was the aircraft in which Oblt. Hannes Trautloft was shot down on 30 August 1936. He baled out safely. In the background of this photo, taken at Escalona airfield, can be seen a Fokker F.VII/3 three-engined transport.

(*Pedros*) unit. When they returned to battle during the second half of October they adopted a role which was to become familiar in the *Luftwaffe* as an 'aerial fire brigade'. On 17 October, for example, Scheele's squadrons operated simultaneously in northern and southern Spain with the main force helping the relief of the Nationalist garrison of Oviedo, while a small force, including the Hs 123 and the floatplanes, attacked airfields around Malaga.

But as Franco's forces approached Madrid in late October Stalin opted to support the Republican Government and Soviet merchantmen began unloading large quantities of military equipment. This included the nimble I-15 biplane fighter, dubbed 'Snub Nose' (*Chato*), the fast I-16 Type 5/6 monoplane fighter nicknamed both Fly (*Mosca*), because of its whining engine noise, and Rat (*Rata*) because of its manoeuvrability. Also arriving were the elegant, modern, twin-engine SB (*Skorostnoi Bombardirovshchik* or Fast Bomber) 2M-100A 'frontal' bomber, which was nicknamed *Katiuska* (Katy) or

Martin because it was confused with the Martin 139 and was 110 km/h faster than the He 51! The Russians were under Yakov Smushkevich, an air commander with political credentials, who would become a senior leader in the Soviet Air Force in 1939 and then be succeeded by Pavel Rychagov, who was the *Chato* unit commander in Spain. The Russians were augmented by Spanish and mercenary aircrew, including German *emigrés* and Austrians, but it was the newcomers who quickly proved superior to the Germans and Italians.

Fears of Russian intervention saw an expansion of the German presence as Berlin now formally recognised Franco's Nationalist Government. German participation in the Spanish Civil War now came under the 'Rügen' Winter Exercise (*Winterübung 'Rügen'*) whose operational element was originally dubbed first 'Iron Rations' (*Eiserne Rationen*) then the 'Iron Legion' (*Eiserne Legion*) but finally, and at the animal-loving Göring's insistence, the *Legion Condor*[6].

This was formed on 7 November by expanding Scheele's force, the *'Feuerzeuber'* commander becoming Air Attaché with the Nationalist Government until January 1939. Tragically, he and eight other veterans were killed when their Ju 52 crashed at Roubilon in France on 24 February 1939. Henke was more fortunate and with the re-organisation finally left Spain and became associated with the new four-engined Focke-Wulf Fw 200 *Condor* airliner. In August 1938 he again teamed with Moreau to set a non-stop record from Berlin to New York in 24 hours and 36 minutes but within two years they were both dead; Moreau testing a Ju 88 on 4 April 1939 at Rechlin, while Henke's *Condor* crashed while taking off from Berlin-Staaken on 22 April 1940.

Given his experience it was logical that Sperrle, now a *Generalmajor* of *Luftkreis V,* would command the *Legion*. His Chief-of-Staff was *Oberstleutnant* Alexander Holle who enlisted in the infantry during the Great War, became a *Reichsheer* officer and transferred to the *Luftwaffe* in 1934. Although very capable, Holle appears to have had trouble delegating authority and to have reacted pessimistically to adversity.

The *Legion Condor* consisted of two *Gruppen* and two *Staffeln*; the *Kampfgruppe* K/88 absorbed *Gruppe Moreau* (as 4.K/88) while the *Jagdgruppe* J/88 absorbed *Gruppe Eberhardt* as 4.J/88. Moreau's reconnaissance aircraft were absorbed by the *Aufklärungsstaffel* A/88 with corps and reconnaissance *Kette*, while the floatplane unit was absorbed by *Küstenfliegerstaffel* AS/88. The *Flak* force was expanded into *Flakabteilung* F/88 with three heavy and two light batteries, while communications came under *Luft-nachrichtenabteilung* Ln/88. A variety of maintenance, base protection and transport units were also created but against an establishment of 5,500 they had only 5,000 Germans. The remainder were Spaniards acting as 'hewers of wood and drawers of water' manning a network of airfields, depots and signal centres throughout the Nationalist zone. While much equipment, including 24 He 51s, 10 He 70Fs, a He 112V and a Ju 87A, came in by sea from the west, the largest aircraft and the leadership came via Italy.

Sperrle flew into Seville on 5 November after a six day journey including a Rome stopover. K/88 received 33 Ju 52/3mg3es which flew from Lechfeld down to Italy and then hopped across the Mediterranean in three or four groups via Sardinia and the Balearics to Serrania de Ronda. Italian warships were stationed along the route to shepherd them.

Most of the men, volunteers and usually bachelors, sailed to Cadiz and Seville from Stettin and Swinemünde wearing civilian clothes until they entered Spanish territorial waters where they received a uniform similar to that of the National Labour Service (*Reichsarbeitsdienst*-RAD) but with Spanish insignia. Their mail would be sent 'care of Mr Max Winkler', who was the Junkers representative in Spain and upon arrival there they would often be promoted a grade. Pay was excellent and to cater for the excesses of the young, there were special arrangements in which the men marched down to specially selected brothels. The surviving veterans would return tanned and with enough savings to buy a motor car[7].

The superior Russian aircraft quickly eroded Sperrle's 120 aircraft as they supported Franco's final assault upon Madrid. The dead included Eberhardt who was replaced by *Major* Hubertus von Merhardt and he informed Sperrle that he would not send his pilots against such overwhelming odds[8]. The shield of J/88 became so leaky that Fuchs temporarily abandoned daylight raids upon Madrid on 26 November, by which time the bombers were carrying five machine guns.

Night attacks by one or two *Staffeln*, as well as individual aircraft upon 'choke points' around Madrid, proved no sinecure. Their aircraft operated from the other side of the 2,500 metre Sierras de Guadaramma and Gredos and the heavily laden bombers frequently had to fly through dense cloud with little meteorological support and in bitter cold, the pilots having one hand on the controls while the other pounded their thighs to keep some semblance of warmth. The bitter weather and lack of any warm clothing meant that many fell victim to influenza and pneumonia, which killed three in January.

By January Sperrle had lost 20 per cent of his front line strength and K/88 had only 26 Ju 52s by the end of the month. Morale plunged and only the

Often known as a 'Curtiss' by pilots of the Legion Condor, the Polikarpov I-15 'Chato' was one of the most successful biplane fighters, outclassing the He 51. Powered by a 700 hp M-25 radial engine, the I-15 possessed a maximum speed of 360 km/h and was highly manoeuvrable. It carried an armament of four 7.62 machine-guns.

General Hugo Sperrle in conversation with Adolf Hitler. Sperrle was born in 1885 and served in the German flying service during the First World War. He remained in the armed forces after the war, joining the Luftwaffe in 1935. This somewhat abrasive officer was appointed the first commander of the Legion Condor in November 1936, leading it until November 1937.

The He 112 V3 arrived in Spain in November 1936 where it was test-flown by Oblt. Günther "Fips" Radusch. The prototype, which had been built without armament, had been fitted with an experimental engine-mounted 20 mm C/30 L cannon for tests. Shown here at Tablada airfield, the aircraft was given the code 5●1 and was later flown operationally against Republican armour by Uffz. Max Schulz of 1./J88 who destroyed three tanks.

Germans' own professionalism and Sperrle's leadership prevented a collapse. Despite having the hopelessly inferior He 51, the veterans of 4.J/88 claimed five SBs on the northern front on 12

Two He 51s with Oblt. Dietrich 'Philipp' von Bothmer of J/88 standing in the foreground. Von Bothmer was credited with two victories in Spain: a Curtiss on 13 November 1936 (the Legion Condor's 29th kill) and a Rata on 8 December 1936 (the 32nd kill).

December. Nevertheless J/88 was reduced to a bomber escort role and the *Legion Condor* began 1937 operating on fronts where Russian opposition was weakest.

On 6 February Sperrle returned to the Madrid front to support a new Nationalist offensive south of the city in the Jarama valley and sought to interdict roads. The Russians reacted fiercely, twice breaking up K/88 formations and forcing the He 51 escorts to shelter behind the bombers' guns and after four days the bombers reverted to night attacks. J/88 had only a single victory in February and returned to the ground-attack missions it had begun the previous month, although even here it was initially confined to the quieter sectors. Only F/88 distinguished itself providing direct fire support for the Nationalist troops and this would become its secondary role.

The *Legion Condor* needed modern aircraft urgently. The development unit received three Bf 109 prototypes in December, which returned to Germany in February, and accompanying them was Richthofen who supervised their operational evaluation. The Spanish conflict had stirred his blood and when he returned to Berlin before Christmas he began pulling strings to get a permanent posting.

On 6 January a top-level conference involving Milch, Kesselring (Wever's successor), Udet and Wilberg apparently agreed that the *Legion* should have modern aircraft and also that Richthofen should replace Holle, who departed on 22 January. Holle received a *Stukagruppe* (a Ju 87A was operating in Spain and would remain until July) and then became *Luftwaffenkommando Ostpreussen* Chief-of-Staff during the Munich Crisis. In 1940 he became IV. *Fliegerkorps* Chief-of-Staff and the following year commander of X. *Fliegerkorps* in the Mediterranean. In 1944 he replaced Sperrle as commander of *Luftflotte 3*, which was promptly renamed *Luftwaffenkommando West*[9].

If Sperrle had played a part in removing one thorn in his side, the new appointment merely replaced it. He and Richthofen had many disputes about the quality of aircraft in 1934 and as a reflection

of his own feelings of social inferiority, he may have regarded Richthofen as an aristocratic snob[10].

For his part Richthofen disliked his fastidious superior's table manners and coarse wit, but despite the tensions, they formed a working partnership helped by a mutual interest in cards. Furthermore, Richthofen had linguistic skills including Italian which eased relations with the *Aviación Legionaria*, Mussolini's *Legion Condor*. He also learned Spanish which helped him quickly to develop a good working relationship with Franco, allowing Sperrle to leave daily affairs in his capable hands.

Richthofen was followed by a stream of new aircraft. Moreau's 4.K/88 veterans received a total of 12 Do 17E-1s, He 111B-1s and Ju 86D-1s and was renamed Experimental Bomber Squadron (*Versuchsbomben Staffel*) 88 (VB/88) earning its baptism of fire on 9 March when the Heinkels struck enemy airfields in support of the disastrous Italian offensive at Guadalajara/Brihuega. The veterans of 4.J/88 received 16 Bf 109B-1s two weeks later and were renamed 2.J/88 under *Oberleutnant* Günther 'Franzl' Lützow, a scion of a very distinguished military family and a Lipetsk veteran. A man who would stand up to anyone, including Göring, and described as 'the best fighter leader in the *Luftwaffe*' by future Inspector of Fighters (and *Legion Condor* veteran), Adolf Galland, he now took a leaf from the book of the wartime ace Boelcke. Just as Boelcke had kept *Jasta 2* (including Manfred von Richthofen) out of the firing line until his 'cubs' familiarised themselves with their new aircraft, so did Lützow, who appears to have introduced the tactic of operating in pairs or Chained Dogs (*Kettehunde*) rather than trios[11].

Their debut came on a quieter front. Having failed to seize Madrid, Franco decided to eliminate the Republic's northern enclave along the Bay of Biscay based upon Bilbao, Santander and Gijon, whose conquest would provide him with a much-needed industrial base, manpower as well as minerals, to trade for foreign weapons. Richthofen was briefed by the Nationalist air force commander General Alfredo Kindélan who would nominally control 150 German, Italian and Spanish aircraft. Kindélan promised Richthofen that if he provided integrated air and artillery bombardments and close-air support, they would exploit the attacks. In the past they had watched Merhart's fighters strafe and bomb enemy positions and emerged from their trenches only to applaud!

Sperrle's headquarters transferred to Vitoria while 62 aircraft had moved to Burgos by 21 March. The enemy had only 30 aircraft and to prevent reinforcement the *Legion Condor's* bombers, including six Heinkels and Dorniers, struck airfields. The main offensive began on 31 March with Sperrle providing both battlefield interdiction and close-air support around Orchandiano[12].

The latter missions were often delayed by showers while ground fire destroyed or damaged seven aircraft but, despite Kindélan's promise, they were not exploited. Worse, Mola seemed uninterested

A Junkers Ju 52/3m g3e bomber of 3.K/88 releases a 250 kg bomb over Spain. The unit's Ju 52s had overall pale-grey finish with the exception of the undercarriage and the front section of the engine cowlings. The emblem of the 3.Staffel, a white stylised diving eagle on a black circle, was painted on the nose.

in these missions and demanded attacks on Bilbao's factories, leading to a bad-tempered exchange on 2 April with Richthofen who regarded such attacks as 'nonsense'.

A face-saving compromise continued close-air support while Richthofen promised to strike an explosives factory during a lull. The Germans were already irritated with Mola; Sperrle disliked his step-by-step attacks and was also annoyed that a bombing raid, which the Spaniard had requested upon enemy reserves reported to be assembling at Durango, had proved a propaganda disaster. The reserves had gone by the time K/88 struck and the 750 casualties were all civilians – a waste of resources in Sperrle's book!

Sperrle protested to Franco and vainly pressed his Spanish allies to conduct a battle of envelopment which German air power could influence. By 25 April Richthofen had moved his command post to Durango and could see an opportunity developing some 16 kilometres to the north-west.

The Republican centre was being driven towards the River Oca and to reach safety would have to pass over the bridge running from Rentaria into the town of Guernica on the west bank. But first they would have to pass through the 'choke point' town of Guerricaiz (which he called Guerricaiz in his diary), 9 kilometres from Rentaria. Here his bombers could annihilate them and by destroying the Rentaria bridge he could bottle the defenders up on the wrong side of the Oca[13].

Although the Astra-Unecta small arms factory lay in south-eastern Guernica with a rail station to the north, there was no target folder; indeed when Richthofen asked if any of his staff knew anything about the town they all shook their heads[14]. On the evening of 25 April Richthofen decided to strike Guerricaiz.

But that morning A/88 reported the assembly of large enemy forces (actually they were civilians on their way to the market) around Guernica. Richthofen saw an opportunity to use air power to isolate and destroy these 'reserves' and rushed to see Mola's Chief-of-Staff, *Coronel* Juan Vigón, who gave him permission to abandon other missions and strike the new target. VB/88 and K/88 (together with Italian bombers whom he roped in for the mission) were to

strike what he believed were enemy troops on the roads immediately east of Guernica, and in the nearby suburbs as well as the Rentaria Bridge, while J/88 and A/88 interdicted the roads east of the river to herd the defenders into the Guerricaiz killing ground[15].

But in communicating this concept from Durango 160 kilometres over mountains to Burgos there appears to have been confusion. Despite the best efforts of Ln 88 the message was interpreted as an attack *upon* Guernica and 26 bombers of K/88 and VB/88, escorted by 16 fighters of 1. and 2. J/88, took off. VB/88 dropped nearly eight tonnes of bombs around the bridge and K/88 added 37 tonnes, most of which struck the centre and south of the town while a burning olive oil plant caused dense clouds of smoke, confusing the later waves. Between 250 and 1,500 people were killed or wounded, some being strafed by the fighters as they tried to flee the holocaust.

Bombs straddled the bridge (Richthofen wrote '*Guernica is isolated*' in his diary that night) but did not hit it or any other military target except for the rail station. The small-arms factory and convents used by two Republican battalions were unscathed as were the

The ruins of the Basque town of Guernica which was heavily damaged on 26 April 1937 by the bombers of VB/88 and K/88. Whatever the rights and wrongs of the operation, the name of Guernica was to become synonymous with indiscriminate bombing and later formed the subject of one of Picasso's most famous paintings.

'Guernica is isolated...': Wolfram Freiherr von Richthofen (standing in the foreground with binoculars) watches as his bombers fly an operation. A distant cousin of the famous 'Red Baron' Manfred von Richthofen, he served as a fighter pilot in the First World War, and was credited with eight victories. After the war, he gained a Doctorate in engineering, and eventually transferred to the new Luftwaffe in 1933. In 1936 he was appointed Chief-of-Staff to the Legion Condor, but following several disagreements with its commander, Hugo Sperrle, he returned to Germany. Von Richthofen was to become one of the great advocates of the dive-bomber, leading the VIII. Fliegerkorps from July 1939 to June 1942 through Poland, the West, the Balkans and Russia.

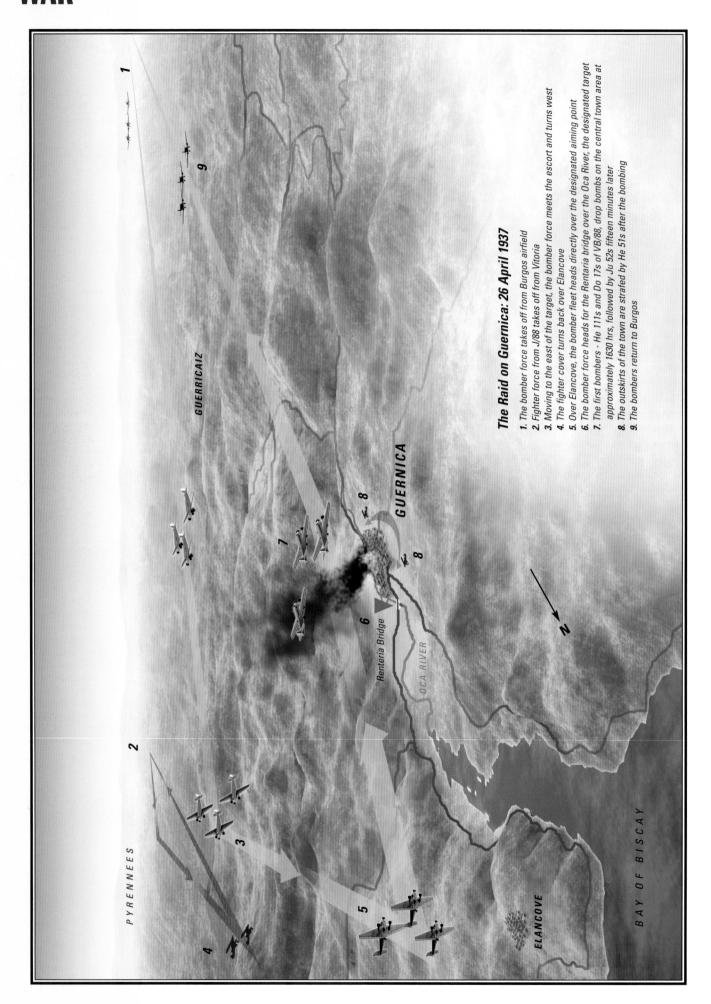

The Raid on Guernica: 26 April 1937

1. The bomber force takes off from Burgos airfield
2. Fighter force from J/88 takes off from Vitoria
3. Moving to the east of the target, the bomber force meets the escort and turns west
4. The fighter cover turns back over Elancove
5. Over Elancove, the bomber fleet heads directly over the designated aiming point
6. The bomber force heads for the Rentaria bridge over the Oca River, the designated target
7. The first bombers - He 111s and Do 17s of VB/88, drop bombs on the central town area at approximately 1630 hrs, followed by Ju 52s fifteen minutes later
8. The outskirts of the town are strafed by He 51s after the bombing
9. The bombers return to Burgos

PYRENNEES

GUERRICAIZ

GUERNICA

Rentería Bridge

OCA RIVER

ELANCOVE

BAY OF BISCAY

N

town's two hospitals. Guernica's destruction horrified the world and provoked a storm of controversy, the Republicans claiming it was an attempt to terrorise the Basques and the Nationalists claiming the defenders had blown up the town. In fact Richthofen had no time for 'terror' attacks and he was at first as bewildered about the town's destruction as everyone else[16].

When Nationalist troops occupied the town on 29 April they learned the truth and a furious Mola banned further attacks upon towns or villages. For propaganda reasons the Germans denied bombing the town both to the world and even themselves. Meanwhile, once across the Oca, Mola's troops closed upon Bilbao which was defended by fortifications dubbed The Ring of Iron (*Cinturón de Hierro*). The *Legion Condor*'s bombers began pounding this, dropping 681 tonnes of bombs by 10 May sometimes flying three sorties a day. This was made possible by the ground crews, called 'Black Men' (*Schwarze Männer*) because of their black, often oil-streaked overalls, who ensured serviceability rates of up to 90 per cent.

The He 51s pounded enemy positions using a new Nationalist Air Force tactic called *cadenas* (chains), with continuous low-level attacks made until ammunition was exhausted[17]. On 11 June the Ring of Iron was assaulted, 5. *(Leicht)/F/88* breaking up a counter-attack, and as the defences collapsed the Germans intensified their operations; some flew seven sorties a day. On 19 June the city surrendered to the *Legion*'s liaison officer *Leutnant* Gockel ending an 11-week campaign which had cost the Germans eight aircraft and 25 men, including nine aircrew, of whom two were executed at Orchandiano on 6 April. The majority of *Legion* airmen who baled out behind enemy lines were well treated and some were exchanged for Russian airmen, but retreating Republican troops sometimes shot prisoners out of hand. However, in January 1939 10 were escorted into France. After Bilbao fell Fuchs was replaced at K/88 by *Major* Karl Mehnart while at the beginning of July Merhardt was replaced at J/88 by *Major* Karl Hermann Gotthard Handrick, who had won the Modern Pentathlon Gold in the 1936 Olympic Games, and joined the Legion as it returned to the Madrid front.

Here, on 6 July the Republic attempted to envelop the enemy salient pointing into the heart of the capital. The southern arm was quickly stopped, but the northern one took the town of Brunete close to the Nationalist supply line then prevented General José Enrique Varela from creating a new line, which quickly contained them. Sperrle, whose *nom de guerre* was 'Sanders', immediately despatched two squadrons but, as the scale of the operation became apparent, he assumed command of German and Nationalist units as *Grupo Aéro Sanders* which incorporated the whole of the *Legion Condor* at Avila and Salamanca[18]. Establishing a command post close to Varela, he assumed command of all Nationalist air power over the battlefield, some 161 aircraft of which he provided half, while facing some 250[19].

From 8 July he maintained pressure upon the enemy bridgehead using small formations of bombers to interdict communications and to strike troop assemblies. Corps aircraft roamed the battlefield and called down modern bombers such as the Do 17 and He 111 (the Ju 86 was withdrawn in June while the He 70s of A/88 were replaced by the Do 17F) on targets of opportunity along the roads, a tactic first used by the British during the autumn of 1918. Fighter-bombers struck enemy positions, including anti-aircraft batteries, under blazing skies and, during the oppressively hot nights, the older bombers (including Ju 52s) struck 'choke points' and supply dumps.

Although the first Bf 109 was lost on 12 July the new fighters had now overcome their teething troubles and established superiority over the *Chatos* and *Moscas*, boosted by a brief foray against enemy airfields on 10 July. Sperrle also provided powerful air support for Varela's counter-offensive on 18 July which regained most of the lost ground after six days of ferocious fighting.

Sperrle's campaign cost the Nationalists 23 aircraft, the *Legion* lost eight and nine aircrew, but the Republic lost about 100 aircraft; and 2.J/88's Bf 109s claimed 16, four by *Feldwebel* Peter Boddem, whose tour would eventually end with a tally of 10.

Sperrle returned but his losses over the past four months were not immediately replaced, leaving him with only 68 aircraft, and with J/88 down to 27 fighters it was little wonder that *Oberleutnant* Douglas Pitcairn, *Staffelkapitän* of 3.J/88, observed: "We had a feeling we had been sent to Spain and then deserted[20]". The *Schwarze Männer* kept serviceability rates high, although sometimes they had to cannibalise wrecked aircraft. For the advance on Santander, which fell on 27 August, the Bf 109s and He 111s penetrated deep into enemy air space and the former were now proving a match for the *Ratas* to strengthen Nationalist air dominance[21].

General Alfredo Kindélan y Duany, the head of the Spanish Nationalist Air Force. Kindélan was often heard to remark that the Nationalists could get along well without the Legion Condor.

Coronel Juan Vigón, Chief-of-Staff to General Emilio Mola, worked well with von Richthofen and was one of the relatively few Spanish commanders who earned the German commander's respect.

Two Do 17 E-1s of VB/88 photographed in Spain during the summer of 1937 with an He 70 reconnaissance aircraft of A/88 in the background.

The experimental bomber unit VB/88 under Oblt. Rudolf Freiherr von Moreau joined the Legion Condor late in 1936. It was equipped initially with four Do 17 E-1s (including 27/3), four He 111 Bs (including 25/2) and four Ju 86s. The Dornier in the foreground carries the distinctive Nationalist tailplane markings.

The northern campaign, which consumed 2,500 tonnes of bombs, ended on 21 October with the fall of Gijon. The He 51s, now fitted with racks for six 10 kg bombs and sometimes using improvised napalm bombs, flew up to seven sorties a day in weather so hot the pilots wore only shorts or swimming trunks, striking enemy positions from the rear by flying up valleys and over crests. Ground fire proved deadlier than fighters and six aircraft were shot down or badly damaged, representing 50 per cent of the total losses, including *Oberleutnant* Hans-Detlef von Kessel, *Staffelkapitän* of A/88.

Ten days after Gijon fell, Sperrle returned to Germany, having fallen out with Richthofen whom he refused to allow to make a farewell address. Sperrle spent the next three months on leave and writing reports before becoming commander of *Luftwaffen-gruppenkommando* 3 when it was created from *Luftkreiskommando* 5 on 4 February 1938. His replacement was being considered as the Brunete battle raged; Blomberg wanted to send Kesselring who would certainly have been a good choice. But the former chief-of-staff had just assumed command of *Luftkreiskommando* 3 and Göring wisely decided against a sudden change in command. Instead, he decided to send his chief military administrator, *Generalmajor* Helmuth Volkmann who needed a front line command after 'flying a desk' for three years [22].

Volkmann was 48 and had joined the Pioneers in 1907 then transferred to the air service during the Great War. At one time he was a squadron commander but mostly commanded fighter schools or had administrative assignments. He joined the *Reichsheer* after the war and worked for the *Heereswaffenamt*, helping to produce requirements for new aircraft. He did not transfer to the *Luftwaffe* until September 1934 and had various administrative posts culminating with his appointment as Head of the Administrative Office (*Chef der Luftwaffen-Verwaltungsamt*) in October 1936, when he was also promoted from *Oberst*.

He was clearly an administrator rather than a combat commander and appears to have been 'ticket punching'. However, when he assumed command on 1 November he retained the veteran Richthofen who was himself scheduled for replacement but remained for three months to ensure continuity. He departed on 11 January 1938 and was replaced by the 36-year-old broad-shouldered Swabian, *Major* Hermann Plocher. An *Offizieranwärter* during the closing weeks of the Great War he was commissioned in 1921 and served in the same infantry regiment as Erwin Rommel, later 'The Desert Fox'. He had been one of the first students at Lipetsk and then became a staff officer, transferring to the *Luftwaffe* only in 1935 and then working as an organiser.

Volkmann's arrival also marked Hitler's renewed commitment to the Nationalist cause with the delivery of new aircraft and equipment raising the *Legion's* strength to 100 aircraft. K/88 re-equipped two *Staffeln* with He 111s and absorbed VB/88 which became 3.K/88. A second *Staffel* in J/88 received the Bf 109B and the He 51s were used to create 4.J/88 'Ace of Spades' ('*Pik As*') whose 'parent' was the naval I./JG 136 [23]. A/88 replaced all of its He 70s with Do 17s while *Flak/88* received another two heavy batteries as well as two platoons (*Züge*) of 3.7cm *Flak 28* guns. However, the new aircraft required high-energy (100 octane) fuel, when most aircraft in Spain relied upon 87 octane, and the *Reich* provided only a trickle forcing Volkmann to pay considerable attention to fuel economy in his planning.

He arrived as the *Legion* concentrated around Soria ready to support alternate strategies: Franco wanted to assault Madrid while his allies preferred striking eastwards into Aragon. Enemy air power had been boosted by the arrival of the I-152 or *Super Chato*, but this proved less formidable than fog and snow which disrupted operations and caused both a Bf 109 and a He 111 to force-land behind enemy lines during the first half of December. The Republican Government permitted its French and Russian friends to evaluate the aircraft, which were then shipped to the Soviet Union[24].

On 15 December the Republic pre-empted the strategic argument by attacking at Teruel, 180 kilometres south-east of Soria. The garrison held out until 8 January, but a week elapsed before Franco reluctantly abandoned plans for his Madrid offensive and took up the gauntlet. He reinforced the Teruel front (including two heavy batteries of *F/88*), despite advice from his allies, including Volkmann, and at a planning conference attended by Richthofen, he announced that a counter-offensive would begin on 29 December[25].

Volkmann's headquarters moved to Bronchales, 35 kilometres north-west of Teruel which confirmed its reputation as the coldest city in Spain. The *Schwarze Männer* had to build temporary shelters to warm aircraft engines before take-off and operations, mostly close-air support and attacks upon reserves, were further hampered by snow until the counter-offensive was buried by a blizzard on 31 December.

Impeded by snow it resumed on 17 January forcing the Republicans to strip troops from the Alfambra valley to the north and on 7 February the Nationalists exploited this weakness with a day-long offensive that took the valley. The *Legion Condor* softened up the defences and each day for four days flew 100 sorties and dropped 120 tonnes of bombs. The Republican air force, now almost exclusively Spanish, replied vigorously, striking Volkmann's base at Almazan and damaging many aircraft. *J/88* held its own and in one engagement on 7 February shot down 10 out of a force of twelve SBs and two *Moscas*, *Oberleutnant* Wilhelm Balthasar accounting for four *Katiuskas*. In the face of overwhelming air superiority the Republican defence collapsed, exposing Teruel, which fell on 17 February when K/88 and A/88 dropped 65 tonnes of bombs. *Leutnant* Eckehart Priebe's He 51 just missed a tank carrying the famous Republican general Valentín González, better known as 'The Peasant' (*El Campesino*) to safety[26].

This also marked the debut of the Ju 87 B, a trio of which under *Leutnant* Hermann Haas were transferred from 11.(*St*)/*Lehrgeschwader Greifswald* in mid-January officially forming 5.J/88, but usually known as the *Stuka Kette* replacing the Hs 123. They were used for precision attacks upon strong points and demonstrated their ability to put bombs within five metres of the target[27]. This brought about a triumphant conclusion to the *Legion's* Teruel campaign which had cost it only five aircraft and 10 dead.

Teruel decimated the Republican forces and Franco decided to exploit the situation with a series of successive thrusts into Aragon north of Teruel, these being broken off whenever resistance grew too strong and renewed on nearby sectors.

With 460 aircraft (220 Italian and 100 German) the Nationalists achieved air superiority over the 550 Republican aircraft, including the latest I-16 Type 10. Franco's air support consisted of both Tactical and

Operational-level missions, the latter striking reserves and communications deep in the enemy rear and arousing great fear in the Republican ranks[28].

The campaign began south of the River Ebro on 9 March when K/88 dropped 88 tonnes of bombs to leave the surviving defenders quivering, weeping and unable to resist. The front again collapsed and the *Legion* rapidly assumed the traditional role of cavalry, with K/88 dropping 45.5 tonnes of bombs on communications and the *Stukas* flying twelve sorties while J/88's Bf 109s strafed the enemy to help the He 51s wreck every enemy counter-attack. This brought the total tonnage of bombs on the first day to 210, a record for the Civil War. Within a week A/88 was unable to locate useful targets and Volkmann was switched north of the Ebro, leaving support south of the river to the lumbering He 59 floatplanes of AS/88.

The air support ensured steady progress allowing the Nationalists to reach the sea and split the Republic on 15 April. The *Luftwaffe* then conducted *Unternehmen 'Neptun'* against the Republican Fleet's

A group of pilots photographed at Santander during the summer of 1937. Many of the pilots show here went on to achieve fame during the Second World War. From left to right are: Gotthard Handrick (commander of J/88), Peter Boddem (10 victories in Spain), Günther Lützow (Kapitän of 2.J/88), Joachim Schlichting (the next leader of 2.J/88), Walter Ehle, Harro Harder (Kapitän of 1.J/88), Erich Woitke and Rolf Pingel.

One side of the spinner of Hptm. Gotthard Handrick's Bf 109 D-1 was marked with the five Olympic rings to commemorate his winning a Gold Medal in the 1936 Berlin Games together with the legend '1936' and a laurel wreath. This photograph was taken after the aircraft had been decorated by his ground crew to commemorate his return to Germany in September 1938. The German inscription 'Scheiden tut weh' means 'Parting is painful'. The other side of the spinner of Handrick's aircraft was adorned with the five Olympic rings and the legend '1940?' This recorded Handrick's hope that he would win a second Olympic Gold Medal at the 1940 Games scheduled to take place in Tokyo. The nose of the spinner was painted in concentric red, yellow and red bands.

Generalmajor Hellmuth Volkmann (code named 'Vieth' in Spain), took over from Sperrle as commander of the Legion Condor in October 1937. He was not particularly popular, constantly pressing for the Legion's withdrawal. He returned to Germany in December 1938, but was killed in a car accident on 21 August 1940 while leading an Infantry Division in France.

A group of pilots gathered around a He 51 of the 4.Staffel of J/88 at Calamocha. The tall figure on the left is Oblt. Eberhardt Trützschler-d'Élsa, Kapitän of 4.J/88 with, in the centre facing the camera: Ufw. Heinrich Torner (killed on 19 February 1938), Lt. Fritz Awe (killed on 4 April 1938) and, first from right, Lt. Kurt Müller (3 victories).

bases, which involved 59 sorties and 82.5 tonnes of bombs for the loss of one aircraft. This, like almost all German bombing during the Spanish Civil War, was an Operational Level mission.

This was a brief interlude because from 22 March Volkmann supported operations north of the Ebro but these were hamstrung by bad weather. His headquarters moved close to the mouth of the Ebro at Benicarlo with bombers and reconnaissance aircraft operating from Saragossa, while his single-engined aircraft operated from La Cenia and Vinaroz. From 25 April the Nationalists swung southwards into the Levante towards Valencia and for two months they crawled forward against fierce resistance and the *Legion Condor* suffered severe attrition from a resurgent enemy air force.

Volkmann was recalled to Berlin late in May but was left to cool his heels until a meeting at the RLM was held on 10 June. He told his masters that he had lost 20 per cent of his strength since 9 March with 20 aircraft destroyed and seven badly damaged, while 38 crew were dead or missing. Only 16 Bf 109s remained serviceable, the He 51s could barely fly and most of the *Flakkanone* had been worn smooth. He demanded either reinforcement or withdrawal but received no decision. Back in Spain he warned his commanders on 16 June that operations might have to be restricted.

He was already under a cloud for expressing his fears of isolation if a general European conflict erupted. He first expressed them when Hitler created a union (*Anschluss*) with Austria at bayonet point in March 1938 and again during the summer when the

largely German population of Czechoslovakia's Sudetenland demanded absorption into the *Reich*.

The *Anschluss* crisis saw Wilberg 'bowler-hatted' to be replaced at *Sonderstab W* on 1 April by 54-year-old *Generalleutnant* (*General der Flieger* from 1 June) Karl-Friedrich Schweickhard, a pre-war pilot who ended the war as a *Grufl*, having served in the *Reichsheer's* infantry then as a *Luftkreis* commander[29]. In addition to Volkmann's want of nerve, Berlin was also concerned about friction between him and Franco and with the Sudetenland crisis the RLM was slow to respond, apart from despatching a band!

On 17 June Berlin finally decided to send more Bf 109 Bs and some Bf 109 Cs to make J/88 into a Bf 109 unit, 4.J/88 and its He 51s being disbanded, with the aircraft passed to the Spanish. The unit which most benefited was 3.J/88 under *Oberleutnant* Werner 'Daddy' ('*Vati*') Mölders who is widely credited with introducing '*Kettehunde*' tactics. The *Jagdgruppe* began to conduct sweeps of up to 32 fighters and usually triumphed in air battles.

While AS/88's floatplanes were briefly used over land during March, their greatest contribution during the spring and early summer was interdicting the Republic's maritime communications[30]. Created under *Major* Karl-Heinz Wolff purely as a recon-naissance force they began to carry torpedoes (nicknamed 'Eels') from January 1937 and *Oberleutnant* Werner Klümper (*Kommodore* of the torpedo-bomber KG 26 in 1943-1944) damaged the 1,253 GRT freighter *Delfin* on 30 January. There was then a lull of several months before an anti-shipping campaign began during the second half of 1937 with the He 59s using bombs and 20 mm cannon rather than torpedoes, most of the attacks taking place around Cartagena and Valencia[31].

With the arrival in November of *Major* Martin 'Iron Gustav' Harlinghausen the campaign intensified with up to 16 sorties a day being flown by August 1938, until he was relieved by *Hauptmann* Smidt in March 1939. Harlinghausen, aged 36, was a short, slim man who combined a sense of humour with nerves of steel. He came from inland Westphalia, but joined the Navy as a seaman in 1923 serving in torpedo boats until 1931. He was commissioned in 1929 and two years later became a pilot so it was no surprise when he transferred to the *Luftwaffe* in 1933. He qualified as an observer in October 1934 and then spent most of his time until late 1937 in the training organisation[32].

Under Harlinghausen ships were usually attacked in the approaches to ports whose facilities were also bombed. A favourite tactic was to begin from high altitude, switch off the engines and glide down towards the target, drop up to a tonne of bombs from 300 metres, restart the engines and fly away. The 'Big

A line-up of six He 111s of K/88 ready to take part in 'Operation Neptune,' a concentrated attack against Republican naval forces in the ports of Cartagena and Almeria in April 1938.

Shoes' (*Zatapones*) He 59s sank 23 ships (55,161 GRT) during the Spanish Civil War and many small sailing vessels and fishing boats but 12 He 59s were lost in 1938 and 1939 including three night fighters[33].

As the Sudetenland Crisis intensified Volkmann had more pressing problems. During July A/88 began to bring disturbing images of Republican preparations for their own offensive across the Ebro towards Gandesa, but Franco's headquarters ignored the warnings. On the night of 24/25 July the enemy crossed the river supported by 260 aircraft and Gandesa was quickly under threat[34]. Reinforcements, including 434 aircraft, were despatched and from 6 August the Nationalists, through limited offensives, waged a battle of attrition which began in stifling heat and ended with the last Republican troops withdrawing through falling snow on 18 November.

With its forward bases under threat Volkmann immediately committed the *Legion*'s 70 aircraft. During the first week the airmen were flying two or three sorties a day with 587 bomber sorties mounted by K/88 and A/88 who dropped more than 566 tonnes of bombs, while the *Stukakette* flew 77 sorties and dropped 37.5 tonnes of bombs[35]. The bridges were the prime target and in August alone the Republican umbilical received more than 1,564 tonnes of bombs from K/88 supported by the *Stukas* and three Ar 68Es, although the A/88 reverted to a pure reconnaissance role[36]. The Germans alone would drop 1,713 tonnes of bombs during the campaign but, while they hindered the movement of enemy supplies and forced the Republicans to build bridges just under the water, Nationalist air power failed to isolate the battlefield.

Fighter sweeps quickly established air superiority over the bridgehead although the *Katiuskas* would make occasional attacks upon their bases, destroying or damaging five Bf 109s at La Cenia on 4 October. Yet the same month J/88 claimed 23 victories, but by then significant changes were affecting the *Legion Condor*.

With the Sudetenland Crisis bringing Europe to the verge of war, Volkmann was ordered to strip his squadrons to supply the Reich and 246 experienced aircrew returned to German shores. This robbed him of both *Kommandeure* Handrick, being replaced by *Hauptmann* Walter Grabmann in J/88, while Mehnert was replaced by *Major* Fritz Härle at K/88. Having lost half his fighter pilots and bomber crews as well as a quarter of his reconnaissance and seaplane crews, Volkmann was forced to replace them with Spanish airmen, who luckily proved very capable.

This led him to pen a highly critical and pessimistic letter to Berlin about the Spanish conduct of the war. For the RLM this was the final straw but it waited until the Munich Agreement was signed before recalling him. He departed on 13 November to join the *Luftkriegsakademie* but he clearly realised his

A line-up of He 51 B-1s photographed at Calamocha airfield in January 1938. The aircraft in the foreground is 2-73 with 2-70 behind. This aircraft was flown by Lt. Helmut Henz of 4.J/88 who was taken prisoner on 14 June 1938 after his He 51 was shot up by a Rata south of Castellon. Note the auxilliary tanks and the personal white script marking under the cockpit of the aircraft in the foreground.

The Ju 87 As, which had arrived in Spain in December 1937, proved disappointing and were later withdrawn and replaced by the improved Ju 87 B-1. This particular Ju 87 A-1, coded 29-4, originally belonged to St.G 163 and, together with the Ju 87 Bs, was flown by a large number of personnel in order to provide as many crews as possible with combat experience.

A flight of Ju 52/3ms of the Spanish Nationalist Air Force. These aircraft could be distinguished by the white diagonal cross painted over the black circle on the fuselage, most Condor Legion aircraft having plain black discs in this position.

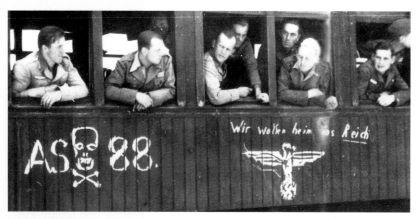

Members of the naval reconnaissance squadron AS/88 on their way back to Germany at the end of the war. The words chalked on the side of the train can be translated as: "We want to go back in the Reich"!

career was under a cloud and he returned to the Army in May 1940 as a *General der Infanterie*. He was given an infantry division, which failed to distinguish itself in the Western campaigns of 1940, and died on 21 August from car accident injuries.

He was briefly replaced by Plocher, who supervised the final stages of air support for the Ebro battle, aided by the arrival of five Ju 87 Bs which entered the fray on 30 October. The Ebro campaign cost the *Legion* 10 aircraft, most to accidents, while 14 were badly damaged and there were 18 aircrew casualties. There was then a brief respite and, with the end of the Sudetenland Crisis, reinforcements of men and machines arrived to replace many of the Spanish airmen. The *Legion* expanded to 96 aircraft, a fifth of total Nationalist air strength, including Bf 109 Es, He 111 E/Js and the Hs 126.

Volkmann's replacement on 1 December was *Generalmajor* von Richthofen, accompanied by 37-year-old *Oberstleutnant* Hans Seidemann who replaced Plocher in what became a military marriage. Parson's son Seidemann had been an *Offiziersanwärter* when the Great War ended and then joined a *Freikorps* unit which was later absorbed by the *Reichsheer* as an infantry battalion. He was commissioned in 1922 and from 1926 to 1928 trained as a pilot at Lipetsk. In 1933 he went on a staff officers' training course and after qualifying he promptly transferred to the *Luftwaffe* in 1935, serving with *Oberstleutnant* Hans Jeschonnek's Operations Department in the *Luftwaffe* General Staff before joining Richthofen. He would end the war as a *General der Flieger* leading Richthofen's old command, VIII. *Fliegerkorps*[37].

They had three weeks to plan the next campaign, the occupation of Catalonia which began on 23 December[38]. The Republican air force had lost 150 aircraft over the Ebro but remained aggressive and elusive to the end. But when its bases were discovered by A/88 devastating attacks followed, with 26 aircraft destroyed or damaged beyond repair at Vilajuiga on 6 February. The bombers and *Stukas* focused their fury on communications, striking targets around Figueras at hourly intervals and contributing to the Nationalist's rapid advance, despite snow, with the French frontier reached on 9 February.

Losses were heavy: 11 aircraft or nearly 11.5 per cent of strength, and some 30 airmen of whom 21 were German, mostly due to accidents. Richthofen then moved to Toledo for the final assault upon Madrid. Fighter sweeps sought out the last remnants of Republican air power and *Oberleutnant* Hubertus von Bonin, commander of 3.J/88 since the Ebro battle, shot down a *Chato* over Alicante for the Legion's 314th and last aerial victory on 5 March. But the previous day Härle, *Kommandeur* of K/88 was killed when his He 111 exploded in mid air over Madrid, apparently the victim of a faulty electric fuze in the bombs. Three K/88 '*Schwarze Männer*' were killed by two explosions during the Bilbao campaign and during 1938 two aircraft suffered the same fate as Härle's. Indeed, it was a problem which plagued the

Generalleutnant Karl-Friedrich Schweickhard replaced Wilberg as head of 'Sonderstab W' on 1 April 1938. He would later serve in senior training positions and as an officer judge at the Reich Court of War.

Photographed at Escratón airfield during the Aragón offensive, this group of Bf 109 B-1s carry the later style of marking system, with the aircraft type number forward of the black national insignia disc and the individual number aft. Previously, Bf 109s had both numbers painted behind the disc, with a hyphen between. 6●6 in the foreground was flown by Lt. Herbert Ihlefeld before being written off by Uffz. Franz Jaenisch in July 1938.

Gathered in an assortment of leather overcoats and hybrid uniforms, the crew and ground crew of Heinkel He 111 B-2, 25-57, of 1.K/88 wait while a Spanish refuelling team attend to their aircraft, before lining up for an inspection by a senior officer at Armilla, 1938.

Luftwaffe, accounting for at least 12 aircraft and 24 lives between September 1939 and May 1940!

In the event, the Spanish Civil War ended in farcical anti-climax with the Republic collapsing in internecine fighting and surrendering to Franco on 26 March. Tragically, before the *Legion*'s final parade on 26 May there were several fatal accidents, but on that day 5,136 men departed from Vigo taking with them some 700 tonnes of equipment including all their modern aircraft.

Some 19,000 men served in the *Legion Condor* which lost 226 dead (including 41 aircrew) and 139 wounded, while 449 had been injured in accidents! The material losses were 232 aircraft, 72 to enemy action, and the expenditure of munitions may be

This Bf 109 B-2 was flown by Oblt. Walter Oesau who led the Stabskette of J/88. Oesau scored nine victories in Spain before returning to Germany to command III./JG 51, III./JG 3, JG 2 and finally JG 1. He was killed in combat on 11 May 1944. The spinner of his aircraft had a small shield painted on one side.

gauged from the fact that K/88 alone dropped more than 21,000 tonnes of bombs. The small training mission had produced 500 Spanish aircrew trained in Spain while another 40 pilots were trained in Germany[39].

While Spain apparently confirmed the supremacy of the high-performance bomber, and the value of dive-bombing, it also showed the need to strengthen defensive armament, which influenced Ju 88 development. However, experience also led Udet to increase the fighter-bomber production ratio from 25 per cent to 33 per cent while strengthening the armament through the introduction of the 20 mm Oerlikon MG FF/M cannon[40].

The need for a long-range fighter underlined development of the Bf 110, although none was sent to Spain. There was also a requirement for an armoured ground-attack aircraft issued in December 1937 and leading to the Henschel Hs 129, while in Moscow a similar requirement a few months later led to the Ilyushin Il 2.

Yet some of the after-action reports included words of caution. Lützow noted: "The fact that we suffered only slight losses despite being outnumbered is due to the inadequate training and erratic leadership of the enemy airmen, and to the greater speed of our own fighters…" Another noted: "It proved impossible to inflict lasting damage on, or to put out of action completely, any enemy air force ground installation. It also proved impossible to knock out enemy air forces on the ground because of the high degree of flexibility of enemy formations." Both would prove prophetic in the coming months.

Richthofen also recognised the problem of providing air support for mechanised formations striking deep into enemy territory. Upon his return to Berlin in 1937 he campaigned for the Luftwaffe to address this problem but with little initial success although *Wehrmacht* exercises that year demonstrated his perception[41].

NOTES TO CHAPTER FOUR

1. For German air operations during the Spanish Civil War the essential sources are Proctor and Ries & Ring. See also Hugh Thomas' classic history, Howson, Mombeek, Smith & Creek, Salas Larrazabel Hooton pp.120-145 and Schliephake pp.41-44. BA MA RL 35/7-8, 39-41.

2. Hermann pp.25-26. Proctor pp.3-23. Ries & Ring pp.12-14.
3. Proctor pp.20-22. The first airlift was by the RAF who flew 586 people of 20 nationalities out of Kabul, Afghanistan, over a two-month period during the winter of 1928-1929. See Baker.
4. Hooton p.122. Proctor pp.25-33. Ries & Ring pp. 14-16.Green, *Warplanes* p.407.
5. Proctor pp.28-29. Ries & Ring p17. See also Dr Osborne's essay.
6. Proctor pp.53-70. Ries & Ring pp.35, 37-41.
7. Mombeek, Smith and Creek pp.136, 138. Ries & Ring pp.170-171.
8. For the Madrid campaign Hooton pp.125-129. Mombeek, Smith and Creek p.107.Proctor pp.80-116. Ries & Ring pp.42-49).
9. Mitcham p.293. Collins and Miller's website.
10. For Sperrle and Richthofen see Corum pp.192, 215. Thomas & Witts pp.30, 42-43, 53. Also BA MA N 671/1.
11. For Lützow see Braatz pp.148ff. It should be noted that the term 'Kettehunde' was also an uncomplimentary term for the Military Police.
12. For the Bilbao campaign see Proctor pp116-144. Ries & Ring pp.56-67. See also Martínez Bande.
13. For Guernica see Kappe-Hardenberg, Martínez Bande (with excellent sketch maps), Thomas and Witts. Also Proctor pp.127-130. Ries &Ring pp. 62-64. Thomas pp.624-629.
14. Thomas & Witts p.106.
15. Richthofen diary.
16. The French *Général* Maurice Duval, who commanded the French Air Force from 1917-1918, perceptively described Guernica as "…an experimental bombardment by the *Legion Condor* on a communication centre and an army in retreat". Quoted Martínez Bande p.111 n.174.
17. The Russians developed a similar tactic in Spain and called it 'The Conveyer Belt'. For *Luftwaffe* ground-attack operations in Spain see Weal pp.8-16.
18. Howson p.233.
19. For Brunete see Proctor pp.145-155. Riese & Ring pp.68-82.
20. Proctor p.171.
21. For the northern campaigns see Proctor pp.157-169. Ries & Ring pp. 87-104. 22.
22. Proctor pp.157-158. Collins & Miller's website.
23. Ries & Ring p.117.
24. The French evaluation is in SHAA, 2B78 Dossier 2.
25. For Teruel see Proctor pp.170-186. Ries & Ring pp.110-127.
26. Mombeek, Smith, Creek p.138.
27. BA MA RL 35/39.
28. For the Spring-Summer 1938 campaigns see Proctor pp.187-219. Ries & Ring pp.127-178. Thomas p.801.
29. See Collins & Miller's website.
30. Ries & Ring pp.135-142.
31. Thiele pp.11, 14.
32. Mitcham p.111. Collins & Miller's website.
33. See Hooton pp.138-141. Articles by Dr Osborne and Torroba. In addition *K/88* and *VB/88* sank 11 ships (27,335 grt) attacking ports.
34. For the Battle of the Ebro see Henry. For air operations see Hooton pp.140-142. Proctor pp.221-236. Ries & Ring pp.178-200.

Hptm. Werner Mölders (left), Staffelkapitän of 3.J/88, stands by his Bf 109 D-1, coded 6●79. At this time the aircraft has three victory bars painted on the rudder, Mölders having claimed these, including an I-16 Rata, on 19 July 1938. The name 'Luchs' (Lynx) was painted on both sides of the fuselage in white.

[35.] IWM Microfilm Ger/Misc/MCR./19 (1A).

[36.] Italian Breda Ba 65 ground-attack aircraft were also used to dive bomb the bridges. Howson p.65. This air offensive mirrored the Allied operations on the Marne in July 1918.

[37.] Mitcham p.209. Collins & Miller's website (Prignitzlexikon website.).

[38.] For the last air operations of the Spanish Civil War see Proctor pp.237-249. Ries & Ring pp.201-224.

[39.] Proctor p. 253. Ries & Ring Appendix L & M. Salas p.206. Westwall in Axis History Fact Book website.

[40.] Proctor pp.251-266.

[41.] Corum pp.223, 234. Murray, *Effectiveness* pp.104-105.

Loaded with bombs or equipped with heavy machine guns, the He 59 'Zapatones' flew aggressive patrols or attacks against enemy harbours. The first five He 59s arrived at the end of 1936 and were delivered to AS/88. Around twenty of the type were used in Spain, its main success being the sinking of the battleship 'Jamie I' in Almeria airfield on the night of 24/25 May 1937. Seven or so He 59s were lost in the fighting in Spain and about five survived to serve with the Spanish Navy into the later 1940s.

CHAPTER FIVE

THE BIG STICK

1936–1939

*Oberst Ernst Udet, Chief of the Technisches Amt (Technical Office)
of the RLM from June 1936, strides away from his open-topped saloon
during a visit to an airbase.*

Within a week of Wever's well-publicised death on 3 June the *Luftwaffe* suffered a greater disaster, but did not recognise it at the time[1].

On the morning of 9 June Richthofen went to see Wimmer to express doubts about the *Stuka* concept and to recommend its abandonment. But that day, after 'flying a desk' so successfully for so many years, Wimmer was given command of *Luftkreis* III[2]. He was replaced by the *Stuka* enthusiast, the stocky, balding, Ernst Udet.

Udet was one of the most popular in the *Luftwaffe* leadership and with 62 victories was the highest scoring German fighter ace to survive the war. His Bohemian post-war years saw public romances interspersed with hair-raising flying stunts as he barnstormed around Germany and later the United States. His popularity owed much to his abilities as a self-deprecating raconteur and cartoonist, often using restaurant tablecloths. However, his preference for rare steaks and refusal to eat green vegetables meant that he appears to have suffered from scurvy and certainly when he celebrated his 40th birthday in April 1936 he looked 50[3]!

He was one of the last 'Old Eagles' to join the colours, in 1935, attracted by a steady income, although Göring also promised to let him pursue his fascination with the dive-bomber[4]. He knew little about aircraft development, indeed his 'test flights' involved throwing the aircraft around the sky and, although he was one of the few senior members of the *Luftwaffe* who was a Party member (from 1933), the *Gestapo* watched him, partly because he had anti-Nazi friends.

Udet was reluctant to accept greater responsibilities and told Göring: "This isn't for me. I don't know anything about production and big aircraft." It was probably on account of his technical ignorance that Göring appointed him since he would not show up 'Fatty's' own ignorance, while Göring was confident that Wimmer's organisation would carry its boss. The Nazis believed that the strong should rule the weak uninhibited by moral or legal considerations – indeed it was brawn rather than legality which defined the leadership of Party organisations from top to bottom.

Udet was a close friend of Milch and Göring wanted to exploit this to counter-balance the *Staatssekretär* as relations between the two surviving members of the *Luftwaffe* triumvirate deteriorated[5]. There were heated rows over the telephone and Milch would often end them by slamming the telephone down; so knowing that the *Staatssekretär*'s ego was harnessed to control of aircraft production, the new appointment undoubtedly gave the *Luftwaffe*'s commander much private enjoyment. In turn Milch soon began to exploit Udet's inadequacies in intrigues, which gradually grew in effectiveness until in November 1941 Udet shot himself, leaving a note which blamed 'the Jew Milch.'

The engineers in the *Technische Amt* also followed Göring's 'divide and rule' policy. To improve their status, and to permit them to indulge their interests in technical discussion and development, they got Udet to rubber stamp a reorganisation into 13 highly specialised departments created between March and May 1938. In practice this blinkered the various departments and increased development times because manufacturers had to deal with numerous private little empires whose activities Udet was unable to co-ordinate[6].

Despite his inadequacies Udet developed ambition late in life and proposed an air production ministry in all but name similar to the wartime *Flugzeugmeisterei*. On 29 January 1939 *Generalmajor* Udet (he was promoted in April 1937) became the *Generalluftzeugmeister* controlling the *Technisches Amt*, Supply and Economic Directorates, the Industrial Group as well as development establishments. Milch must have been green with envy that his former friend was holding the position he coveted but even he would have found it hard controlling an organisation of 19 departments.

Milch's frustrations grew following Wever's death. The *Luftwaffe*'s growing status fed Göring's megalomania and he wanted a greater say in 'his' service. Before 1936 he rarely visited the RLM more than four times a year but his promotion to *Generaloberst* on 20 April 1936 (when Milch was promoted to *General der Flieger*) dictated a more active role as he moved from Minister to Commander-in-Chief (*Oberbefehlshaber*). Milch saw himself as Wever's replacement but Göring had no intention of making his rival stronger. Blomberg's proposed Bavarian *Generalmajor* Franz Halder opted

Man of the people: throughout the mid-and late 1930s, Göring worked hard and with considerable energy to cultivate a positive profile with the German people through whistle-stop tours of factories and schools. Those who worked closely with him however, experienced a darker, more autocratic personality driven with megalomania. The Generaloberst is seen here signing autographs and collecting pocket money from apparently adoring children to go towards industrial funds.

Generalleutnant Albert Kesselring, Göring's choice to head the Luftkommandoamt in June 1936. An immensely capable staff officer with good administrative skills and, outwardly at least, good humour. He would enjoy promotion to the highest levels of the wartime Luftwaffe.

to remain in the Army where he became Chief of the Army Staff two years later.

Göring then selected another Bavarian, his administrative chief *Generalleutnant* Albert Kesselring, to head the *Luftkommandoamt*. Kesselring was a former gunner who qualified as a balloon observer before the war but remained with the guns. Also balding and stocky, his optimism earned the nickname of 'Smiling Albert', although few realised that his was a loveless marriage to Pauline, which saw a son adopted three years after their marriage, and which his Catholic background prevented him from ending. He was an immensely capable staff officer who seemed effortlessly to create order from chaos but on a personal level displayed an interest in his subordinates' welfare which some felt was an attempt to create a substitute family[7].

Out of pique the snubbed Milch, who retained authority for the *Luftkommandoamt*, began sniping at Kesselring and interfered on every possible occasion. Once Milch wished to court-martial his former adjutant, *Major* Hans Jeschonnek, now *Kommodore* of *Lehrgeschwader Greifswald*, after a series of accidents. Kesselring slapped him down leaving Milch to add Jeschonnek to his long list of enemies through a personal reprimand. Yet even the optimistic Kesselring tired of the constant petty struggles in which he was obviously piggy-in-the-middle between Göring and Milch. He resigned to assume, with great relief, command of *Luftkreiskommando* III on 1 June 1937.

The struggles with Milch limited Kesselring's impact upon *Luftwaffe* development with the *Staatssekretär* opposing development of a *Bomber B* heavy bomber successor until the day after Kesselring's departure, when the RLM pettily authorised a programme using a Heinkel design. Yet Kesselring strengthened the *Luftwaffe's* supply organisation to support rapid advances and in April 1937 took the first steps to creating night fighters by producing a manual on the subject[8].

But before Kesselring departed he fired a Parthian shot. He played on Göring's vanity to persuade him to place the *Luftkommandoamt* under his personal control and finally to rename it the *Luftwaffengeneralstab* (*Luftwaffe* General Staff)[9]. Its reluctant first *Chef* on 1 June was *Generalmajor* Stumpff, who retained the post until the end of January 1939 but achieved little except to hold the line. However, he did oversee the *Luftwaffe's* part in September 1937 in the *Wehrmacht's* largest peacetime exercise which involved several *Panzer* divisions and more than 62,000 men and 1,337 aircraft[10].

Ritter von Greim replaced Stumpff at the *Luftwaffenpersonalamt* and, while both he and Udet were nominally under Milch, by mid-July 1937 Göring was meeting them without bothering to inform the *Staatssekretär*. When he learned what was happening Milch, in September 1937, replaced the acting head (since April) of the *Luftwaffenführungsstabes* (the *Luftwaffe* General Staff's operational command element), and *de facto* deputy *Luftwaffe* Chief-of-Staff, *General* Paul Deichmann, with *Generalmajor* Kühl, its first head, who would remain until 28 February 1939. The wily Bavarian air ace retaliated by placing *Oberstleutnant* Jeschonnek as head of the *Luftwaffenführungsstabes* Operations[11].

For Milch 1937 was the *annus horribilus* in which he lost not only power but also his appendix and the following year also began badly. It was clear that the *Luftwaffe* was becoming too unwieldy for Milch and the RLM to control directly and, on 1 February 1938 it was reorganised, with Udet and Greim formally becoming Göring's subordinates. The remaining administrative departments were placed under the *Chef der Luftwehr* (Chief of Air Defence), 55-year-old *General der Flakartillerie* Otto Günther Rüdel leaving Milch, now appointed *Generalinspekteur der Luftwaffe*, in a largely ceremonial role, although he did share with Stumpff responsibility for the 10 inspectorates.

The new organisation lasted less than a year for it was too unwieldy for any one man to control, especially the lazy Göring whose fat fingers were in far too many pies. He was forced to recognise Milch's administrative skills and another re-organisation took effect on 1 February 1939. Essentially it followed the wartime principle of splitting leadership between the operational and administrative/industrial, with Göring taking control of the former while Milch controlled the latter (aping *Kogenluft* and *Idflieg* in the Great War).

The operational element consisted of the *Generalstab der Luftwaffe* whose chief now controlled the *Führungs-* (Operations), *Fremde Luftmächte* (Intelligence) and *Taktischeabteilungen* (Support) directorates, leaving the *Organization-*, *Quartiermeister-* (Supply), and *Rüstungsabteilungen* (Replacements) Departments under a separate *Generalquartiermeister.* Milch now controlled the organisations of Udet, Rüdel (who replaced Greim in the *Personalamt*), and Martini as well as the inspectorates which were combined under Kühl, who was promoted *General der Flieger* when Chief of Training Resources (*Chef des Ausbildungswesens*) and who had become redundant following the disbanding of the *Luftwaffenführungsstabes.* Kühl, whose first Chief-of-Staff was *Oberstleutnant* Deichmann, would hold this position until July 1943, gradually centralising training. He retired in October 1943 and was captured by the Russians and died, like Haehnelt, in Sachsenhausen concentration camp in early 1946[12].

Of equal importance was the appointment on the same day of *Oberst* Hans Jeschonnek as Chief-of-Staff. Jeschonnek was 39-years-old and one of ten children born to an East Prussian headmaster, and the youngest son of the headmaster's first wife. He enlisted at 15 and, with his elder brother Paul acting as Wilberg's operations officer in 1917, he became a pilot with *Jasta* 40. Like many young soldiers the Armistice brought him no peace and he served with the *Freikorps* against the Poles before joining a *Reichsheer* cavalry regiment, at one time serving in the same squadron as Richthofen.[13]

After working under Student at the *Heereswaffenamt* he went on a staff training course from which he emerged top of his class in 1928. He went straight to Felmy's organisation and wrote a number of important papers and became friendly with Milch, becoming his adjutant in January 1933. Then they fell out and in October 1935 Jeschonnek was sent off to become *Kommandeur* of *Fliegergruppe Greifswald* (II./KG 152) to get him out of the way. In April 1937 the *Gruppe* became part of the newly created *Lehrgeschwader Greifswald* to develop new operational techniques with Jeschonnek as its *Kommodore*.

As head of *Luftwaffenführungsstabes* Operations, Jeschonnek's influence grew because he drafted operational requirements and his *Lehrgeschwader* experience aroused his concern about bombing accuracy. This gave him a special interest in dive-bombing which he applied to the He 177 heavy bomber – but he was not unique. The contemporary Royal Air Force Specification P.13/36 for a new medium bomber included a similar requirement and led to the Avro Manchester (which became the Lancaster) and Handley Page Halifax. While the dive-bomber requirement was abandoned it meant

that the Lancaster and Halifax were strong enough to make surprisingly violent manoeuvres without threat to their airframes[14].

Milch's enmity helped propel Jeschonnek into the Chief-of-Staff role. In October 1938 Hitler demanded a huge expansion of the *Luftwaffe* and on 9 November Jeschonnek produced a plan for 10,700 first-line aircraft by New Year's Day 1942. Although wiser heads in the RLM, including the Organisation head, *Oberst* Josef Kammhuber, believed only a 4,000-strong force was possible, Jeschonnek retorted: "In my opinion it is our duty to support the *Führer* and not oppose his wishes."

Milch mockingly raised the issue with Göring to humiliate his former friend but under-estimated both 'Fatty's' loyalty to Hitler and his dislike of his *Staatssekretär*. Göring supported Jeschonnek and soon propelled him to the heights of *Luftwaffe* leadership while Kammhuber promptly requested transfer to a front line command and, after a few months, replaced *Oberst* Heinz-Helmutt von Wühlisch as Chief-of-Staff of Felmy's *Luftflotte* 2.

Göring selected Jeschonnek partly because he anticipated less opposition from younger and less experienced officers but, as happened in this case, such officers tended to defer to older and wiser heads and lacked the seniority to override them. Unfortunately, Jeschonnek shared Milch's ability to make enemies for, while he possessed a near-English reserve he was also capable of sarcastically berating his subordinates and making comments which were deeply wounding.

He appointed his friend *Oberst* Otto Hoffmann von Waldau to replace him as Operations Chief. It was a good choice for von Waldau was a perceptive staff officer but he would not hold his tongue and he quickly clashed with Jeschonnek over the Ju 88. Soon the relationship between the two men, who had once addressed each other by their Christian names, became icily correct. In April 1942 Waldau became *Fliegerführer Afrika* then commander of X. *Fliegerkorps* and was killed in an air crash in May 1943. His former friend refused to attend the funeral.

Jeschonnek's professional failings, above all his lack of experience, overshadowed his personal ones, for he was promoted far beyond his capabilities. Like many *Luftwaffe* leaders he held technicians in low esteem; indeed less than 5 per cent of *Luftwaffe* generals and staff officers actually held technical degrees, for most came from classically biased schools (*Humanistische Gymnasien*) rather than the technical schools (*Realgymnasien*). The impact of technical developments such as radar, were therefore

Rising star: Oberst Hans Jeschonnek (right) seen here at a meeting with Göring at Carinhall, was appointed as Luftwaffe Chief-of-Staff on 1 February 1939. A strategic thinker, he made himself noticed by writing reports and papers on a variety of issues from dive-bombing to production. But his later difficult relations with many senior officers, including Milch, caused both himself and those around him problems. Loyal to Hitler, he would nevertheless have a troubled tenure.

Former artillery man General der Flakartillerie Otto Günther Rüdel, as Chef der Luftwehr, was in charge of air defence in the late 1930s. He would remain in senior air defence and Flak appointments until his retirement in November 1942.

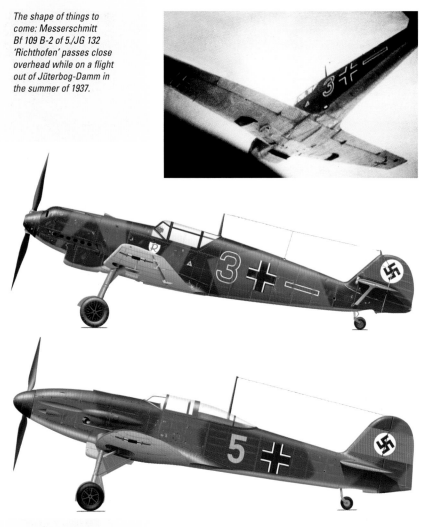

The shape of things to come: Messerschmitt Bf 109 B-2 of 5./JG 132 'Richthofen' passes close overhead while on a flight out of Jüterbog-Damm in the summer of 1937.

Heinkel He 112 B-0 of 12./JG 132 based at Oschatz in September 1938. It competed with the Bf 109 but was used operationally for only a short time.

tended to raid the training organisation. However, even as Operations chief he had recognised the need to provide stronger support for the mechanised forces and it was apparently thanks to him that a dedicated strike force or *Nahkämpfkorps* (Close Air-Support Corps) *Fliegerdivision zbV* was created in August 1938, being renamed *Fliegerführer zbV* on 19 July 1939 under Richthofen.

Richthofen's new command completed a pre-war process of reorganisation as the *Luftwaffe* steadily expanded *(see Tables below left)*.

The six *Luftkreiskommandos* at Wever's death were joined on 6 October 1936 by *Luftkreiskommando* VII created under Felmy from *Luftgau-Kommando Braunschweig* (Brunswick). The organisation was fragmented and cumbersome but allowed many officers to familiarise themselves with the roles and responsibilities of command, although Felmy was one of the minority of *Luftkreis* commanders who were actually airmen[15]. The remainder were retired Army officers such as 59-year-old former gunner and staff officer *General der Flieger* Leonhard Kaupisch of the Berlin-based *Luftkreis* II, who returned to the Army in 1939 and would command an army corps in Denmark until 1942 when he again retired[16].

These elderly gentlemen needed to be replaced with young airmen and this became more urgent following a meeting on 5 November 1937 when Hitler informed his military leaders that he planned to expand the *Reich* into Austria and Czechoslovakia, even if this meant war. Many Army leaders, including Blomberg, protested and Hitler decided to purge the 'defeatists'. He did so on 4 February 1938 immediately before the Austria Crisis broke out and Göring, who helped to execute the purge against the Army leadership which included Blomberg, extended it to remove those who were more 'old' than 'eagle' including the *Luftkreise's* flightless 'birds'.

But also thrown out with the bath water were the monocled *General der Flieger* Otto von Stülpnagel, commander of the *Luftkriegsakademie* which trained staff officers and now absorbed the *Lufttechnischen Akademie*, founded at the same time to train technical officers and whose commander, *Generalleutnant* Erich Karlewski, was also bowler-hatted. Stülpnagel rejoined the army at the outbreak of war and eventually became Military Commander, France, from October 1940 to February 1942. After the war he faced war crimes charges, but committed suicide in February 1948. Karlewski remained retired but was arrested by the Russians after the war and died in a prison camp in January 1947. Wilberg, at 57, was also shown the door from *Sonderstab W* and did not return until war was imminent. He was given a training command (*Höhere Fliegerausbildungskommando* 4) which he held until his death in an air crash on 20 November 1941[17].

The purge occurred as Göring and Stumpff rationalised the air command organisation to create

underestimated and there was also a tendency to neglect both intelligence and supply.

Compounding this in the Chief-of-Staff's case was a tendency to seek short-term solutions and when shortfalls occurred, especially in transport, he

Luftwaffe expansion in Staffeln 1937–1939

Type	1937	1938	1939
Fighter	42	54	73
Bomber	94	90	95
Stuka/Schlacht	15	19	29
Reconnaissance	17	14	24
Corps	17	23	34
Transport	6	9	9
Naval	10	16	18
Total	**201**	**227**	**282**

All strengths on April 1 of each year. It should be noted that these figures include *Staffeln* raised on that date.

Flak expansion in batteries 1937–1939

Type	1937	1938	1939
Gun Batteries	147	192	321
S/L Batteries	40	55	49
Total	**187**	**247**	**370**

Generaloberst Hermann Göring visits trainee pilots at a Fliegerführerschule in 1937. He had expressed concern at the rising number of flying accidents that year labelling it 'a plague', as evidenced by 'White 12' (above right), an Arado Ar 68, seen following a landing accident at Mecklenburg on 26 September 1937 and a belly-landed Bf 109 D (right) of II./JG 234 carrying the chevron markings of the Kommandeur of II. Gruppe, Major Eduard von Schleich - though it is believed he was not flying it at the time. The increase in the accident rate was reflected in the significant increase in flying hours over the previous two years.

Purged: General der Flieger Otto von Stülpnagel (above), commander of the Luftkriegsakademie and Generalleutnant Erich Karlewski (below), head of the Lufttechnischen Akademie both became victims of Göring's 'reshuffle' in February 1938. Soldiers of the first war, they were nevertheless deemed to be too old to offer value to the young Luftwaffe and were retired... initially. Karlewski, who retired twice – in 1932 and 1938 – died in Soviet captivity in January 1947, while von Stülpnagel, who also retired twice – in 1939 and 1942 – committed suicide in French captivity the year after Karlewski whilst awaiting trial for war crimes.

stronger and better-balanced Air Group Commands (*Luftwaffengruppenkommandos*) to meet the new operational requirements more efficiently. In the east *Luftkreis* 2 and 3 were merged to create Kesselring's Berlin-based *Luftwaffengruppenkommando* 1. In the north-west *Luftkreis* 4 and 7 became Felmy's *Luftwaffengruppenkommando* 2 in Brunswick while in the south-west Sperrle, newly returned from Spain, headed *Luftwaffengruppenkommando* 3, created from *Luftkreis* 5 with headquarters in Munich. Geography and roles dictated that two autonomous commands remained: *Luftkreis* 1 in East Prussia now became Keller's *Luftwaffenkommando Ostpreussen* while the Navy retained its operational command *Luftkreis* 6 which remained under Zander but became *Luftwaffenkommando See*. They would be joined on 1 August by a separate command created in Austria under Löhr as *Luftwaffenkommando Österreich* (also known as *Luftwaffenkommando Ostmark*).

The expansion of the *Luftwaffe* required more generals and led to a wry story circulating in the *Luftwaffe* about a caged lion which Göring was supposed to keep in the RLM. One evening the lion managed to open the lock, strolled around the RLM, encountered a general, gobbled him up then returned to the cage and reset the lock. Every few days he would unlock his cage and find another general to eat but it was six months before anyone noticed!

The *Luftwaffe* expanded from 84,000 officers and men by the summer of 1937 to 220,500 a year later as conscription took hold, although there were many volunteers[18]. A mixture of motives spurred recruitment: there was the glamour of aviation and the promise of a less rigid relationship between the ranks while spearheading the resurgence of national pride.

Many were also encouraged by the prospect of learning to drive because the *Luftwaffe* was the only fully motorised service and driving was as much a dream of young men then as now. There were also plenty of inducements to join the *Luftwaffe* including special labour certificates, subsidies and loans and the prospect of remaining in aviation after being demobbed.

While the closer relationship between the ranks reflected the Nazi ethos of dissolving class barriers, at this time relatively few of the junior officers, NCOs and enlisted men were Nazis, although future fighter ace (258 victories) Walter 'Nowi' Nowotny regularly wore a Party pin. The *Luftwaffe* was certainly associated with the Nazi Party; conservatives referred to the Royal Army, the Imperial Navy and the Party Air Force; but it appears to have been no more committed to the Party than the remainder of the *Wehrmacht*. However, every recruiting draft included one or two *HJ Quex* who were 'asked to report on my comrades by the authorities[19]'. There also remained some Army traditions such as officers' committees in which senior officers vetted not only their juniors but also their fiancées[20].

Young men usually joined the paramilitary *Reichs Arbeitsdienst* (RAD) which was used for largely

Flight discipline was improved with the creation of an Inspector for Flight Security and Equipment (Luftwaffeninspektion für Flugsicherheit und Gerät) under Oberst Dipl.Ing. Robert Fuchs, who is seen here to the right in civilian dress with his brothers, Otto, (left) a glider pilot and Director of the DFS at Munich-Riem, and Ottfried, a founding member of the Ring der Flieger. Robert Fuchs would go on to command KG 26, two Luftwaffe field regiments and finally, from early November 1943 to the end of the war, the 1. Fliegerdivision.

manual tasks (its uniform included a spade) including farming and road construction[21]. This was followed by basic training at the FEA/FAR which lasted between six months and a year and was followed by two years with the colours.

Men with an aptitude for flying were transferred to the FEA's Candidate Pilot Company (*Fluganwärterkompanie*) for two months *ab initio* training. Potential aircrew were then transferred to the FEA's *Fliegerführerschule* A/B for 100-150 hours' training, although this was hindered by a chronic lack of instructors with one for every six pupils instead of one for every four[22].

This was one reason for a 'plague' (to use Göring's words) of accidents with 108 aircraft destroyed and 1,290 damaged in 1937 at the cost of 147 men killed and 2,422 injured. Of course this also reflected an increase in flying hours, especially by the squadrons, from 603,000 in 1935 (40,000 by squadrons) to 750,000 in 1936 (290,000 by squadrons), and the technical sophistication of the new generation of aircraft and wheels-up landings undoubtedly accounted for the 75 Bf 109s, He 111s and Do 17s damaged in 1937. However, the chronic unreliability of the Ju 86's Jumo 205 diesels was also a factor and 'The Flying Coffee Grinder', as it was called, was involved in 56 accidents during 1937, although the leaders tended to blame the pilots rather than the aircraft[23].

Yet throughout the war the *Luftwaffe* suffered a very high number of landing accidents, suggesting a more profound problem possibly related to the instructor ratio. There was also a shortage of both instructors and facilities to train instrument flying and with the rapid expansion of the *Luftwaffe* many pilots received only cursory instruction. This was a cause of many accidents in Spain and upon his return to *Luftkreis* 5 at the end of 1937 Sperrle

ordered his *Kommodore* and *Kommandeure* to intensify instrument flying training throughout the winter[24]. Youthful high spirits and slack flight discipline also contributed to the depressing figures. Many were lost stunting over the homes of parents or girlfriends, and some young officers had barely paid their mark to the first enlisted man to salute them. Eventually flight discipline was improved with the creation of an Inspector for Flight Security and Equipment (*Luftwaffeninspektion für Flugsicherheit und Gerät*) under *Oberst Dipl.Ing* Fuchs[25].

Specialist training was given at *Waffenschule* where fighter and *Stuka* pilots received three and four months instruction respectively. Bomber crews also received three months instruction after navigators and radio operators had received specialist training, while the pilots received 60 hours at a *Fliegerschule C* and between 50 and 60 hours at an Instrument Training School (*Blindflugschule*). Considerable attention was given to Observer training due to the status of these officers with the *Luftwaffe*, who were expected to be capable of every aircrew task. They received pilot training to *Fliegerschule C* standard and their 9-12 month course at *Aufklärungsfliegerschule* included instrument training.

Until 1937 each *Flugzeugführerschule* conducted the complete range of flying training at which time the 18 land-based schools became specialised. Single-engine training was assigned to *Flugzeugführerschulen* A (*ab initio*) and *Flugzeugführerschulen* B (advanced) while advanced multi-engined training was by *Flugzeugführerschulen* C and the Navy had three *Flugzeugführerschulen See*. From November 1938 the A and B courses were combined at *Flugzeugführerschulen* A/B of which there were 16 by the outbreak of war together with 11 *Flugzeugführerschulen* C, two *Blindflugschule* (augmented by *Streckenschule Berlin*) and 10 *Waffenschule* with some 2,700 aircraft as well as 27 FAR. Christiansen's *Kommando der Schulen* controlled training until it was

The first intake, 'Lehrgang', of Jagdfliegerschule 1 at Werneuchen pose in front of one of their Ar 68 E-1s during the autumn of 1937. Sitting, second from the left, is Leutnant Otto Böhner with the Jagdlehrer, Oblt. Hannes Trautloft, next but one.

An officer shouts above the noise of one of the two 750 hp BMW VI 12-cylinder engines of a Do 23 with its huge four-blade wooden propellers as he directs two crews prior to a training flight. The aircraft carried a crew of four comprising pilot, navigator/bomb-aimer, ventral and dorsal gunners with a defensive armament of three 7.9 mm machine guns.

disbanded on 28 February 1937 when flying training came under Stumpff's control through the inspectorates[26].

Oberst Fischer now became *Inspekteur der Schulen* (later *Flugzeugführerschulen*), but as the training organisation continued to expand it was clear that rationalisation was required. With the creation of the *Luftwaffengruppenkommandos* flying training was now devolved to six *Kommandos der Fliegerschulen und Ersatzabteilungen*, but even this organisation did not last. In February 1939 Kühl became *Chef des Ausbildungswesens* (Chief of Training Resources) to co-ordinate the inspectorates, but he was primarily interested in operational training. Responsibility for flying training was devolved to the *Luftgaue* which in turn devolved this to newly-established Senior Flying Training Commands (*Höhere Fliegerausbildungskommandos*).

The *Luftwaffe's* expansion and its new equipment increased the confidence of the Nazi leadership who expected great things. The aircraft were its sword while its shield was the *Flak* arm which also expanded steadily with personnel strength rising from 46,140 in October 1937 to 98,600 in July 1939. The *Flakwaffe* had not only an excellent range of weapons from the 8.8cm *Flak* 18 and 36, through the 3.7cm *Flak* 18 and 36 to the 2 cm *Flak* 30, all supported by electro-mechanical fire control computers[27].

Such was Göring's confidence that he famously claimed that if any bombs fell on Germany then people could call him by the Jewish name 'Meyer'. Curiously enough, when people raised this point during the war he never took offence. Nevertheless he had good cause for his confidence for an anti-aircraft barrier was built parallel to the Rhine from June 1938 as part of the *West Wall* defences as *Luftverteidigungszone West* under *Generalleutnant* Karl Kitzinger. It was some 600 kilometres long and 10-30 kilometres deep and reportedly consisted of some 1,500 concrete positions with 1,300 guns and

incorporated the 245 static weapons of the Wiesbaden-based *Hohere Kommandeur der Festungsflakartillerie* III. Other *Luftverteidigungszonen* were established around Berlin, Dusseldorf, Hamburg, Leipzig, Stettin and later Vienna[28].

But Göring, the blustering bully, preferred the more aggressive use of air power and the next opportunity came in March 1938 in Austria. There had long been a move for a German-Austrian union (*Anschluss*) and Hitler was determined to bring the land of his birth within the *Reich*. The Austrian Nazi party under Dr Arthur Seyss-Inquart instigated a crisis and the Chancellor, Dr Kurt Schushnigg, visited Berchtesgaden in February to defuse the situation. But he was coerced, with the aid of Sperrle's brooding presence, into accepting Seyss-Inquart as the Interior Minister.

He decided on 9 March to resolve the *Anschluss* issue with a plebiscite, an announcement which provoked Hitler to new heights of fury. The *Führer* demanded military intervention which had already been anticipated in Contingency Plan 'Otto' (*Sonderfall 'Otto'*) with the mobilisation of 8. *Armee* with Sperrle's *Luftkreis* 5 and Kesselring's *Luftkreis* 3 which was to seize the country after a telephone ultimatum to Schuschnigg. While some bombers were to be kept in reserve it was expected †that the *Luftwaffe* would merely support the advance, capture airfields and drop leaflets. Göring recalled Milch from a skiing holiday and personally briefed him so that he could smooth the logistical arrangements for Sperrle[29].

Certainly the *Österreichische Luftstreitkräfte* (LStrKr) was in no condition to oppose the *Luftwaffe*. In January 1936 it had only 151 aircraft and while Löhr had ambitious plans for some 15 and later 20 *Staffeln* by March 1938, it had only six *Jagdstaffeln* with Fiat CR.20bis/30/32s, two *Bombenstaffeln* with Caproni Ca.133s and two *Aufklärungsstaffeln* with Fiat A120s and Romeo Ro 37s. While most of these aircraft were from Italy,

A contemporary German watercolour depicting a pilots' briefing on a typical Jagdgruppe flightline in the late 1930s with He 51s behind.

Above left: A He 51 B-1 of 3./JG 135 has its engine cowling finished in pale blue, a similar colour being used to paint the forward half of the spinner. The centre of the propeller was finished in varnished polished wood colour, but the blades were painted pale grey, with the Schwarz company's logo on the front of each blade.

Generalmajor Wolff (centre) and Generaloberst Alexander Löhr salute Göring after German forces entered Linz in March 1938. In Löhr, the previous commander of the Austrian Air Force, Germany was to gain a very able leader who later led Luftflotte 4. He is seen here in his Austrian Air Force uniform.

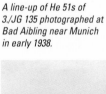

A line-up of He 51s of 3./JG 135 photographed at Bad Aibling near Munich in early 1938.

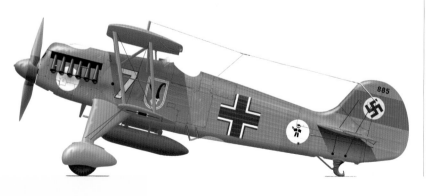

German aircraft had been evaluated and the He 112 and Ju 86 selected, but limited funds reduced the numbers of both aircrew and spares so that on 11 March Löhr had only 210 aircraft of which only 33 were serviceable[30].

Sperrle had the active role, assembling a *Jagdgruppe* (I./JG 135) with He 51, three *Kampfgruppen* from KG 155 and 255 with Do 17 E and five *Staffeln* from *Aufklärungsgruppen* 15 and 25, most of which were assigned to *Generalmajor* Ludwig Wolff's *Höhere Fliegerkommandeur* 5, apart from three corps *Staffeln* which were assigned to *Stabsoffizier der Flieger* (*Stofl*) 8. *Armee* together with six *Flakabteilungen*. Kesselring's role was purely support and he raised *Transportgruppen Chamier* and *Fleischhauer* together with *Kampfgruppe zbV Ziervogel* to fly in troops and equipment, his *Staffeln* having been fleshed out with *Lufthansa* Ju 52s.

Aerial demonstrations began on 10 March as Schuschnigg resigned in favour of President Wilhelm Miklas, who rejected Hitler's call to appoint Seyss-Inquart as chancellor. The following morning Löhr ordered day and night reconnaissance flights along the border but that afternoon there were ominous reports of German aircraft flying over Austrian territory. The blustering Göring directed a barrage of telephone calls upon the unfortunate Miklas who capitulated that evening and at a diplomatic ball Milch was ordered to begin the *Luftwaffe* occupation the following morning.

Ironically it was the trainers of *Oberst* Vierling, Sperrle's training commander, who appeared first over Vienna on 12 March dropping leaflets, followed by KG 155's Do 17 Es on a similar mission, one of them then landing at the city's Aspern airfield. It was quickly followed by Wolff with two infantry companies who secured the airfield. As leaflets rained down on Austrian towns other transports followed bringing in some 2,000 troops, allowing Wolff to move first to Löhr's headquarters and ultimately to more salubrious quarters in Vienna's Hotel Astoria.

By the end of the first day nine *Luftwaffe Staffeln* landed unopposed in Austrian air bases, being not only welcomed but actively assisted by the *Luftstreitkräfte*. Austria was quickly secured and on 15 March there was a massive fly-past of 720 German and Austrian aircraft led by Wolff with Löhr in the co-pilot's seat. Although only three aircraft were lost in accidents during '*Otto*' the operation had demonstrated that the *Wehrmacht* had serious weaknesses. Staff work was poor and this especially hindered the mobilisation of reservists and, despite Milch's best efforts, civilian vehicles had to be impressed to transfer fuel in large drums due to the lack of petrol bowsers. Worst of all, these problems were obvious to foreign observers[31].

The *Luftwaffe* learned from its mistakes and received a substantial reinforcement when it absorbed nearly 4,100 LStrKr and Austrian Army men on 12 April. However, many senior officers were dismissed including Yllam who retired, to die amid his memories at Klagenfurt in January 1942[32]. The Austrian *JaGeschw* I was split between JG 132 and *134*, *JaGeschw* II became I./JG 138 retaining its Fiat CR. 32s while the *BombGeschw* was absorbed by KG 155 and was then renamed KG 158. The reconnaissance units became *AufKl Gr* 18.

Löhr, now a *Generalleutnant*, provided continuity by assuming command of the new *Luftwaffenkommando Ostmark* (or *Österreich*) whose terrestrial infrastructure was under the newly created *Luftgau* XVII. However, he was given a German Chief-of-Staff in 39-year-old *Oberstleutnant* Günther Korten. Born in Cologne, Korten had volunteered for the Army when war broke out and spent most of his career in the Pioneers. He became an officer during the war and remained one, despite participating in Hitler's Beerhall *Putsch* of 1923; indeed he received flying training at Lipetsk between 1928 and 1929. He was one of the first officers to be transferred to the *Luftwaffe* and was on the service's first staff course before commanding *Aufklärungsgruppe 122* and then joining the *Luftwaffenpersonalamt*. He would ultimately replace Jeschonnek as *Luftwaffe* Chief-of-Staff[33].

Hitler now turned on Czechoslovakia which, together with Poland, was a key element of the perceived eastern strategic threat. Hitler decided to destroy the stronger Czechs first using the Sudetenland, with a largely German populace, as the wedge, partly because the Czech equivalent of the Maginot Line ran through this region. From the *Luftwaffe*'s viewpoint it was especially important because since 1934 France had arranged to station heavy bombers in Bohemia (western Czechoslovakia) and had assembled 400 tonnes of bombs for them[34]. There was also the Soviet-Czech mutual assistance pact of March 1935 which had provided the Czech air force with Tupolev SB bombers which became the Avia B.71.

As Goebbels' propaganda shrilled claims of Czech persecution, Hitler called his military leadership to a conference and announced that he

After Austria was incorporated into Germany in March 1938, Hitler led a parade through the capital, Vienna. To Hitler's right in this picture is General Erhard Milch, Secretary of State in the new German Air Ministry while, to his left, is Generaloberst Fedor von Bock, commander of the troops entering Austria. Von Bock subsequently had several army commands, but was dismissed by Hitler and died in an air attack raid in 1945.

Austrian fighters from the Österreiche Jagdgruppe based at Vienna-Schwechat seen during a visit to Berlin-Döberitz in early 1938. The aircraft, coded '182', in the foreground is an Italian Fiat CR. 30 B while the machines behind are CR. 32 B two-seaters.

Ju 52/3ms of KGrzbV 2 seen sometime between early 1938 and March 1939 wearing markings typical of the period in which Germany occupied Austria, annexed the Sudetenland and occupied Czechoslovakia. KGrzbV 2 was one of six Transportfliegergruppen assigned to the operation against Czechoslovakia.

wanted the country 'wiped off the map.' Two days later a directive for an invasion was issued with preparations to be complete by 1 October and, while Czechoslovakia was the prime target, no-one was under any delusions that France, and possibly Britain, would not become involved.

The Army had long had contingency plans for Czechoslovakia and this was updated after the *Anschluss* as *Planstudie 1938*. As *Luftwaffen-gruppenkommando* 1 was on Czechoslovakia's northern border in June 1938 Kesselring began drafting a support plan which was published on 11 July as *Planstudie Grün* (Study Plan Green) with detailed planning assigned to the *Höherer Fliegerkommandeuren* (*Fliegerdivisionen* from 1 August) and the *Luftgaue*. Later planning was extended southwards to Sperrle and Löhr[35].

The *Luftwaffe* plan envisaged a knock-out blow to destroy the Czech air force then to offer direct and indirect support to the Army's advance. However, on 30 May Hitler ordered industrial centres to be spared where possible so they might support the *Reich*'s war efforts. A notable feature of the later stages of the campaign was the creation, probably on 1 August, of *Fliegerdivision zbV* using three *Schlachtfliegergruppen* (SFGr 10, 30, 50) with Hs 123 light dive-bombers while another two, with He 45 close-air support aircraft (SFGr 20, 40), were assigned to Sperrle. These *Gruppen* were created by *Oberleutnant* Adolf Galland exploiting his experience in Spain[36].

For the first time the *Luftwaffe* also planned an airborne operation. Paratroop units were created as part of *Regiment General Göring* from October 1935 and Kesselring had encouraged development of the arm which participated in the 1937 *Wehrmacht* manoeuvres[37]. Fittingly they were now assigned to Kesselring who would place them, on 1 September, under the newly created 7. *Fliegerdivision* led by the *Luftwaffeninspekteur der Luftlande und Fallschirmtruppe Generalmajor* Kurt Student with six *Transport-fliegergruppen* (KGrzbV 1-6) to augment the two *Gruppen* of KG zbV 172. This unit was to be used in

Exercise (*Übung*) '*Freudenthal*' with paratroops dropped 250 kilometres behind the Czech fortifications.

The Czech Air Force was not regarded as a major problem; indeed Jeschonnek referred to '...those ridiculous Hussites'. With 54 squadrons and 800 largely obsolescent aircraft it was a slender reed as was its potential ally, the Russian VVS-RKKA, which was numerically strong (some 7,000 aircraft) but had been ravaged by Stalin's purges which had decimated its leadership.

But Hitler discovered on 12 August the *Luftwaffe*'s feet of clay when he received a *Wehrmacht* survey. On 1 August it had an impressive 2,928 aircraft, including 81 transports, with the latest Bf 109 D, He 111 H and D 17 M/P entering service, yet production was less than 500 aircraft a month. While the *Kampfgruppen* mostly had modern aircraft, including some Ju 86 'Coffee Grinders', the *Jagdgruppen* had not received the Bf 110; indeed the Heavy Fighter Groups (*Jagdgruppen, Schwere*) were not formed until 1 November. Most *Jagdgruppen* had Bf 109s but were under strength, averaging only 26 aircraft, many of which lacked radios; seven (31 per cent) had biplanes (mostly Ar 68s) and the recently formed IV./JG 132 was equipped with requisitioned Japanese He 112s. From training formations two *Staffel*-sized *Reservejagdgruppen* were created and assigned to Sperrle.

Other serious problems eroded German air power. Inadequate spares production reduced serviceability to 57 per cent and while 60 per cent of the aircraft required an overhaul, maintenance depots held engine stocks at only 4-5 per cent of front line strength. It was later estimated that the supply of spares and tools would have supported barely a month's operations, with most *Jagd*- and *Stukageschwader* having only one set of technical

The second highest scoring ace in the Legion Condor, Hptm. Wolfgang Schellmann (left), gives instructions to the pilots of 1./JG 131 prior to a training flight during the winter of 1938/39.

Friends of the Gräfin (Countess) Siersdorf (furthest in the group seen here) interrupt their al fresco drinks to look up into the sky from their deckchairs as aircraft fly over 2./JG 131's airfield at Oppeln just after the Munich Crisis in the autumn of 1938. Behind the onlookers is Bf 109 'Red 5' of I./JG 131.

This view of a Ju 86 D of 4./KG 253 gives an excellent view of the 'splinter' pattern of dark brown, medium green and pale grey uppersurface camouflage. The unit's code 33+E24 has been painted on both sides of the fuselage and repeated above and below the wings.

Lt. Herbert Huppertz (third from the left) photographed late in 1938 during his training on the Bf 109, probably with IV./JG 132. Entering the Luftwaffe in the autumn of 1937, Huppertz achieved his first victories with 3./JG 77 in 1940. He was eventually appointed Gruppenkommandeur of II./JG 2 in March 1944 but was killed just after D-Day when his Fw 190 was shot down over Normandy by American fighters.

equipment (*T-Sätze*), while the 'pampered' *Kampfgeschwader* had three. The serviceability rate was raised by 26 September to 94 per cent due to careful organisation and a severe reduction in flying hours, which hit training badly.

This aggravated the problem of inexperienced aircrew. The *Luftwaffe* had only two-thirds of the men it was supposed to have and of 2,577 aircrew barely a third (1,432) were fully qualified. Göring's sword was especially brittle with only 27 per cent of aircrew regarded as qualified, many bomber pilots were not instrument-qualified while many Stuka 'back seaters' did not know how to use either radios or the MG 15 machine gun. Effectively this reduced the *Kampfgruppen* to 378 aircraft and the *Jagdgruppen* to 537, 32.5 per cent and 83.5 per cent of their strength.

Undaunted by their problems, the *Luftwaffe* leadership accelerated preparations for *Fall Grün*, the invasion of Czechoslovakia whose main blow would come from the north and the north-west supported by 1,200 aircraft of Kesselring's 1. and 2. *Fliegerdivisionen* and *Fliegerdivision zbV*, whose airfields in Silesia, Saxony and Thuringia were shielded by two borrowed Naval *Freya* radars. Kesselring would also be responsible for the airborne assault by 7. *Fliegerdivision* which had 400 transports although there was considerable opposition from the Army leadership to 'Freudenthal'.

Sperrle would support 12. *Armee's* attack from the south-west with 650 aircraft of 4. *Fliegerdivision* whose SFGr 20 and 40 were assigned to the newly created *Fliegergeschwader* 100. Löhr had 180 aircraft to support 14. *Armee's* attack from the south. The Western defences were stripped to 400 aircraft (excluding *Luftwaffenkommando See*) mostly under Felmy who had only 175 bombers. Some 500 fighters were assembled for *Grün*, but a third were assigned home defence duties.

Fortunately for the *Luftwaffe* its opposite numbers in Great Britain and France were even weaker. The British estimated their front line strength on 1 October at 1,606 aircraft with a 25 per cent reserve while the French had 1,454 with a 50 per cent reserve and of their combined 700 fighters, only 71 were modern. In March, London and Paris audited their air forces and their Chiefs of Air Staff, Marshal of the Royal Air Force Sir Cyril Newall and *Général* Joseph Vuillemin stated that their bombers were incapable of effective offensive operations. In his annual report on 10 March, Air Chief Marshall Sir Edgar Ludlow-Hewitt opined that '...our bomber force is, judged from a war standard, practically useless'[38].

Both had a concise picture of *Luftwaffe* strength, which they estimated accurately at 3,000, and the French certainly had detailed orders of battle. Vuillemin assessed the accuracy of his intelligence between 16-21 August during his

On 29 September 1938, Sir Neville Chamberlain flew to Munich and was met at the airport by the German Foreign Minister, Joachim von Ribbentrop and other high-ranking Nazi Party officials. He is seen here being escorted to his meeting with Hitler in the 'Führerhaus' in the Königplatz.

The American aviator Charles Lindbergh (third from the left) watches as machine gun calibration tests are carried out on a He 51 A-1 of 2./JG 132 during a visit he paid to the unit at Berlin-Döberitz during the summer of 1936. Lindbergh became famous after completing the first solo flight of the Atlantic Ocean on 21 May 1927 in his 'Spirit of St.Louis'. From 1935 he moved to Europe, making tours of several countries. In 1938 he was to receive a decoration from Hitler, praising the Luftwaffe as "...superior to that of any other European country".

famous visit to the German aircraft industry. Although his report was later dismissed as defeatism, aggravated by fear, it was actually an extremely pragmatic assessment which led to an acceleration of French aerial re-armament[39]. But the politicians and the general public were also influenced by 'Jeremiahs' such as the famous aviator, Charles A. Lindbergh.

As the Sudetenland Crisis grew, the dread of aerial bombardment and the knowledge of their national military unpreparedness influenced the British and French politicians and led to Chamberlain's first flight to Munich on 14 September in a desperate effort to negotiate a peaceful solution. But six days later the *Luftwaffe's Gruppen* moved to their operational airfields as Europe seemed poised upon another bloody war. Göring's nerves were hardly soothed by pessimistic reports from Felmy about the prospects of an air war against Great Britain. Astonishingly it was not until the *Anschluss* Crisis that Felmy, whose command was closest to the British Isles, was asked to investigate the challenge and he concluded that without bases in the Low Countries his *Kampfgruppen* could not strike British industry until they received heavy bombers[40].

This report arrived on 22 September and Göring promptly reprimanded Felmy, planning to replace Felmy's Chief-of-Staff, *Oberst* Heinz von Wühlisch, with his old friend *Oberst* Ulrich Kessler who was Deputy Air Attaché in London, to put more backbone into *Luftwaffenkommando* 2. But when Kessler met Göring in Carinhall on 17 September he begged him to avoid war with the British and in November he became *Kommodore* of KG 152.

Chamberlain was willing to betray the Czechs and signed the Munich Agreement on 30 September giving Berlin control of the Sudetenland. The unopposed occupation lasted from 1–10 October supported by 500 aircraft, some of which demonstrated over Czech cities. Sperrle flew into Ach-Eger airfield on 3 October to create a forward command post, but four aircraft were lost and eight

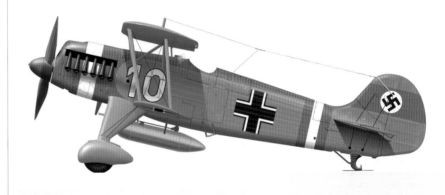

Taken at Berlin-Döberitz during the Czechoslovakian crisis of March 1939, this photograph shows Bf 109 D, 'White 3' piloted by Lt. Hermann Reifferscheidt of 1./JG 131. Reifferscheidt was one of the Schwarmführer of this Staffel, his aircraft carrying large white crosses on the wings and fuselage sides with white question marks above the horizontal tail surfaces to indicate this function.

men killed: three in accidents and one had the misfortune to become the *Luftwaffe's* first combat loss outside Spain when trigger-happy *Flak* gunners in Vienna shot down a courier aircraft.

From 13 October the *Luftwaffe* began to stand down but first it demonstrated its growing proficiency in airborne operations. Some 300 aircraft and gliders landed in the Sudetenland in front of Hitler on 6 October; civilians had earlier cleared the landing zone of all obstacles. The *Gruppen* hastily created to augment *Luftwaffe* strength were mostly disbanded, but the Hs 123 units were retained and on 1 November SFGr 10 became II.(Schlacht)/ LG 2, SFGr 30 became I./St.G 162 while SFGr 50 became II./St.G 163. The opportunity was also taken to redesignate the *Aufklärungsgruppen* and to create *Aufklärungsgruppe* 120 (see following Table).

Aufklärungsgruppen redesignation
1 November 1938

Old designation	New designation
Aufklärungsgruppe 11	Aufklärungsgruppe 10
Aufklärungsgruppe 12	Aufklärungsgruppe 21
Aufklärungsgruppe 13	Aufklärungsgruppe 31
Aufklärungsgruppe 15	Aufklärungsgruppe 13
Aufklärungsgruppe 18	Aufklärungsgruppe 14
Aufklärungsgruppe 22	Aufklärungsgruppe 121
Aufklärungsgruppe 23	Aufklärungsgruppe 11
Aufklärungsgruppe 24	Aufklärungsgruppe 22
Aufklärungsgruppe 25	Aufklärungsgruppe 123
Aufklärungsgruppe 27	Aufklärungsgruppe 122
Aufklärungsgruppe 28	Aufklärungsgruppe 124
Aufklärungsgruppe 52	Aufklärungsgruppe 41

Simultaneously three *Aufklärungsgeschwader* were created to control the Army's reconnaissance squadrons and to allow the headquarters of the *Luftwaffe* commander-in-chief (*Oberbefehlshaber der Luftwaffe* – ObdL) to focus upon Operational/Strategic operations. *Luftwaffe* Generals with Army and Navy headquarters (*Luftwaffe Generale beim Oberbefehlshaber das Heeres* (ObdH), *Oberbefehlshaber der Kriegsmarine* (ObdM) were established under former gunner *Generalmajor* Rudolf Bogatsch and former seaplane pilot *Generalmajor* Hans Ritter to give the services tactical control of units, providing direct support while Göring retained control in all other aspects; indeed at this time the Navy lost its fighter squadrons to ObdL control.

Although Hitler claimed he had no further territorial ambitions after the Munich Agreement his warped mind felt cheated by Chamberlain. By encouraging the Slovaks in the east of the country to demand independence by March 1939 he had a political wedge. The elderly Czech president, Emile Hácha, went to Berlin on 14 March to seek a negotiated solution and found Göring threatening to bomb Prague, although with flying conditions deteriorating with every hour he knew this was an increasingly hollow threat.

Hácha reluctantly signed away his country's independence on 15 March; the Slovaks confirmed

their independence but quickly became a 'protectorate' of the *Reich*, and German troops promptly moved in supported by 500 aircraft drawn largely from Sperrle's command, which lost two aircraft and seven men in accidents[41]. The *Luftwaffe* gained vital strategic air bases while the Army swelled by a third by gorging on looted military equipment. Three days later Germany occupied the former German port of Memel (Klaipeda), with *Luftwaffenkommando Ostpreussen* demonstrating over the city for an hour to dissuade resistance[42]. The German aggression now steeled hearts in both Paris and London, who pledged military support for Poland if it was similarly threatened, with Chamberlain publicly warning on 31 March that aggression against Poland would lead to war.

The following day the *Luftwaffe* was again re-organised. Kesselring's, Felmy's and Sperrle's *Luftwaffengruppenkommandos* were renamed *Luftflotten* while Löhr's was upgraded to *Luftflotte* 4. At the same time there was a wholesale redesignation of units (see Table 5-4), the *Jagdgruppen* (*Schwere*) having been redesignated Destroyer Groups (*Zerstörergruppen*) on 1 January. The same day Rowehl's secret strategic reconnaissance unit was renamed *Aufklärungsgruppe ObdL* with a second *Staffel*.

Geschwader redesignation – 1 May 1939

Old designation	New designation
JG 130	JG 1
JG 131	JG 2
JG 132	JG 26
JG 133	JG 53
JG 231	JG 3
JG 233	JG 51
JG 331	JG 77
JG 333	JG 54
JG 433	JG 52
ZG 141	ZG 1
ZG 142	ZG 26
ZG 143	ZG 52
ZG 144	ZG 76
KG 152	KG 1
KG 153	KG 3
KG 155	KG 55
KG 157	KG 27
KG 158	KG 76
KG 252	KG 2
KG 253	KG 4
KG 254	KG 54
KG 255	KG 51
KG 257	KG 26
KG 355	KG 53
St.G 160	St.G 1
St.G 162 & 163	St.G 2
St.G 165	St.G 77
St.G 168	St.G 76

The *Luftwaffe* now began planning operations against Great Britain although Felmy's latest pessimistic appreciation, *Planstudie 1939*, further irritated Göring. To help Felmy interdict Britain's sea lanes, *Generalmajor* Joachim Coeler was appointed Air Corps Commander (*Führer der Luftstreitkräfte*) for minelaying operations while *Generalleutnant* Hans Geisler became General for Special Employment with *Luftflotte* 2 (*General zbv der Luftflotte 2*) for bombing and torpedo attacks. During the early summer, British radar monitored Geisler's North Sea exercises; one *Gruppe*-sized formation approached Norfolk at 80 kilometres away but it turned back some 10 kilometres off the coast.

Only now did the *Luftwaffe* General Staff finally receive a proper air intelligence organisation with the creation of a Foreign Air Power Directorate (*Fremde Luftmächteabteilung*) under 37-year-old *Oberstleutnant* Josef 'Beppo' Schmid. Previously *Luftwaffe* intelligence had a low status, largely relying upon the Army's organisation *Abwehr*, and it was not until June 1935 that the *Luftwaffeführungsstab* created an intelligence office under *Oberst Freiherr* von Bülow. But it was manned by reservists and civilians and its activities consisted of assembling newspaper clippings and it had no access to Martini's seven communications intelligence (comint) stations or Rowehl's photographs and no reports from diplomatic attachés.

Schmid was poorly qualified for the post; he was not an airman, had no intelligence experience and spoke no foreign languages, but he was a friend of Göring! A Bavarian (his nickname '*Beppo*' was Bavarian slang for 'Boy') he was just too young to serve in the Great War, but had joined *Freikorps Epp* then entered the Army in 1921 as a *Fähnrich* and was commissioned at the end of 1924. He qualified as an Army general staff officer in June 1935 and promptly transferred to the *Luftwaffe*, becoming an advisor in the Operations Directorate. His staff training may have helped him to recognise the weaknesses of the Intelligence organisation and he defined his role, established priorities and began acquiring information.

The *Abwehr* provided him with spy data augmented by reports from the attachés and he took over both Martini's comint organisation and Rowehl. Schmid had good relations with Milch who would provide industrial insight, and regarded himself as an expert on the British, but *Luftwaffe* technical intelligence remained weak until the end of the war; indeed it was apparently on Martini's initiative that three inconclusive signals intelligence missions were flown in the retired commercial airship LZ 130 *Graf Zeppelin II* to investigate British radar activity[43]. The new Intelligence organisation retained its lowly status, for Schmid's opposite number in the Royal Air Force was equivalent to a *Generalmajor*.

Martini was slower to develop radar and by September 1939 was still evaluating a naval *Freya* (FuMG 39) search radar; two were on order while a contract for two *Würzburg* (FuMG 62) anti-aircraft fire control radars had been signed. But he had provided the *Luftwaffe* with an electronic precision bombing system in *X-Gerät*, based upon the radio navigation technology, and this had equipped an operational unit, *Luftnachrichtenabteilung* 100, for nearly a year while another system, *Y-Gerät*, was at an advanced stage of development when war broke out.

The *X-Gerät* would soon see action. Schmid produced three detailed studies on enemy air power in Poland (*Studie Grün*), France (*Rot*) and Great Britain (*Blau*), the latter being updated until the end of the war, with input from specialists and academics. *Studie Grün* was especially relevant, for two days after the *Luftwaffe* reorganisation, Hitler began planning an invasion of Poland – Contingency White (*Fall Weiss*).

To support '*Weiss*' Jeschonnek created the Air Commander for Special Employment (*Fliegerführer zbV*) under Richthofen, based on experience gained with the ad hoc *Fliegerdivision zbV*. But where this had followed the *Schlachtflieger* tradition of the Great War in offering only tactical or close-air support the new command had *Stukagruppen* to provide an operational level of support.

As the beautiful summer of 1939 reached its peak the *Luftwaffe* prepared to go to war as Goebbel's propaganda machine shrieked once more about the persecution of Germans by the evil Slavs. While thousands of *Luftwaffe* men hoped against hope for another peaceful solution, their leaders were less optimistic and waited with bated breath. Göring, who had made every effort to establish good relations with Poland's leaders, was appalled and tried to dissuade the *Führer*, who called him 'an old woman.' Göring would seek a political agreement through backdoor links almost to the moment when the first shots were fired, and his ultimate commitment to military action was largely due to German Foreign Minister Joachim Ribbentrop negotiating a non-aggression agreement with the Soviet Union on 23 August.

From 1 June 1939 Generalleutnant Hans Geisler was appointed 'General zbV' with Luftflotte 2 and tasked with responsibility for conducting bombing and torpedo attacks against British shipping. Geisler was an experienced naval man, having served in the Kriegsmarine in the First World War and in various minesweeping commands. Promoted to Korvettenkapitän, he was one of the first commanders of the Funkversuchskommando (experimental wireless detachment) at Warnemünde, co-located with the Warnemünde Verkehrsfliegerschule ('civilian' flying school) and, like many other Naval officers, he transferred to the Luftwaffe on 1 September 1933.

On 24 August 1939, von Ribbentrop returned from signing a non-aggression agreement with the Soviet Union under conditions of great secrecy. He is seen here accompanied by military and Party dignitaries, walking away from the just-landed Focke-Wulf Fw 200, W.Nr. 3098, D-ACVH, 'Grenzmark'.

Even by the autumn of 1939, the Luftwaffe placed relatively little importance on an organised intelligence-gathering infrastructure. What it did do was to form the Fremde Luftmächteabteilung – the Foreign Air Power Directorate – under a Bavarian Freikorps veteran with no previous intelligence experience, Oberstleutnant Josef 'Beppo' Schmid. The Luftmächteabteilung was manned by reservists and civilians and its activities consisted of assembling newspaper clippings, though Schmid did recognise the weaknesses of his organisation and defined his role, established priorities and began acquiring information. Schmid is seen here in 1944 when he was commander of I. Jagdkorps.

ORDERS OF BATTLE
April 1 1938

Höherer Kommandeur der Lehrtruppen der Luftwaffe:
Generalmajor Helmuth Förster
> Garz: I.(J)/LG Greifswald
> Tutow: II.(J)/LG Greifswald
> Greifswald: Stab, III.(K)/LG Greifswald
> Barth: IV.(Stuka)/LG Greifswald
> I., II., III./Flak LehrRegt

Luftwaffengruppenkommando 1 (Berlin): General der Flieger Albert Kesselring
Höherer Fliegerkommandeure 2 (Berlin): Generalmajor Ulrich Grauert
> Berlin-Döberitz: Stab, I./JG 132
> Jüterbog-Damm: II./JG 132
> Bernburg: I./JG 232
> Neubrandenburg: Stab, I./KG 152
> Schwerin: III./ KG 152
> Kolberg: IV./KG 152
> Prenzlau: 1., 2., 3. (F)/AufklGr 22
> Berlin-Staaken: Fliegerstaffel zbV
> Kottbus: 1., 2. (H)/AufklGr 52
> Stargard: Stab, 1., 2. (H)/AufklGr 12
> Jüterbog-Damm: Stab, 1.,2., 3. (H) AufklGr Jüterbog
> Berlin-Tempelhof: Stab KG zbV 172
> Tutow: I./KG zbV 172
> Fassberg: II./KG zbV 172
> Fürstenwalde: KGrzbV 1

Höherer Fliegerkommandeure 3 (Dresden): Generalleutnant Wilhelm Wimmer
> Merseburg: Stab, I./ KG 153
> Finsterwalde: II./KG 153
> Heiligenbeil: III./KG 153
> Liegnitz: IV./KG 153
> Gotha: Stab, I KG 253
> Erfurt: II./KG 253
> Nordhausen: III./KG 253
> Breslau: I./StG 163
> Grossenhain: Stab, 2., 3. (H)/AufklGr 23
> Brieg: Stab, 1., 2. , 3.(H)/AufklGr 13

Höherer Kommandeur der Flakartillerie *2* (Berlin): Generalmajor Hubert Weise
> I., II./FlakRegt 12; I., II./FlakRegt 22; I./FlakRegt 32; I., II./Regt General Göring

Höherer Kommandeur der Flakartillerie *3* (Dresden): Oberst Alexander Kolb
> I./FlakRegt 3, II./FlakRegt 3; I./FlakRegt 10; I., II./FlakRegt 13; I./FlakRegt 20;
> I., II./FlakRegt 23; I., II./FlakRegt 33; I./FlakRegt 43

Luftgaukommando III (Berlin)
Luftgaukommando IV (Dresden)
Luftgaukommando VIII (Breslau)
Luftgaukommando IX (Weimar)
Luftnachrichten Regimenter 11, 12, 13

Luftwaffengruppenkommando 2 (Brunswick:) General der Flieger Hellmuth Felmy

Höherer Fliegerkommandeure 4 (Münster): Generalmajor Helmuth Bienick
> Dortmund: Stab, I./JG 134
> Werl: II./JG 134
> Cologne-Ostheim: I./JG 234
> Dusseldorf: II./JG 234
> Wiesbaden-Erbenheim: Stab, I./JG 334
> Mannheim-Sandhofen: II./JG 334
> Lippstadt: Stab, I./KG 254

> Giessen: II./KG 254
> Fritzlar: III./KG 254
> Gütersloh: IV./KG 254
> Kassel-Rothwesten: Stab, 1., 2.,3. (F)/AufkIGr 24
> Munster: Stab, 1., 2., 3. (H)/AufklGr 14

Höherer Fliegerkommandeure 7 (Brunswick): Generalmajor Kurt Student
> Bernburg: I./JG 137
> Hannover-Langenhagen: Stab, I./KG 157
> Wunstorf: II./KG 157
> Delmenhorst: III./KG 157
> Lubeck-Blankensee: I./KG 257
> Lüneburg: Stab, II./KG 257
> Goslar: Stab AufKlGr (F) 27

Höherer Kommandeur der Flakartillerie 4 (Munster): Generalleutnant Johannes Lentzsch
> I., II./FlakRegt 4; I., II./FlakRegt 14; I., II./FlakRegt 24; I./FlakRegt 34;
> I., II./FlakRegt 44; I./FlakRegt 64

Höherer Kommandeur der Flakartillerie 7 (Brunswick): Oberstleutnant Dr. Eugen Weissmann
> I., II./FlakRegt 6; I., II./FlakRegt 7; I., II./FlakRegt 26; I./FlakRegt 27

Luftgaukommando VI (Munster)
Luftgaukommando X (Hamburg)
Luftgaukommando XI (Hannover)
Luftnachrichten Regimenter 14, 17

Luftwaffengruppenkommando 3 (Munich): General der Flieger Hugo Sperrle
Höherer Fliegerkommandeure 5 (Munich): Generalmajor Ludwig Wolff
> Bad Aibling: I., II./JG 135
> Landsberg: Stab, I./KG 255
> Leipheim: II./KG 255
> Memmingen: III./KG 255
> Gablingen: Stab, I./KG 355
> Schwäbisch-Hall: II./KG 355
> Illesheim:III./KG355
> Kitzingen: I./StG 165
> Schweinfurt: Stab, II./StG 165
> Wertheim: III./StG 165
> Kassel-Rothwesten: Stab, 1., 2., 3 (F)/AufklGr 25
> Göppingen: Stab, 1., 2., 3.,4.(H)/AufklGr 15

Höherer Kommandeur der Flakartillerie *5* (Munich): Oberst Friedrich Heilingbrunner
> I./FlakRegt 5; I., II./FlakRegt 9; I., II./FlakRegt 25; I./FlakRegt 28
> I./FlakRegt 29; I./FlakRegt 49

Luftgaukommando V (Stuttgart)
Luftgaukommando VII (Munich)
Luftgaukommando XII (Giessen/Wiesbaden)
Luftgaukommando XIII (Nuremburg)
Luftnachrichten Regiment 15

Luftwaffenkommando Östmark (Vienna): Generalleutnant Alexander Löhr
> Vienna-Aspern: I./JG 138
> Wiener-Neustadt: Stab, I., II./KG 158
> Wels: III./KG 158
> Graz: I./StG 168
> Köttingbrunn: 1., 2., 3. (H), 4. (F)/AufKlGr 18
> Luftgaukommando XVII (Vienna)
> I./FlakRegt 8

Luftwaffenkommando Ostpreussen: Generalleutnant
Alfred Keller
       Jesau: I./JG 131
       Insterburg: Stab,1.(H), 2., 3. (F)/AufklGr 11
Höherer Kommandeur der Flakartillerie 1
(Konigsberg): Oberst Walter Feyerabend
       I./FlakRegt 1; I., II./FlakRegt 11
       Luftgaukommando I (Konigsberg)
       Luftnachrichtenabteilung 6

Luftwaffenkommando See (Kiel): General der Flieger
Konrad Zander
Führer der Seeluftstreitkräfte: Generalmajor Hans Geisler
       Jever: I./JG 136
       Nordenay: Stab, 1./ KüFlGr 106
       Hörnum: 2./ KüFlGr 106
       Borkum: 3./ KüFlGr 106
       Kiel-Holtenau: 5./BordFlGr 196

List/Sylt: Stab, 1., 2., 3./ KüFlGr 406
Dievenow: Stab, 1., 2. KüFlGr 306
Stab, 1./ KüFlGr 506
Kamp: 2./ KüFlGr 506
Stab, 2./ KüFlGr 706
Pillau: 3./ KüFlGr 506
Nest: 1./ KüFlGr 706
Wilhelmshaven: 1./BordFlGr 196

Flakkommandeur Kiel: Oberst Kurt Steudemann
       I./FlakRegt 61; I./FlakRegt 62
       Luftnachrichten Regiment 16

Legion Condor (Spain): Generalmajor HelmuthVolkmann

J/88	AS/88
K/88	F/88
A/88	Ln/88

NOTES TO CHAPTER FIVE

1. For the *Luftwaffe* 1936-1939 see Corum, *Luftwaffe* pp.224-270. Homze pp.139-256. Hooton pp.146-174. Schliephacke pp.49-51, 53-58, Appendix G; Suchenwirth pp. 61-73, 82-90;Völker, *Luftwaffe* pp.71-147, 159-214 (Hereafter Völker). Again for aircraft see Green's *Warplanes* and for units see both Rosch as well as Holm's website. See also Ries, *Luftwaffen-Story.*

2. Wimmer succeeded Keller as commander of *Luftwaffenkommando Ostpreussen* in April 1939 and later commander *Luftflotte* 1 during the winter of 1939/1940 before being assigned command of *Lufgau Belgien Nord Frankreich*, replacing his former production assistant *Major* Friedrich Loeb.When forced to retreat in 1944 he was threatened with a court-martial by Göring but narrowly escaped. Collins & Miller's website.

3. For Udet see Ishoven's biography. Also Faber pp. 61-72.

4. Corum p.331 f/n 4. Hooton p.152.

5. Hooton p.147.

6. Corum pp.225-6. Hooton pp.151-153.

7. For Kesselring see Macksay's biography. Corum 331 f/n 1. Faber pp.24-25.Homze p.60. Hooton p.118 f/n 10. Mason p.216. Mitcham pp.17-19. Also Collins & Miller's website.

8. Corum pp.154, 235.

9. Macksey pp.52-54.

10. Völker p.158.

11. Deichmann p.87.

12. See Collins & Miller's website.

13. For Jeschonnek see Mitcham pp.27-28, Faber pp.26-27, 73-93. Irving, Milch pp.68-69. Collins and Miller's website. I am also grateful to *Admiral* Gert Jeschonnek for personal information.

14. Goulding and Moyes pp.50-59.

15. The others were Kesselring, Sperrle and Zander but Sperrle would soon depart for Spain.

16. Taylor, Sword & Swastika pp.172. Taylor, Munich pp.324-326.Völker pp.96-97. Collins & Miller's website.

17. Collins & Miller 's website.

18. Blandford pp.11-37.Völker pp.120, 122, 125.

19. *HJ Quex* (*Hitlerjunge Quex*) was a Goebbel's propaganda movie about the son of Communists who joins the Hitler Boys (*Hitlerjunge*) organisation and betrays the dastardly Bolshevik plots to his new friends.

20. One of those who faced such a veto was future air ace *Major* Helmut Wick who was the top *Experte* (56 victories) when he was killed in November 1940. Steinhilper pp.108-109.

21. The RAD was created in June 1935 from a scheme established in 1931 but following a wartime precedent. Men and women were subject to conscription from the age of 18 for at least six months' service although few women joined its ranks.

22. For flying training see Hooton pp.158-159. Reis *Fliegerführerschulen.*

23. Hermann pp.44-45. Hooton p.159.

24. Corum p.223.

25. Not to be confused with *Oberst* Robert Fuchs who was in charge of Technical Training and later *Kommodore* of KG 26.

26. Völker p.145-146.

27. Völker pp.108, 110, 112, 178.

28. For *Luftverteidigungszone West* see Kaufmann & Kaufmann, pp.133, 138-139. Short, pp.18-19.

29. For the *Anschluss* air operations see Haubner and Tudor. Also Hooton pp.160-162. Schliephake pp.47-48.Völker p.154.

30. For the Austrian air force orbat March 1938 see Wendel's website. *Österreichisches Bundesheer.*

31. See UKNA FO 371/21710, C 2354.There were only 77 qualified staff officers in the *Luftwaffe*.Völker p.124 f/n 240. Information kindly supplied by Dr Erich Gabriel of the *Heeresgeschichtliches Museum.*

33. Mitcham pp.237-245. Collins & Miller's website.

34. SHAA 2B97. Taylor, Munich p.463.

35. For Munich see Taylor, *Munich.* Homze pp.149, 158-159, 229-230.Hooton pp.163-169. Schliephake p.48.Völker p. 154-156. Murray's article and BA MA RL7/1.

36. Weal pp.15-16. At this time the Spanish Nationalist Air Force were already using He 45s in the *Schlacht* role. Green, *Warplanes* p.260.

37. Corum pp.236-238. Kuhn pp.9,14,16.

38. Jones pp.129-130. UKNA Air 9/90.

39. Christienne & Lissarague p. 300. Hooton pp.164-165. Patric Façon's article. SHAA, 2B61.

40. A similar conclusion was reached at about the same time by Group Captain John Slessor of the British Air Ministry. UKNA Air 9/90.

41. Hooton p.170. Irving, *Göring* pp.244-245. Schliephake p.52. BA MA RL7/85.

42. Schliephake, p.52.

43. Pritchard pp.55-56. Wood & Dempster pp.17-21. The *Graf Zeppelin* flew some 30 missions for the *Luftwaffe* before being laid up on 20 August 1939.

CHAPTER SIX

THE FIRST CAMPAIGN: POLAND

September 1939

Troops of the SS Leibstandarte Adolf Hitler Regiment advance through a Polish town shattered by German bombing.

Throughout the Weimar Republic's existence Warsaw, underwritten by Paris, was viewed as a threat to Germany's eastern borders but as the Third Reich grew in power a settling of accounts became only a matter of time.

On 18 April 1939 Göring returned from an Italian vacation and dined with the *Führer*, who quickly ruined the meal by revealing that a fortnight earlier he had ordered preparations for *Fall 'Weiss'*, an attack upon Poland. Knowing the weakness of Germany's industry, and aware that France and Britain regarded such action as *causus belli*, Göring sought to dissuade Hitler. But the *Führer* sharply dismissed him as 'an old woman[1]'.

It was with mounting disquiet that Göring received a briefing from Jeschonnek a week later and, as the pace of war preparations increased, Göring used personal intermediaries to the British and French in a vain bid to avoid war while allowing Berlin a free hand in the East. It was only the signing of the Russo-German Pact on 25 August, which secretly carved up Poland like a piece of meat, that restored his confidence in Hitler but he sought to keep open his options with London until war was declared.

Even as Göring's digestion was being ruined, Schmid was directing the intelligence effort. With German troops now occupying territory all around Poland he was able to use a network of 74 comint stations to assess the Polish air force's (*Polskie Lotnictwo Wojskowe* or PLW) order of battle and intentions, with *Abwehr* agents supplementing the information. Rowehl's *Aufklärungsgruppe* Ob.d.L. began to assemble key photographic images about the same time but it was not until July that the *Fernaufklärungsstaffeln* began to penetrate Polish air space.

They were soon flying up to 160 kilometres beyond the German frontier to build up a detailed picture of Poland's communications system and industrial base. From 31 August they also followed the mobilisation of the Polish Army which was organised into six reinforced corps, designated 'armies' (*Armii*). Three were in the north; *Armia Poznan* facing Pomerania, *Pomorze* in the Polish Corridor and *Modlin* (augmented by a smaller group) facing East Prussia. In the south *Armii Lódz* and *Kraków* faced Silesia while *Armia Karpaty* faced

Slovakia and Polish strategy was to hold out until enemy pressure was relieved by a French offensive upon the *West Wall*[2].

Schmid overestimated PLW strength at 740 aircraft (315 fighters, 130 bombers), when it was 494 aircraft of which 392 were combat aircraft. It had a traditional structure with 32 squadrons supporting the 'armies' piecemeal, the 253 fighters, reconnaissance/light bombers and corps aircraft providing an illusion of air support in an air force whose prime function was reconnaissance. A Pursuit (Fighter) Brigade had five squadrons (53 fighters) and, shortly before mobilisation, a Bomber Brigade was created with nine squadrons with 50 PZL P.23B *Karas* light bombers and 36 PZL P.37 *Los* medium bombers, but no attempt was made to co-ordinate their operations[3].

The *Wehrmacht's* battle plan was developed from early May under cover of the 'General Staff's Silesian journey' (*Generalstabsübung Schlesien*) at Bad Salzbrunn. *Generaloberst* Fedor von Bock's *Heeresgruppe Nord* in the north was given a subordinate role with 4. *Armee* in Pomerania and 3. *Armee* in East Prussia; the former would cut the Polish Corridor and take Danzig (Gdynia) while the latter would drive southward on the Polish capital of Warsaw. The main blow was to be launched from Silesia by *Generaloberst* Gerd von Rundstedt's

On 18 April 1939 Göring returned from an Italian vacation to dine with the Führer. The General-feldmarschall – who was known for his considerable appetite – was put off his meal when Hitler chose to reveal that a fortnight earlier he had ordered preparations for Fall 'Weiss', an attack upon Poland.

Major Theodor Rowehl (third from left) and other officers of the Aufklärungsgruppe Ob.d.L. in conversation in the final days of peace before the oubreak of the Second World War. The unit gathered critical photographic intelligence prior to operations against Poland.

A Polish PZL P-23b Karas reconnaissance aircraft prepares to take off. A total of 205 such machines were available to the Polish Air Force at the time of the German invasion.

Heeresgruppe Süd whose spearhead would be *General der Artillerie* Walter von Reichenau's 10. *Armée*, with 8. *Armée* to the north and 14. *Armée* to the south. The forces would comprise three mechanised corps to drive some 480 kilometres north-eastwards to Warsaw ignoring their flanks and rear to reach the Vistula before the enemy could retreat across the river.

Bock would be supported by Kesselring's *Luftflotte* 1 and Rundstedt by Löhr's *Luftflotte* 4, augmented by the Slovak Air Force (*Slovenske Vzousne Zbrane-SVZ*) with 30 aircraft. More than 70 per cent of the *Luftwaffe*'s 1,176 bombers, and all of its *Stuka-* and *Schlachtgruppen*, were in the East (see order of battle) and, in accordance with *Luftwaffe* doctrine, the aerial campaign was to open with a pulverising double blow, the most important being the destruction of the PLW on the ground followed by a massive attack upon Warsaw, Operation 'Seaside' (*Unternehmen 'Wasserkante'*) to erode both Poland's industrial base and its political will. Once these operations were complete the *Luftwaffe* would provide the army with unlimited Tactical and Operational support.

Kesselring's subordinates, who received a verbal briefing on 31 August, were Grauert's *Fliegerdivision* 1, Förster's *Lehrdivision* and Wimmer's *Luftwaffen-kommando Ostpreussen* in East Prussia. Löhr had Loerzer's 2. *Fliegerdivision*, to which Richthofen's

Fliegerführer zbV was attached to support 10. *Armée* under the Anglophile *Nazi* (and International Olympic Committee member) Reichenau, whom Richthofen met shortly before the campaign together with his colourless Chief-of-Staff, *Oberst* Friedrich Paulus, who would later command the renamed 6. *Armée*.

Grauert and Förster were both 50-year-old Prussians, the former from Berlin the latter from Upper Silesia, who joined the *Fliegertruppen* but their careers were very different. Grauert was the 'old sweat' who served first as an observer before transferring to a multi-role combat *Kagohl*. He held a variety of posts and ended the war supporting 18. *Armée* opposite the British before leading *Freikorps* squadron FFA 420. He joined the *Reichsheer*, serving mostly as a gunner but secretly having various aviation roles (he received refresher training at Lipetsk). Between 1928 and 1931 he was an aviation 'advisor' at the *Reichswehrministerium* and in 1930 he made some indiscreet remarks to the British air attaché. In September 1933 he became one of the first officers to transfer to the *Luftwaffe* and from his appointment as *Höhere Flieger-kommandeur* II in July 1937 until his death in 1941 he held front line commands.

Förster, a former railway troops officer, was one of the first officers to volunteer for flying training and spent most of the war as a staff officer, working with Hoeppner and helping to demobilise the *Luftstreitkräfte* in 1919 before he retired. His staff experience proved invaluable when he returned to the *Luftwaffe* in March 1934 but he remained largely in the background until appointed commander of the *Lehrdivision* in February 1938. After the Poland campaign he would work with Milch and become *Luftflotte* 5's Chief-of-Staff.

From July the pace of preparation increased with more intensive reconnaissance and the stocking of 155 airfields and airstrips. There was also a last-minute 30 per cent expansion of the fighter force through the creation of 26 *Staffeln*, including 12 night fighter (*Nachtjagd*) and three *Zerstörer*. It was easier to create *Zerstörerstaffeln* than to equip them; indeed on 1 September there were only 102 Bf 110s in service and *Major* Walter Grabmann, *Kommandeur* of I.(Z)/LG 1 (and last *Kommandeur* of J/88) later noted that many *Staffeln* had only seven serviceable aircraft due to a spares shortage[4]. Only three of the 10 *Zerstörergruppen* (I./ZG 1, I.(Z)/LG 1 and I./ZG 76) were genuine units, with the others flying false colours using the Bf 109 *Dora* (Bf 109D) which lead to them receiving temporary *Jagdgruppe* designations.

Most *Jagdgruppen* had their full establishment of Bf 109E (*Emils*) but to preserve them the *Doras* were used for training until mobilisation and 3./JG 54 reportedly used former Czech Avia B.534 biplanes until just before 'Weiss' began[5]. To support the advance the *Luftgaukommandos* on the Polish border created Special Employment Air District Staffs (*Luftgaustaben zbV*) which were to provide logistics, communications and air defence but Richthofen,

'The Air War against Poland': A contemporary German map showing dispositions of the German and Polish armies and air forces.

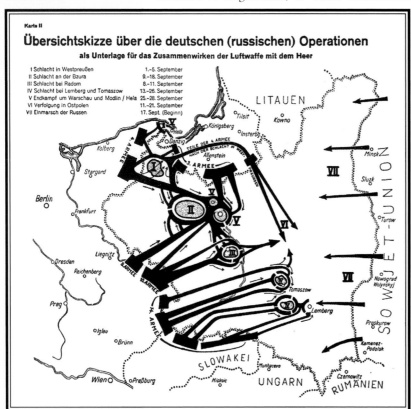

whose *Fliegerführer zbV* would be reined to the mechanised forces, was unconvinced and his concern would prove well-founded. Nominally he was under Loerzer's 2. *Fliegerdivision* but he received no responses to his concerns from the former cigar salesman nor from Jeschonnek whom he met on 28 August.

In fact Jeschonnek had anticipated the problem and two days earlier created a new transport *Geschwader*, KG zbV 2, under *Oberst Dipl.Ing* Gerhard Conrad, to support Löhr, KGzbV 172 having been assigned to support Kesselring. Between them the two *Geschwader* had some 270 aircraft, including a proportion of *Lufthansa's* 147-strong fleet, but these moves proved to be little more than an aspirin to cure pneumonia.

Planning is never smooth but during August the *Luftwaffe* was shaken by a series of events[6]. On 15 August during an unwise demonstration in dense cloud and ground fog at Neuhammer, I./St.G 76 lost 26 airmen when all of 2./St.G 76 flew straight into the ground together with four more from the remainder of the *Gruppe*. One of the few to escape was the *Staffelführer* of 1./St.G 76, *Oberleutnant* Dietrich Peltz, who remained in St.G 76 until the summer of 1940 before transferring to bombers and becoming *Inspekteur der Kampfflieger* in 1943[7].

With only the 1937 exercise to demonstrate the validity of *Luftwaffe* doctrine the generals took counsel of their fears and in the closing weeks of August demanded a greater degree of air support during the opening hours of the campaign. Hitler backed them on 31 August leaving a grumbling Jeschonnek to make major last-minute revisions of ObdL's plans, diverting half the strike force to attack enemy communications. '*Wasserkante*' now slipped to the latter part of A-Day (the German equivalent of D-Day) although now augmented by LnAbt 100's night precision attacks.

The Navy then got into the act and persuaded Hitler to demand a greater effort against the Polish Navy, stretching even Kesselring's patience. Half of Grauert's squadrons were now diverted to Gdynia and the Hela naval base although there was the prospect of reinforcement by *Oberst* Hans Behrendt's Hannover-based KG 27.

Finally, on 28 August, there was a mutiny in the lukewarm Slovak forces. The Slovak armed forces harboured strong nationalistic elements and in June five pilots defected to Poland and Yugoslavia while on 5 August, the commander of the SVZ, Lieutenant Colonel Jan Ambru? followed suit and would later lead a Czech squadron in the Royal Air Force[8]. The new mutiny threatened Zipser Neudorf airfield, home of *Stab* and II./St.G 77 which was secured by a paratroop battalion. It was an unwelcome distraction for Student's 7. *Fliegerdivision*, which desperately sought a role in the forthcoming campaign. At the last minute it was assigned the role of opening the Polish Corridor by seizing the bridges at Tczew (Dirschau) and Grudziadz (Graudenz) near the German border but these later

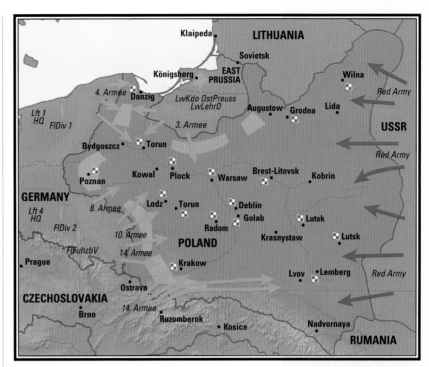

proved to be bridges too far and the operation was replaced by *Stuka* attacks.

Under sunny August skies the *Luftwaffe* completed its preparations having assigned 2,315 combat aircraft to 'Weiss'. The superior bases in northern Germany meant that Kesselring had the bulk of the *Gruppen* (807 aircraft), augmented by eight *Staffeln* (92 seaplanes) of Coeler's *Fliegerführer der Seeluftstreitkräfte Ost* to support operations against the minuscule Polish Navy. Löhr had 627 aircraft and 30 Slovaks and the remainder were under the *Luftgaue* or ObdL.

The scattered nature of the Polish defence is clearly shown in this map. On land and in the air the Polish forces were individually too weak to offer prolonged resistance to the German offensive and this made them vulnerable to the Russian invasion.

Distribution of Staffeln: 1 September 1939

Luftflotte	Fighter	Zerstörer	Bomber	Stuka/Schlacht	Reconnaissance
1	6 (90)	6 (67)	30 (407)	16 (172)	5 (71)
4	3 (48)	3 (35)	27 (303)	15 (194)	3 (47)
Total	**9 (138)**	**9 (102)**	**57 (710)**	**31 (366)**	**8 (118)**

The structure of the *Luftwaffe* was clearly for offensive operations, but nearly two-thirds of the fighter force in the East (406 fighters) were retained for home defence, augmented by 456 *Flak* batteries.

Home defence forces in the East: 1 September 1939

Luftgau	Jagdstaffeln	Heavy Flak	Light Flak	Searchlight
I (Konigsberg)	6	33	24	6
III (Berlin)	4	79	33	23
IV (Dresden)	6	72	52	25
VIII (Breslau)	–	24	27	6
XVII (Vienna)	–	22	25	5
Total	**16**	**230**	**161**	**65**

The Army also had its own air support, with 333 reconnaissance and corps aircraft under *Kommandeur der Luftwaffe* (*Koluft*) attached to each *Heeresgruppe* and *Armee Oberkommando* together with 109 *Flak* batteries, *Koluft Heeresgruppe Süd* being the staff of *Aufklärungsgeschwader* 11 from 26 August while *Koluft 14. Armee* was the staff of *Aufklärungsgeschwader* 12. (The staff of

Aufklärungsgeschwader 13 became *Koluft Heeresgruppe* C on the Rhine).

Koluft forces in the East: 1 September 1939

Heeresgruppe	Reconnaissance	Corps	Heavy Flak	Light/Medium Flak
Nord	3 (36)	5 (57)	15	16
Süd	3 (36)	17 (204)	36	42
Total	**6 (72)**	**22 (261)**	**51**	**58**

Generalmajor Helmut Förster, commander of the Luftwaffenlehrdivision, whose command, together with those of Generalleutnant Ulrich Grauert and Generalleutnant Wilhelm Wimmer, would form part of Generaloberst Kesselring's Luftflotte 1 strike force. Förster, a former railway troops officer, was one of the first officers to volunteer for flying training and spent most of the war as a staff officer, working with Hoeppner and helping to demobilise the Luftstreitkräfte in 1919 before he retired. His staff experience proved invaluable when he returned to the Luftwaffe in March 1934. He served as Kommodore of KG 253 'General Wever' between 1935 and 1937. He was awarded the Knights Cross in February 1942 as commander of I. Fliegerkorps. He was captured by the Allies in May 1945 and remained in captivity until June 1947.

Diplomatic efforts to contain the conflict meant frequent postponements to A-Day although mobilisation was formally authorised on 25 August. All civilian air movements were banned on the late afternoon of 26 August but only five days later did Hitler authorise the invasion, ObdL issuing the code warning at 1255 to the *Luftflotten* for the surprise attack on the Polish air force, '*Ostmarkflug 1 September 0445*' involving half the strike force. By then the PLW had dispersed to wartime airstrips and the *Aufklärungsstaffeln*, which had been monitoring the peacetime bases since 25 August, now discovered that the birds had flown!

Yet the *Luftflotten* staffs hoped that something would turn up and rigidly stuck to their plans. But what Man proposes, God disposes and many airmen awoke on 1 September to find their bases covered by dense, clammy fog with the weather 'prophets' warning of dense cloud down to 180 metres in northern Poland. The fog cleared slowly from south to north and only five of Kesselring's 15 *Kampf-* and *Stukagruppen* took off on schedule while '*Wasserkante*' was postponed.

Löhr's airfields cleared first and generally he had the better weather allowing *Oberst* Martin

Air and ground crew of 1.(schwere Jagd)/LG 1 relax on the grass beneath the wing of one of their Messerschmitt Bf 110 C-1s in the summer of 1939 – the last summer of peace before the outbreak of war. The Bf 110 would perform well in the air superiority role against the Polish Air Force in the first days of the campaign.

Fiebig's KG 4 to fly all day, although cloud forced KG 76 to abandon its mission. As the fog cleared, the pace picked up from midday and during the afternoon some *Gruppen* flew two missions. Löhr committed St.G 77 (half Richthofen's strike force) to counter-air missions. *Luftflotte* 4's strike force flew some 1,200 sorties to deliver some 389 tonnes of bombs (200 tonnes on Cracow) and as targets disappeared in smoke and dust the follow-up missions had to be flown low; indeed several of KG 77's Dorniers were damaged by splinters from their own bombs. It was during the first attack upon Cracow that I./St.G 2 achieved the first German air victory when *Oberleutnant* Frank Neubert blew apart a P.11c fighter of Captain Mieczyslaw Medwecki, commander of Group III./2 [9]. In the deeper raids the Germans used Russian radio stations at Minsk and Kiev as navigation aids and there was some night bombing by ordinary *Kampfgruppen* [10].

The few *Zerstörer* distinguished themselves, especially supporting attacks upon Warsaw's airfields, including KG 27's which involved a 725 kilometres flight from bases in Hannover to East Prussia. The Warsaw missions encountered fierce resistance from Colonel Stefan Pawlikowski's Pursuit Brigade but with each *Kampfstaffel* covered by a Bf 110 *Rotte*, the attackers were well-shielded and, by the end of the day, Pawlikowski had lost 17 per cent of his strength which rose to 72 per cent over the next five days. Grabmann's I(Z)./LG 1 was prominent on the first day and claimed 30 victories, including four by *Leutnant* Werner Methfessel, who would become the leading ace of the campaign with a total of eight victories. Even the nominal *Zerstörergruppen* were successful, with *Hauptmann* Hannes Gentzen's JGr 102 claiming 28 aerial victories as well as 50 aircraft on the ground.

The mountain had laboured and brought forth a mouse! Most of the counter-air campaign was wasted because of the PLW dispersal, leaving only 'several dozen derelict or obsolete aircraft' to become sacrificial lambs, including 28 unserviceable trainers at Cracow-Rakowice. German after-action reports concluded that the *Luftwaffe* failed to wreck the enemy bases and often left their runways intact but at least its losses were light at only 25 aircraft [11].

Reconnaissance discovered 15 empty airfields and, with the dispersal of the PLW weakening its response, the *Luftwaffe* achieved air superiority by default. On 2 September *Stab*, I. and II./KG 55 reinforced Loerzer but the counter-air effort was downgraded as concern about enemy bombers meant that even AufklGr ObdL was committed to search for them.

Consequently, there were only 364 strike sorties, 28 per cent of the total effort on that day and Löhr devoted more than a third of his sorties to facilitate the army's advance. Loerzer was especially active with 13 *Staffeln*-size missions against airfields around Deblin, which received 180 tonnes of bombs, mostly from KG 4, although it housed only trainers of which 11 were claimed on the ground by *Hauptman* Günther Reinecke's I./ZG 76.

With the need to restrain the *Kampfgruppen* until the enemy bombers were discovered, '*Wasserkante*' was again postponed, yet the same day Colonel Wladyslaw Heller's Bomber Brigade finally appeared and over the next five days flew 157 sorties and lost 26 bombers (16.5 per cent casualties). Most fell in suicidally low-level attacks to a hurricane of *Flak* cannon fire as they tried to prevent Reichenau's armoured spearhead pushing back *Armii Lódz* in its drive on Warsaw[12].

The destruction of their main base on A-Day meant the *Los* medium bombers could not be repaired, while salt was rubbed into the wound on 5 September when two bombers were destroyed on the ground at Kuciny. The *Zerstörergruppen* crushed *Armii Lódz*'s fighter shield; Reinecke's men claimed nine of its fighters for the loss of three Bf 110s on 2 September and two days later Gentzen finished it off by shooting down another five.

On the third day of the campaign ObdL changed tack in its counter-air missions and planned to strike the Polish aircraft industry, only for Göring to change his mind. Instead only occupied airfields were to be struck with KG 27 held in reserve as ObdL's strike force. It returned to Kesselring later in the day and bombed rail targets east of Warsaw. Although the *Luftflotten* had been ordered to conserve the *Zerstörergruppen*, Grabmann again shielded the *Kampfgruppen*.

By 5 September, the *Luftwaffe* regarded its counter-air mission as largely concluded. Airfields were attacked, usually by *Kampfstaffeln*, but occasionally by *Kampfgruppen*, only if the *Aufklärungsstaffeln* confirmed the presence of enemy aircraft. The most successful raid was on 14–15 September when 17 *Karas* were destroyed at Hutniki and the absence of aerial resistance meant that three days later *Luftflotte* 4 made the *Luftwaffe*'s last airfield attack.

Polish fighters remained active and took a steady toll of corps aircraft; the first *Luftwaffe* prisoners of war were from a Hs 126 of 1.(H)/AufklGr 10[13]. But sweeps by the *Jagdgruppen* kept these to manageable levels. As the threat eased the *Jagd-* and *Zerstörergruppen* were increasingly committed to ground-attack missions while *Flak* batteries were transferred from the Eastern *Luftgauen* either into Poland or to bolster the western air defences.

Ironically it was indirect, rather than direct, air support which was the key to air superiority. By striking communications the *Luftwaffe* accelerated the speed of the German advance, which overran airstrips and the early warning network, while also disrupting command, control and logistics. By 6 September the PLW squadrons were running out of supplies, forcing the abandonment of numerous aircraft and on 18 September the surviving 98 combat aircraft withdrew to Romania.

The Pursuit Brigade was hounded from airfield to airfield and by 6 September was down to 16 serviceable fighters and four days later it would absorb the remaining Army fighters before moving to Lublin. There it joined Heller's bombers, which had lost 38 aircraft, or nearly a quarter the strength! The scattered Army squadrons suffered even more, the fighter units losing 41 aircraft, half (34) of their *Karas* reconnaissance-bombers and 60 per cent (37) of the corps aircraft, many to 'friendly' ground fire. The defiant Poles fought on as the odds mounted; Heller's airmen flew 147 sorties between 7 and 16 September dropping 47 tonnes of bombs but losing 49 aircraft while the augmented Pursuit Brigade was down to 54 fighters by 14 September.

As the Polish air threat dissolved, indirect and direct attacks to support the Army became an increasing function of *Luftwaffe* operations. The first *Luftwaffe* strike mission of the war was by *Oberleutnant* Bruno Dilley's *Kette* of 3./St.G 1 to prevent the destruction of the Tczew (Dirschau) railway bridge over the Vistula on the Poland/East Prussian border. Flying in at tree-top height Dilley hit a blockhouse controlling the bridge demolition system 10 minutes before war was officially declared[14]. The control wires were cut and a follow-up raid was made by III./KG 3 but the Poles repaired the wires and blew up the bridge two hours later.

The *Luftwaffe*'s indirect support of the Army initially focused upon struck railway lines and marshalling yards as well as crossroads but during the campaign these targets would be alternated with troop concentrations. These physically disrupted the Polish mobilisation while attacks upon towns and cities hamstrung command and control by cutting the civilian telephone and telegraph system upon which the Polish Army depended, leaving communications 'marginal at best'[15].

Kesselring and Löhr each flew some 500 sorties supporting the Army on A-Day with Reichenau receiving the bulk of the latter's support, both indirect and direct as it pushed back *Armii Lódz*. The need for counter-air missions meant that Richthofen at first could provide only three *Gruppen* of fighters, *Stukas* and the Hs 123s (known as *Ein-Zwe-Drei*) of *Major* Werner Spielvogel's II.(Schlacht)/LG 2 who

Messerschmitt Bf 110s of 2./ZG 76 on an unknown airfield during the winter of 1939/40. Elsewhere on the field can be seen a lone Ju 88 and three Ju 52s – the latter possibly transport aircraft attached to the Zerstörerstaffel.

Berlin-born Generaloberst Ulrich Grauert led 1. Fliegerdivision during operations against Poland. Another Freikorps veteran and artilleryman, he subsequently acted as an aviation 'advisor' at the Reichswehrministerium between 1928-1931. He was appointed commander of the I. Fliekerkorps in October 1939, but was shot down and killed by an RAF fighter over St Omer, France on 15 May 1941. He had been awarded the Knights Cross a year earlier.

A Kette of three Hs 123s of 2./St.G 165 in pre-war markings in formation somewhere over Germany. The Hs 123 was also originally designed as a dive-bomber and saw pre-war service with a number of dive-bomber units. When replaced by the Ju 87, the Hs 123 subsequently equipped for a long time the Luftwaffe's only dedicated ground-attack unit with which it performed valuable service in Poland, France, the Balkans and in Russia.

gave almost continuous close-air support to the mechanised XVI. *Armee Korps*. Fortunately, Reichenau was also aided by the remainder of Loerzer's 2. *Fliegerdivision* whose I./St.G 2 and I./KG 77 helped Richthofen's I./St.G 77 to decimate one of *Armii Lódz*'s cavalry brigades.

Koluft demands for very low-level bombing attacks, sometimes down to 20 metres, caused 20 per cent of Richthofen's fighter and *Zerstörer* casualties on the first day and he therefore then ignored the demands. Yet low-level attacks continued to be made and on 6 September, according to *Kommodore Generalmajor* Hans Siburg, three He 111s of KG 26 fell to their own bomb fragments[16]. The *Kampfstaffeln* also suffered from unreliable bomb fuzes which caused three aircraft to explode in mid-air between 3-6 September, while an airfield accident on 4 September destroyed two of KG 26's bombers and damaged seven.

The swing towards Army support, especially Tactical missions, became apparent on 2 September with strike units increasingly operating in *Staffel*-size formations. Of Kesselring's 575 strike missions on that day, 56 per cent (325) were Tactical and 8 per cent (45) were Operational, Löhr's figures being 43 per cent (295) and 18.5 per cent (125) respectively. The extremely fluid situation meant that Loerzer

despatched reconnaissance aircraft with radio links to the *Kampfgeschwader* which had rapid-response forces, each of one or two *Ketten*, ready to set-off at a few minutes' notice. This proved deadly, interdicting retreating Polish troops whose columns were frequently struck by low-level bombers, but hundreds of civilians also died for, justifiably fearing German reprisals, thousands fled from the front where they became mixed up with the troops, further hindering the defence[17].

But after two days there was a change to Operational Level missions with Kesselring's *Kampf*- and *Stukagruppen* flying 17 (39 *Staffeln*) and nine Tactical (20 *Staffeln*), a third supporting 4. *Armee*'s advance southwards. Löhr was especially active behind *Armii Lódz* and *Kraków* against the rail network to cause congestion at the rail heads, another of *Armii Lódz*'s cavalry brigades detraining in a rain of bombs, and also against the road system[18]. KG 4, KG 55, KG 76 and KG 77 (the last acting as Löhr's fire brigade) would bomb from around 2,000 metres, then the *Stukas* would roll over to make shallow-angle (10-30 degree) attacks.

So successful were these attacks that the *Luftwaffe* began to run out of targets and from the next day increasingly returned to Tactical operations. But ObdL was determined that it would not wear out men and machines in such missions and on 5 September it also ordered each *Luftflotte* to use only two-thirds of its aircraft and to rest the others on rotation, although Kesselring had begun to do so on his own initiative from the previous day.

But extra burdens continued to be placed on the *Luftwaffe*'s shoulders. *Koluft* 14 *Armee*'s comint stations reported radio chatter from British aircraft near the Polish-Romanian border, leading OKW to fear the despatch of Allied reinforcements and material from the Danube valley. ObdL instructed Löhr to interdict the Polish rail network to Romania but, with the support of Reichenau consuming most of its resources, *Luftflotte* 4 reacted half-heartedly and assigned the task to a couple of *Kampfgruppen*.

From 3 September the Polish air threat became a distant memory and ObdL demanded maximum effort to support the Army. Grauert supported *General der Artillerie* Günther Kluge's 4. *Armee* as it cleared the Polish Corridor driving back both *Armia Pomorze* and *Armia Poznan*, while to the east Wimmer sent 15 *Staffeln* of LG 1, KG 2 and I./St.G 1 against *Armia Modlin*'s defences around Mlawa, which had been delaying *General der Artillerie* Georg von Küchler's 3. *Armee*. The *Stukas* were especially effective, diving down to 500 metres and placing their bombs within five metres of bunkers, whose stunned defenders were quickly overrun, allowing 3. *Armee* to approach to within 60 kilometres from Warsaw.

On that day Reichenau's armoured spearhead was some 450 kilometres from Warsaw but Richthofen then destroyed the 7th Polish Division anchoring *Armia Kraków*'s right. The Germans then split the defence isolating *Armia Lódz* west of the

The coming of Blitzkrieg. Mechanics push a Ju 87 A-1 of 4./St.G 165 across the concrete apron at Schweinfurt in 1939. The Stuka – after a faltering start in Spain – would be unleashed to devastating effect in Poland.

This He 111 P piloted by Lt. Scholz of 2./KG 27 took part in bombing raids on Polish rail and road communications in September 1939 from its forward base at Neukuhren. The aircraft, '1G+EK', carries Scholz' personal insignia, a rather crudely painted clown, with the individual letter 'E' in the Staffel colour red.

Vistula as Reichenau's armour drove towards Warsaw, entering its southern suburbs on 8 September. But the advance frequently outstripped supplies and the armoured spearhead received the support of only a single transport *Gruppe* (I./KGzbV 2). This delivered 30 tonnes of fuel to 1. *Panzer Division* on 2 September and 91 tonnes on 5 September, the tanks having a higher priority even than Richthofen's *Staffeln*[19]. The Polish High Command fled to Brest-Litovsk (Brzesc-nad-Bugiem) 200 kilometres to the east, but poor communications meant this increased its isolation.

To keep pace with Reichenau's armour, Richthofen had to move into Polish airfields. *Oberst* Günther Schwartzkopff's St.G 77 occupied 'Tschenstochau' (Czestocowa) on 8 September; Gentzen's JGr 102 moved to Cracow the following day but moved to Debrica on 11 September. The record went to the '*Ein-Zwei-Dreis*' who would occupy Witkowicze and another three Polish airfields in succession by the end of the campaign.

Meanwhile, the *Luftwaffe* was crushing the Polish Navy with Coeler's 'sailors' aided by *Geschwader Kessler* formed around *Generalmajor* Ulrich Kessler's *Stab* KG 1, reinforced by all of Grauert's *Stukas*. On the first day they sank a torpedo boat and a tender as well as damaging the destroyer *Wicher* and the minelayer *Gryf*, which *Hauptmann* Blattner's 4.(St)/TrGr 186 and 3./KüflGr 706 finished off on 3 September. The Polish Navy's air service, which had some 18 seaplanes and had chased off the airship *Graf Zeppelin* during the summer, lasted a little longer but contributed nothing of significance to the defence.

Kessler then supported the army assault upon the Polish Navy's base on the Hel Peninsula which was led by the former *Luftkreiskommando* II commander *General der Artillerie* (formerly *General der Flieger*) Leonhard Kaupisch, who had been retired at the time of the *Anschluss* but rejoined the colours the day war broke out, his 61st birthday. Kaupisch, whose troops would take the Polish base only on 2 October, would become commander of XXXI. *Armee Korps* which later occupied Denmark.

Long before Kaupisch succeeded, Kesselring was facing a problem. Kluge's 4. *Armee* was essentially herding *Armia Pomorze* and *Armia Poznan* into a pen while Küchler's 3. *Armee* was enveloping Warsaw from the north. To support them Kesselring began to transfer squadrons to East Prussia from 3 September when *Major* Joachim-Friederich Huth's I./ZG 1 left its Pomeranian base at Mackfitz and landed at Mühlen.

Most of Förster's *Lehrdivision* followed, causing overcrowding at the handful of airfields as well as confusion over command. The last problem was resolved on 6 September when Kesselring split the East Prussian forces between Wimmer, whose headquarters became *Gruppe West* (KG 3, KG 27, I./St.G 1), and Förster, whose *Lehrdivision* became

These Ju 87 B-1s (top) and crews (above) of I./St.G 1 were photographed during the Polish campaign and were probably deployed against the Polish defences around Mlawa. The aircraft nearest the camera above is AB+BB, a Stab aircraft, and carried a narrow white band around the fuselage for rapid air-to-air identification. Just visible on the starboard wheel fairing is the Gruppe's diving raven badge. This was later repositioned on the engine cowling.

Gruppe Ost (LG 1, KG 2, III./KG 27, I.(Z)/LG 1). On about 10 September Kesselring moved his headquarters to Konigsberg to improve co-ordination. By then his command was being slowly drained to reinforce Löhr, partly due to a change of boundaries, which left Kesselring supporting only 3. *Armee*. Two *Gruppen* of St.G 2 were the first to fly south while *TrägerGruppe* 186 went westward. Many units came from Grauert's 1. *Fliegerdivision* which was finally transferred to Löhr on 6 September. These moves were partly responding to a crisis facing Reichenau due to the failure of Germany's military leaders to learn from the 1918 offensives, which made a mockery of the intensive post-war operational analysis.

As in France two decades earlier, army headquarters lost touch with their forward units and while aircraft proved the most reliable means of finding the spearheads, the *Kolufts* tended to be sidelined, if not ignored completely. The collapse of communications deprived squadrons of orders, a situation exacerbated by the lack of a common radio frequency, and the over-stretched logistics system forced some to scavenge enemy supply depots to survive.

Richthofen was the worse affected and as early as 3 September commented in his diary that the army headquarters never seemed to know the location of the front line; indeed from A-Day he began committing units not in response to Army requests but according to his own interpretation of the situation. This inevitably led to 'friendly fire' incidents while on 8 September Richthofen's *Stukas* destroyed a bridge across the Vistula, unaware that a *Panzer Division* was just about to cross[20]!

The co-ordination of air-ground operations was the responsibility of the *Kolufts* who synthesised data from their own aerial reconnaissance and the forward units, but they were only advisors and, as officers with little experience in air warfare, controlled only the Army *Fern-* and *Nahaufklärungsstaffeln*. They depended upon the *Luftwaffe*'s visiting Air Liaison Officer (*Fliegerverbindungsoffizier* or *Flivo*) for fighter and bomber/*Stuka* support. However the *Flivos* were responsible not to the Army but to the *Luftwaffe* and their role was to keep their commanders constantly informed of the situation on the ground through radio-equipped vehicles[21].

Loerzer would later confess that he had no contact with Reichenau's command post and within three days Richthofen was complaining to Löhr about the former cigar salesman's ignorance. Probably because he wanted to be in the thick of the action, Richthofen from the very beginning began flying personal reconnaissance missions in a Fi 156 *Storch* and as air-ground co-ordination collapsed he sought to co-ordinate them by reporting to army command posts, although his claims were not always believed. This was a waste of his time and exposed him needlessly; indeed the *Storch* of Major Spielvogel, the *Schlachtgruppe Kommandeur* fell to anti-aircraft fire

in Warsaw on 9 September and he was killed[22]. However, from Richthofen's viewpoint there was the advantage that on the afternoon of 4 September Löhr assumed authority for *Fliegerführer zbV* giving it virtual autonomy and allowing him to conduct some spectacular empire-building involving six *Gruppen* within a week.

Even the *Luftwaffe*'s formidable signals network was brought to the verge of ruin. Each *Fliegerdivision* seemed well-endowed with signals support: a telephone company, five liaison platoons, two radio aircraft as well as telephone/teleprinter units. However, the system was designed to follow an army advancing at a pedestrian seven kilometres a day while the *Panzer Divisions* advanced at an average 40 kilometres a day, with the result that land-line communication collapsed and increasing demands on radios meant messages were taking up to three hours to get through[23]! Where possible the Germans had to exploit the surviving elements of the Polish communications network which they had previously sought to wreck.

The supply problems which Richthofen had anticipated rapidly became acute. Despite fuel conservation, by 11 September his *Stukas*, which had begun the campaign flying three sorties a day, were now reduced to one and a frustrated Pflugbeil could only blame bureaucrats in the rear, a favourite German scapegoat. Milch roamed the battlefield trying to help, but the situation eased only from 13 September when a force of 21 *Staffeln* was assembled for Löhr who subordinated them to the *ad hoc Geschwader zbV Ahlefeld* (II. and IV./KG zbV 1, I., III. and IV./KGzbV 2, and *Transportstaffel* 172)[24].

Despite these problems by 8 September Richthofen was preparing to support the final assault on Warsaw for which he received *Oberst* Heinrich Seybald's KG 77, although he sourly described Seybald as 'apparently a comedian'[25]. The assault had barely begun when a new threat emerged behind him as the encircled force of 100,000 men, or nearly a quarter of the Polish Army, sought to break out through *General der Infanterie* Johannes Blaskowitz' 8. *Armee* to reach sanctuary beyond the Vistula.

Reconnaissance aircraft detected the spearhead, assembling in the forests around Ilza south of Radom. Despite supply shortages Richthofen, with Loerzer's assistance, spent the three days pounding them into oblivion with the *Schlachtgruppe*, now under *Hauptmann* Otto Weiss, four *Stukagruppen* (I./St.G 2, I./St.G 77, III./St.G 51 and the newly arrived I./St.G 1) together with three *Kampfgruppen* (I. and II./KG 55 and I./KG 77). Grauert also joined the massacre with a *Stukagruppe* (III./St.G 2) and four *Kampfgruppen* (I./KG 1, I./KG 2, II./KG 26, and I./KG 53) being especially profligate with incendiary bombs, although Löhr had wanted him to use high-explosives.

As the Ilza pocket was hammered a new threat developed to the south on 9 September as the other troops tried to cross the River Bzura, driving back

Blaskowitz and taking 1,500 prisoners. After a week's desperate fighting, Rundstedt contained the threat and steadily reduced the pocket by 20 September. On his own initiative, backed by an ObdL directive on 11 September, Grauert supported Blaskowitz' hard-pressed troops and in perfect flying conditions the *Luftwaffe* gave an awesome demonstration of air power on the battlefield.

The bridges across the Bzura were first cut and as the Polish columns piled up at the river's edge the *Stukas* deluged them with light (50 kg) bombs; in the resulting confusion the bombers followed up to cause huge casualties. The massacre intensified as Richthofen switched from the Ilza pocket, allowing his *Staffeln* no more than 10 minutes over the battlefield, during which they were to expend all their ammunition.

As their anti-aircraft guns ran out of ammunition the Poles sought refuge in the forests but were smoked out with 100 kg incendiaries. Towards the end of the campaign, low cloud brought heavy rain but there was no respite for the Poles and on 17 September alone Richthofen's men flew 750 sorties, some crews flying five missions, and dropped 388 tonnes of bombs to 'break the morale of the enveloped troops completely'.

The *Luftwaffe* had been largely responsible for destroying resistance in the pockets, allowing the Army to mop up. Göring later observed to the *Luftwaffe*: "If you perform in the west as you did in Poland, then the British too, will run". The implications of this success and statement did not become apparent until eight months later. However, even here there were co-ordination problems as Grauert lost touch with the *Flivo* at Blaskowitz' headquarters and his replacement was seriously injured when his *Storch* crashed. The situation was saved by Löhr's Chief-of-Staff, *Oberst* Korten, who managed to restore communications.

The fighting was so confused that the *Luftwaffe* had to defend its positions on the ground. *Flak* played an important role in providing direct support to the troops, the 2 cm and 3.7 cm automatic guns proving even more devastating than machine guns, while the awesome 8.8 cm demonstrated its power and accuracy time and again. *Major* Weisser of I./FlakRegt 22 was posthumously honoured for his part in the Ilza battle while Richthofen's I./FlakRegt 23 helped to defend the airbases, supporting two Airfield Support Companies (*Flughafen-betriebskompanie*); but the situation was so desperate that the paratroops of III./FJR 1 had to be flown in to provide some professional infantry. This provided a way for the paratroops to vent their frustration caused by operations being set up and then cancelled at the last minute. The retreat of the Polish Army presented an opportunity on 7 September with plans to prevent the enemy crossing the Vistula by seizing the Pulavy road bridge at Deblin and holding it for 48 hours until relieved. The troops had actually boarded their aircraft when they learned that the operation had been cancelled, as

A Messerschmitt Bf 109 E-3 of 3.(J)/LG 2 taxies away from its dispersal to take off for another mission over Poland in September 1939. This aircraft, 'Red 15', was named 'Peter' on its nose, the nickname of its pilot, Heinz 'Pietsch' Bretnütz, a Legion Condor veteran who was later awarded the Knights Cross in October 1940.

the *Panzer Divisions* had isolated the enemy west of the river.

Meanwhile, the remainder of *Luftflotte* 4, reinforced by 11 *Kampfgruppen* (KG 1, KG 26, KG 55) supported 14. *Armee* as it pushed through southern Poland to prevent the enemy creating a redoubt backing on Romania. Rail interdiction missions were renewed after a week's lull by an ObdL directive on 14 September, leading KG 76 to send *Rotte* or individual aircraft on low-level missions against choke points such as bridges and cuttings. Attacks upon enemy columns ended with an urgent teletype to both *Luftflotten* on the night of 16/17 September alerting them to a secret clause in the Russo-German Non-Aggression Pact under which the Soviet Union would invade eastern Poland from dawn.

The Byelorussian and Ukrainian Fronts duly crossed the frontier and headed for the agreed demarcation point along the Rivers Bug and Narev (it was later amended). Twelve reconnaissance and corps squadrons (the latter with R-5s) preceded them, covered by 16 fighter regiments or their equivalent of the 18th, 22nd, 56th, 58th, 59th, 66th and 69th Fighter Brigades. Supporting them were a similar number of bomber regiment of the 1st Bomber, 62nd and 70th Light Bomber and 65th Mixed Aviation Brigades and four regiments of the 8th and 51st Ground Attack Brigades. *Legion Condor* veterans would have had little difficulty in recognising the majority of the 2,300 aircraft, including R-Z light bombers and ground-attack aircraft, although there was a new version of the *Chato* with retractable undercarriage (as the I-153) while the 3rd Long-Range Bomber Regiment had the Ilyushin DB-3 medium bomber. Few fired their guns as the remainder of the PLW was ordered into neutral Romania and by 20 September Polish resistance was confined to the 150,00 defenders of Warsaw.

The destruction of the two pockets failed to delay Warsaw's Calvary and actually accelerated it. The city had been under regular air attack from 8 September when *Luftflotte* 1 began striking the Vistula bridges as Reichenau's tanks pushed into the southern suburbs supported by 140 sorties mounted by St.G 77 and III./St.G 51, while KG 77 cut the

Ground crew take a break from servicing the Messerschmitt Bf 109 E-1 of Uffz. Hermann Neuhoff of III./JG 53 in the autumn of 1939. This Gruppe was formed in October of that year under the command of Hptm. Werner Mölders, the most successful fighter pilot in the Legion Condor. The engine cover lying on the grass to the right carries the Geschwader emblem of JG 53 – the famous 'Pik-As' – Ace of Spades.

railways east of the city. There was no relief at night as 2./LnAbt 100 made four precision-bombing forays supported by X-Gerät from 3/4 September to 10/11 September.

But the threat from the pockets whipped the Nazi leadership into a new frenzy with demands for massive attacks upon Warsaw. ObdL briefly dusted off 'Wasserkante' on 10 September due to unspecified crimes against German soldiers, assuming that defeat by the Polish Untermensch was a crime, and Hitler took up the theme the next day. Just after midnight on 12/13 September, Jeschonnek telephoned Löhr with orders for an afternoon incendiary raid by Grauert and Richthofen upon northern Warsaw, centred upon the Ghetto which was due north of the main railway station. The bombers went in, led by Oberst Martin Fiebig's KG 1, carrying a mixture of half high-explosive and half incendiaries while Richthofen despatched 183 sorties (the Luftflotte 4 war diary states 197) towards evening. There was no time to co-ordinate what were undoubtedly terror attacks and several German units narrowly avoided 'friendly bombs' while the dense smoke prevented any form of damage assessment, leading a furious Richthofen to confront Göring at Radom[26]. He demanded unified command for air operations over Warsaw, and strongly hinted that he was the best man for the job, although he did not get his wish until 21 September. His anger was fuelled by the actions of Seybald who ignored demands to bomb the Ghetto and diverted his Dorniers to military targets. Yet, surprisingly, Richthofen did not cite Seybald's failure to obey orders but rather poor leadership and a failure to attend meetings, although Seybald's command post was still in Prague! Also present was Loerzer who observed that he also could not cope with Seybald, who was replaced by the Kommandeur of III./KG 77, Oberst Wolf von Stutterheim.

Preparations for the assault on Warsaw continued as the last embers of the Polish pockets west of the Vistula were extinguished, poor weather delaying the final assault. Having given Richthofen

supreme command for air assault upon the city, ObdL divided it on 22 September: Kesselring was to strike the north, despite the loss of three Stukagruppen to Löhr who was to attack the west and south, the east escaping because it was scheduled to be occupied by the Russians. ObdL's growing preoccupation with preserving the strike force for the western campaign proved a major irritant. Not only did it deprive Richthofen of the He 111 Kampfgeschwader he wanted but also it replaced them with Ju 52s of IV./KG zbV 1; his Stukas were banned from using 250 and 500 kg bombs while bomb loads were confined to 50 kg ordnance.

ObdL had considered a repeat of the 13 September fire raid the following day but suspended judgement and on 18 September leaflets were dropped on Warsaw, demanding its surrender. The city's last links downstream with Modlin were severed on 20 September when Richthofen flew 620 sorties on his own initiative while the corps squadrons sought targets for 1,000 guns and ranged selected batteries. Two days later Richthofen signalled ObdL: "Urgently request exploitation of last opportunity for large-scale experiment as devastation and terror raid…" ominously adding "…every effort will be made to eradicate Warsaw completely."

That day Hitler made his only front line visit of the war, flying into an airstrip north-east of Warsaw, then driving through forests crawling with Polish stragglers to the suburb of Praga. Having seen the situation for himself he issued a directive demanding that Warsaw fall by 3 October.

On 24 September the air and artillery bombardment began, the former hindered by low cloud, and the city's gas, water and electricity were cut. When the weather cleared two days later the full weight of the Luftwaffe fell upon the city with 400 aircraft from five Stukagruppen, a transport Gruppe and a Kampfstaffeln flying 1,150 sorties for the loss of three aircraft, two of them Ju 52s. Some 560 tonnes of high explosive and 72 tonnes of incendiaries fell on the city; many of the latter were carried by the transports, each of which had two 'volunteers' who dug up the incendiaries with potato shovels and threw them out of the open door. Accuracy was impossible, especially with the incendiaries – many of which were pushed from their nominal targets by a strong north-easterly wind and this led to more than half the city's buildings being hit and 10 per cent being destroyed, with 40,000 casualties. Only a pair of Stukas and a Ju 52 were lost[27].

Some bombs hit German positions and the smoke cloud rose to 5,500 metres, concealing targets from the gunners. Blaskowitz was furious and, as Richthofen indignantly noted in his diary, when they met: "I was treated in an extraordinarily unfriendly manner. Neither Blaskowitz… nor Generaloberst (Walther) von Brauchitsch, Oberbefehlshaber des Heeres, took any notice of my reports or offered me their hand." Only Rundstedt was his usual courteous self and laughingly reproved him as: "You old firebug (Sie alter Kokelfritze)[28]".

Blaskowitz took his complaints to the top and demanded an end to the air assaults but Hitler told Richthofen to carry on. Pettily Göring told Richthofen to support only those missions which Blaskowitz requested and the next day *Fliegerführer zbV* flew some 450 sorties against Modlin, which capitulated on 27 September after receiving 318 tonnes of bombs in two days. Warsaw also surrendered and avoided another drenching in bombs which was being planned even as the envoys with white flags entered German lines.

Richthofen and his staff flew to Berlin three days later as the *Staffeln* either returned to their peacetime bases in eastern Germany to lick their wounds or flew to new bases in the West. OKW directives had anticipated the transfer to the West as early as 9 September (*Direktive Nr 3*). Two days later ObdL *Direktive Nr 12* began the flight west with the transfer to *Luftflotte* 2 of Stab, II. and III/LG 1, which went to Greifswald, and II./KG 26 which went to Lübeck-Blankensee. On 15 September I./KG 53 returned to its pre-war *Luftflotte* 3 base of Ansbach.

Grauert's move west was delayed until 20 September by the need to reduce the Ilza and Bzura Pockets, but by then ObdL had begun a major realignment of the *Luftwaffe* with Loerzer following Grauert. By 24 September the two eastern *Luftflotten*, but mostly Löhr, controlled only the *Lehrdivision*, 15 *Gruppen* and five *Aufklärungsstaffeln*. It was decided to leave three *Jagdgruppen*, four *Kampfgruppen* and two *Aufklärungsstaffeln* to secure Poland from Russian interference and for 'police actions'.

The Polish campaign demonstrated the soundness of *Luftwaffe* doctrine and tactics, thus making the *Lehrdivision* redundant. The *Luftwaffe* would create dedicated test commands (*Erprobungskommando*) to test new designs under service conditions and to develop tactics. The writing was on the wall during the spring when an *Erprobungskommando* 88 was created for the new Ju 88 fast bomber (*Schnellbomber*). Much was expected of the new aircraft, despite prolonged development problems, and although only 60 were delivered by the end of 1939, a major re-equipment programme was expected for the *Kampfgruppen*. To facilitate this Förster's headquarters was disbanded on 30 September and was assigned to Milch's staff as *General zbV* [29].

Poland had been annihilated thanks greatly to the *Luftwaffe*, typical activity being that of *Stab* and II./KG 26 together with the attached I./KG 53, which flew a total of 430 sorties for the loss of four bombers, with 18 damaged out of 72 bombers. Only 285 aircraft were lost and 279 suffered damage, in excess of 10 per cent, while aircrew casualties amounted to only 539 (413 dead and missing) out of a *Luftwaffe* 'butchers' bill' of 759. By contrast the PLW lost between 327 and 335 aircraft, of which some 66 per cent fell to the *Luftwaffe*, which accounted for many of the 140 aircraft which crashed on landing [30].

ORDERS OF BATTLE

Luftwaffe in the East: 1 September 1939

Under OKW
Fliegerdivision 7 (Liegnitz): Generalmajor Student
FJR 1 (I-III), 2 (I-II)
KGzvV 1(Liegnitz): Oberstleutnant Morzik
    Schönfeld-Seifersdorf: I., II./KGzbV 1 (Ju 52)
    Aslau: III./KGzbV 1 (Ju 52)
    Attached: KGrzbV 9 (Ju 52)
    Liegnitz u. Lüben: Stab, IV./KGzbV 1 (Ju 52)

Under ObdL
Luftnachtrichtenabteilung 100
    Köthen: 1./LnAbt 100 (Ju 52)
    2./LnAbt 100 (He 111H)
    Aufklärungsgruppe ObdL
    Berlin-Weder: 8.(F)/LG 2 (Do 17P/F)
    Kiel-Holtenau: 10. (See)/LG 2 (Do 18)
    Berlin-Gatow:Westa ObdL (He 111J)

For Luftflotte 4 Luftgau zbV
    KGzbV 2 (Küpper-Sagan): Oberst Conrad
    Sorau: I./KGzbV 2 (Ju 52)
    Freiwaldau: II., III./KGzbV 2 (Ju 52)
    Breslau-Grandau: IV./KGzbV 2 (Ju 52)

For Luftflotte 1 Luftgau zbV
    KGzbV 172 (Berlin-Tempelhof): Major von Gablenz
    Berlin-Tempelhof: Stab, I., II., III./KG zbV 172 (Ju 52)

Luftflotte 1 (Henningsholm bei Stettin):
General der Flieger Kesselring

AufklGr 121 (Prenzlau)
    Stargard-Klützow: 1., 3. (F)/AufklGr 121

Luftgau III (Berlin)
    JG 2 (Fürstenwalde): Oberstleutnant von Massow
    Fürstenwalde: Stab, I./JG 2 (Bf 109E)
    Döberitz: 10.(N)/JG 2 (Bf 109D, Ar 68F)
    Luftverteidigungskommando 1 (Berlin): Generalmajor
    Hoffmann
    Luftverteidigungskommando 2 (Stettin): Generalmajor
    Feyerabend
    Luftverteidigungskommando 3 (Leipzig): Generalmajor
    Sattler

Luftgau IV (Dresden)
    JG 3 (Brandis): Oberstleutnant Ibel
    Brandis: Stab, I./JG 3 (Bf 109E)
    Sprottgau (Attached): I./JG 20 (Bf 109E)
    LuftgauzbV 1, 3
    Ln Regt 1

1. Fliegerdivision (Schönfeld-Crössinsee): Generalleutnant Grauert
> Schönfeld-Crössinsee: 2.(F)/AufklGr 121 (Do 17P/F)
> Malzkow: 1.(J)/LG 2 (Bf 109E)
> Lottin: Stab, 2., 3.(J)/LG 2 (Bf 109E)
> Lichtenau: JGr 101 (Bf 109D/E) (II./ZG 1)
> Mühlen: I./ZG 1 (Bf 110C)
> Stolp-Reitz: II./St.G 2 (Ju 87B, Do 17P)
> IV.(St)/LG 1 (Ju 87B, Do 17P)
> Stolp-West/Annafeld: III./St.G 2 (Ju 87B, Do 17P)
> I., 4. (St)/TrGr 186 (Ju 87B)

KG 1 (Kolberg): Generalmajor Kessler
> Kolberg: Stab, I./KG 1 (He 111H)
> Pinnow-Plathe (Attached): I./KG 152 (He 111H)

KG 26 (Gabbert): Generalmajor Siburg
> Gabert: Stab, II./KG 26 (He 111H)
> Schönfeld-Crössinsee (Attached): I./KG 53 (He 111H)

From Hannover-Langenhagen midday 1 September
> KG 27 (Werneuchen): Oberst Behrendt
> Werneuchen: Stab, I./KG 27 (He 111P) (formerly Hannover-Langenhagen)
> Neuhardenburg: II./KG 27 (He 111P) (formerly Wunstorf)
> Königsberg/Neumark: III./KG 27 (He 111P) (formerly Delmenhorst)

Luftwaffenlehrdivision (Gut Wickbold/Jesau): Generalmajor Förster
> Jessau: I(Z)/LG 1 (Bf 110C)
> 4. (F)/AufklGr 121 (Do 17P/F)
> LG 1 (Neuhausen): Oberst Dr Knauss)
> Powunden: II(K)/LG 1 (He 111H)
> Prowehren: III (K)/LG 1 (He 111H)

KG 2 (Jesau): Oberst Fink
> Gerdauen: I./KG 2 (Do 17M)
> Schippenbeil: II./KG 2 (Do 17Z)

Luftwaffenkommando Ostpreussen (Konigsberg-Ballith): Generalleutnant Wimmer
> Neuhausen: 1.(F)/AufklGr 120 (Do 17P)
> Heiligenbeil (Attached to Luftgau I): Stab, 2./JG 1 (Bf 109E)
> Schippenbeil (Attached to Luftgau I): 1./JG 1 (Bf 109E)
> Arys-Rostken (Attached to Luftgau I): 3./JG 1 (Bf 109E)
> Gutenfeld (Attached to Luftgau I) : I./JG 21 (Bf 109D)
> Grieslienen: I./St.G 1 (Ju 87B, Do 17P)

KG 3 (Elbing): *Oberst* von Chamier-Glisczinski
> Heiligenbeil: II., III./KG 3 (Do 17Z)

Luftgau I (Konigsberg)
> LnAbt 6

Luftflotte 4 (Reihenbach): General der Flieger Löhr
> Schweidnitz: 3.(F)/AufkIGr 123 (Do 17P)

> Luftgau VIII (Breslau)
> Stubendorf: I./JG 76 (Bf 109E)
> Juliusburg-Nord: I./JG 77 (Bf 109E)

Luftgau XVII (Vienna)
Luftgau zbV 4, 8, 16
LnRegt 4

2. Fliegerdivision (Grottkau): Generalmajor Loerzer
> Woisselsdorf: 3.(F)/AufklGr 122 (Do 17P)
> Märzdorf: I./ZG 76 (Bf 110C)
> Welzow: I./St.G 2 (Ju 87B, Do 17P)

> KG 4 (Oels): *Oberst* Fiebig
> Oels: Stab, II./KG 4 (He 111P)
> Langenau: I., III./KG 4 (He 111P)

> KG 76 (Breslau-Schöngarten): Oberst Schultheiss
> Breslau-Schöngarten: Stab, I./KG 76 (Do 17Z)
> Rosenborn: III./KG 76 (Do 17Z)

KG 77 (Prague-Kbely): Oberst Seywald
> Prague-Kbely: *Stab*, I./KG 77 (Do 17Z)
> Brünn/Brno: II./KG 77 (Do 17Z)
> Königgrätz: I., III./KG 77 (Do 17Z)

Fliegerführer zbV (Birkental bei Oppeln): Generalmajor von Richthofen
> Schlosswalden: 1.(F)/AufklGr 124 (Do 17P)

LG 2 (Nieder-Ellguth): Oberstleutnant Baier
> Alt Rosenburg: II.(Schl)/LG 2 (Hs 123)

St.G 77 (Neudorf): Oberst Schwartzkopff
> Neudorf: Stab, I., II./St.G 77 (Ju 87B, Do 17P)
> Nieder-Ellguth (Attached): I./St.G 76 (Ju 87B, Do 17P)
> Gross-Stein (Attached): *Stab*, 1., 3./JGr 102 (Bf 109D) (I./ZG 2)
> Zipser-Neudorff (Attached): 2./JGr 102 (Bf 109D) (I./ZG 2)
> I./FlakRegt 3, I./FlakRegt 23

Slovenske Vzousne Zbrane

38th, 48th Fighter Squadrons (Avia B 534)

16th Corps Squadron (Letov S 328)

Koluft Heeresgruppe Nord: Generalmajor Krocker
> 2.(F)/AufklGr 11 (Do 17P)

Koluft 3. Armee: Generalmajor Zoch
> 3.(F)/AufklGr 10 (Do 17P)
> AK I: 2. (H)/AufklGr 10 (Hs 126)
> II., III./FlakRegt 11
> AK XXI: 1.(H)/AufklGr 10 (Hs 126)

Koluft 4. Armee: Oberst Keiper
> 3.(F)/AufklGr 11 (Do 17P)
> II./421 Light
> AK II: 3.(H)/AufklGr 21 (Hs 126)
> I./FlakLehrRegt
> AK III: 2.(H)/AufklGr 21 (Hs 126)
> I /FlakRegt 411
> AK XIX (Mot): 9.(H)/LG 2 (Hs 126)
> I./FlakRegt 61, II./FlaklehrRegt

THE FIRST CAMPAIGN: POLAND 1939

Koluft Heeresgruppe Süd: Generalmajor Schulz
    4.(F)/AufklGr 11 (Do 17P)
    AK VII: 4.(H)/AufklGr 31 (He 45/46)

Koluft 8. Armee: Oberst von Gerlach
    1.(H)/AufklGr 21 (Hs 126)
    I./FlakRegt 33, I./FlakRegt 52
    AK X: 4.(H)/AufklGr 23 (He 45/46)
    AK XIII: 5.(H)/AufklGr 13 (He 45/46)
    II./FlakRegt 22

Koluft 10. Armee: Oberst Lohmann
    3.(F)/AufklGr 31 (Do 17P)
    I., III./FlakRegt 13, I./FlakRegt 22, I./FlakRegt 43
    AK IV: 1.(H)/AufklGr 41 (Hs 126)
    I./FlakRegt 701
    AK XI: 4.(H)/AufklGr 21 (He 45/46)
    I./FlakRegt 36
    AK XIV (Mot): 3.(H)/AufklGr 12,
    4.(H)/AufklGr 13 (Hs 126, He 46)
    Flakabt 76, 77
    AK XV (Mot): 1.(H)/AufklGr 11,
    3.(H)/AufklGr 41 (Hs 126, He 46)
    Flakabt 93

    AK XVI (Mot): 2.(H)/AufklGr 41 (Hs 126)
    2.(H)/AufklGr 23 (Hs 126, He 46)
    II./FlakRegt 23, Flakabt 83
Koluft 14.Armee: Oberst Pistor
    4.(F)/AufklGr 14 (Do 17F)
    AK VIII: 1.(H)/AufklGr 31 (Hs 126)
    2.(H)/AufklGr 31 (Hs 126, He 46)
    II./FlakRegt 38
    AK XVII: 3.(H)/AufklGr 14 (Hs 126)
    I./FlakRegt 7
    AK XVIII: 1.(H)/AufklGr 14 (Hs 126, He 46)
    2.(H)/AufklGr 14 (Hs 126)
    Flakabt 92, 94

Fliegerführer der Luftstreitkräfte Ost (Dievenow):
Generalmajor Coeler
    Kiel-Holtenau: 5./BordflGr 196 (He 60)
    Dievenow: Stab, 1./ KüflGr 306 (He 60)
    2./ KüflGr 306 (Do 18)
    Pillau: Stab, 1./ KüflGr 506 (He 60)
    3./KüflGr 506 (He 59)
    Kamp: 2./KüflGr 506 (Do 18)
    Stab, 3./KüflGr 706 (He 59)
    Nest: 1./KüflGr 706 (He 60)

NOTES FOR CHAPTER SIX

[1] Irving, *Göring* pp.248-249, 252-266.

[2] For the Poland air campaign see Speidel, *The German Air Force in Poland* (hereafter Monograph 151). Bekker pp.19-59. Blandford pp.47-53. Belcarz & Peczkowski pp.112, 147-221, 247-250. Cynk pp.134-139. Hooton pp.175-189. BAMA RL 2 II./51, RL 7/2, RL 8/102. For German units see Balke, Dierich, Gundelach, Schmidt and Smith. For the ground campaign see Zaloga, Zaloga & Madej.

[3] Belcarz & Peczkowski pp.174-175.

[4] BA MA RL7/2.

[5] Steinhilper p.172. Mombeek, *Jagdwaffe* Volume 1 Section 4 *Attack in the West* p.382. Some Avias would appear in spurious markings as Polish fighters in a movie on the air war in Poland.

[6] For planning and preparation see USNA Microfilm T971 Roll 18: *The planning and preparations for the Air War against Poland 1939.*

[7] Bekker pp.42-43.

[8] Neulen, p.185.

[9] Belcarz & Peczkowski p.200.

[10] Monograph 151.

[11] Cynk pp.134, 137-139. Shores, p.24. Zaloga & Madej pp.116, 147. Monograph 151 pp.183-184.

[12] *Luftflotte 4 Flak* fired the first shots of the campaign on 31 August to warn-off a Polish corps aircraft.

[13] The injured crew were well treated and after the war one, *Leutnant* Wimmer, met one of the victors. Belcarz & Peczkowski pp.182-183.

[14] Dilley was briefly *Kommandeur* of *I./St.G 1* in December 1941 and in early 1942 of I./St.G 2.

[15] Zaloga & Madej p.127.

[16] *Fliegerdivision 1* war diary, BA MA RL8/102. But Schmidt, pp.285, 388, 349, states they fell to enemy fighters. *Koluft 14. Armee, Oberst* Neutitschen, vainly sought direct command of a *Kampfgruppe* and later a *Transportgruppe.* Monograph 151 p.132.

[17] Report by Oberst Wilhelm Speidel, *Die Einsatz der Luftwaffe im Polnischen Feldzug,* IWM AHB6/158 Tin 148. The RAF used similar tactics in the autumn of 1918.

[18] Zaloga & Madej pp.171, 181.

[19] Monograph 151.

[20] Richthofen diary.

[21] Monograph 151 pp.134-137, 147-149. See also Deichmann's *Spearhead for Blitzkrieg.*

[22] Weal p. 19.

[23] Murray pp.108-109. BA MA RL 7/2.

[24] See Rosch p.277.

[25] Richthofen diary.

[26] Bekker p.57. Boog p.373-404. *Fliegerdivision 1* war diary and Richthofen diary entries for September 11 and September 13.

[27] Monograph 151.

[28] Richthofen's diary for September 25. Rundstedt's Saxon accent meant that he actually said 'Sie oller Gokelfritze'.

[29] Green pp.449-450. Windrow p.4. Speidel Monograph 152. pp.89-91

[30] Schmidt pp.302. Shores p.28. Zaloga & Madej p.148.

PERSONNEL INDEX